ENGAGING
ISLAMIC TRADITIONS

Engaging Islamic Traditions: Using the Hadith in Christian Ministry to Muslims

Copyright © 2016 by Bernie Power. All rights reserved.

Published by William Carey Library
1605 E. Elizabeth St.
Pasadena, CA 91104 | www.missionbooks.org

Melissa Hughes, editor
Cheryl Warner, copyeditor
Alyssa Force, graphic design
Jeremy Lind, indexer

William Carey Library is a ministry of
Frontier Ventures
Pasadena, CA | www.frontierventures.org

Published in the United States of America
20 19 18 17 16   5 4 3 2 1 BP300

Library of Congress Cataloging-in-Publication Data
Power, Bernie.
    Engaging Islamic traditions : using the Hadith in Christian ministry to Muslims /
Dr. Bernie Power.
        pages cm
    Includes bibliographical references and index.
    ISBN 978-0-87808-491-3 -- ISBN 0-87808-491-6 1. Missions to Muslims. 2.
Hadith. 3. Christianity and other religions--Islam. 4. Islam--Relations--Christianity.
I. Title.
    BV2625.P69 2015
    297.1'254106--dc23
                                                            2015022507

ENGAGING
ISLAMIC TRADITIONS

Using the Hadith in Christian Ministry to Muslims

BERNIE POWER

WILLIAM CAREY
LIBRARY

Jesus said about the prodigal son: "But while he was still a long way off, his father saw him and was filled with compassion for him; he ran to his son, threw his arms around him and kissed him."

Luke 15:20

"Allah says about every person: 'If my slave . . . comes one span nearer to Me, I go one cubit nearer to him; and if he comes one cubit nearer to Me, I go a distance of two outstretched arms nearer to him; and if he comes to Me walking, I go to him running.'"

Hadith al-Bukhāri 9:267

CONTENTS

I

ABOUT THE HADITH

II

FINDING CONCORD

III
SEEKING CONNECTIONS

IV
USING THE HADITH IN
CHRISTIAN MINISTRY

TRANSLITERATION TABLE

CONSONANTS		
b = ب	z = ز	f = ف
t = ت	s = س	q = ق
th = ث	sh = ش	k = ك
j = ج	ṣ = ص	l = ل
ḥ = ح	ḍ = ض	m = م
kh = خ	ṭ = ط	n = ن
d = د		h = ه
dh = ذ	ẓ = ظ	w = و
r = ر	ʿ = ع	y = ي
	gh = غ	

VOWELS			
SHORT	a = ´	i = ِ	u = ُ
LONG	ā = ا	ī = ي	ū = و
DIPHTONG	ay = اَيْ	aw = اَوْ	

ILLUSTRATIONS

FIGURES

SIDEBARS

TABLES

I

INTRODUCTION

TODAY NEARLY ONE QUARTER of the earth's population sub-
scribes to the Islamic religion, and this number is growing rapidly
mostly due to a high birthrate. The world's only major post-Christian
faith has proved resistant to the Christian message. Compared with
non-Islamic people groups in sub-Saharan Africa, South America,
and parts of Asia, the fruit of Christian ministry among Muslims
has been meager. Professor Dudley Woodberry notes that "no mission work has had less success than Christian mission to Muslims."[1]
Social, political, and cultural factors militate against easy Christian
access. The rate of literacy in the Muslim world is generally low,
minimizing the potential impact of printed resources. Poor infra-
structure, repressive government censorship, and general poverty
have often restricted access by outside electronic mass media and
other forms of outreach into many Muslim countries.[2] Where local
Christian communities live in Muslim-majority countries, their
witness has usually been muted by centuries of "protected" *dhimmi*
status[3] and fear of persecution. Many missiological methods have
been applied[4] to ensure that the message of Jesus Christ receives a
hearing among the followers of the Prophet Muhammad.[5]

Surprisingly, little attention has been paid to the body of literature called the Hadith.[6] After his death, Muhammad's words and
actions or *sunnah* (literally "a trodden path")[7] were collected in the
Hadith (literally a story, a narration, a report) and became considered normative for the lives of Muslims forever. Burton describes the

relationship between Hadith and *sunnah:* "the term *Hadith* refers to a document, the term *sunnah* refers to the usage described in such a document."[8] These ancient documents could be a rich source of material to aid Christians in their task of understanding and responding to Islam. Samuel Zwemer commented that the Hadith "have exercised tremendous power on Moslem thought since the early days of Islam; not only by supplementing but by interpreting the Koran. The *Hadith* are accepted by every Moslem sect, in some form or other, and are indispensable to Islam."[9]

THE PURPOSE OF THIS BOOK

The goal of this book is to evaluate the Hadith for positive Christian approaches to Muslims. The main focus will be an analysis of al-Bukhāri's collection of the Hadith.[10] The vast scope of the Hadith literature necessitates some selection. Al-Bukhāri's collection is not only representative of the Hadith genre, it is one of the *sahīhayn* (two authentic) books, considered by Muslims to be the apex of the most widely accepted Hadith collections.

Although the Hadith constitute a major part to the preaching in many mosques and inform and regulate much of the everyday life of many Muslims, Christian workers rarely utilize them as part of their ministry to Muslims. This book attempts to redress that imbalance. Parshall comments: "It is my opinion that it is permissible to utilize Hadith passages in witness to Muslims."[11] The potential success of such a venture is mooted by no less a figure than the missiologist J. H. Bavinck. "There never has been a system so tightly woven that God did not leave providentially some cracks through which the dynamic of God could find its way in."[12] The use of the Hadith may be one of the keys to ensure that the Christian message receives a positive hearing by Muslims.

NOTES

1. Woodberry, "Failure," 121.

2. Notwithstanding the efforts of organizations like Middle East Media (MEM) and the TV station Sat-7.

3. Many Christians and Jews question the positive perception of *dhimmi* status as "protection" as it is sometimes portrayed by Muslim writers. See Durie, *Third Choice.*

4. Terry, "Approaches."

5. In this book, Muhāmmad is sometimes referred to as "the Prophet." This is based on the biblical precedent of applying the title of "prophet" to anyone, false or true, Jewish or pagan, who claimed to speak publicly for his deity, e.g., 1 Kings 18:19, Nehemiah 6:14, and Titus 1:12. However, the prayer for Muhammad recited by devout Muslims after each mention of his name, often abbreviated as PBUH (Peace be upon him), will not be written. This follows the precedent of Tariq Ramadhan who, noting that he writes for a wide audience, suggests: "Let the Muslim reader personally and inwardly formulate this prayer as he or she reads." Ramadhan, *Messenger,* 217.

6. The term "hadith" will be used in this book as both an individual and collective noun, following standard academic practice. Occasionally the plural "hadiths" will be used. The Arabic word *hadīth* is singular, and its plural is *ahādīth.* Since it is a commonly accepted term in English it, like the words "Muhammad," "Islam," and "Qur'an," will not be transliterated.

7. The plural of *sunnah* is *sunan.* Some Hadith collections have this title.

8. Burton, *Introduction,* ix.

9. Zwemer, *God,* 8.

10. The Hadith pericopes (individual accounts) will be referred to by their number, e.g., B.1:37, which refers to al-Bukhāri vol. 1, Hadith account no. 37. Al-Bukhari's collection has nine volumes, with the number of pericopes varying from 582 (vol. 6) to 895 (vol. 3).

11. Parshall, *Inside the Community,* 14.

12. Bavinck cited in Peters, "Overview," 401–02.

I

ABOUT THE HADITH

AN AFRICAN WRITER ASSERTS, "As Muslims, our knowledge of Islam would be incomplete and shaky if we did not study and follow the *Hadith*. Similarly an outsider cannot understand Islam if he ignores the *Hadith*."[1] Brown notes that "although it stands second to the Quran in terms of reverence, it is the lens through which the holy book is interpreted and understood. In this sense, in Islamic civilization the Sunna has ruled over the Quran, shaping, specifying, and adding to the revealed book."[2]

This section discusses how the body of literature known as the Hadith came to be, what it is, how it is structured, and the role it fills in the lives of Muslims. Each separate hadith can be categorized in various ways, and chapter 2 will touch on the complexities of these classifications. Lastly, this section prepares the reader for both a comparative and a biblical analysis of the Hadith.

NOTES

1. Kateregga and Shenk, *Islam and Christianity*, 31.
2. Brown, *Hadith*, 3.

WHAT IS THE HADITH?

1. HOW AND WHY DID THE HADITH ARISE?

Muslims claim that their religion is all-inclusive: "Islam was not satisfied with preaching only broad principles. . . It is a complete code of life."[1] Sayyid Qutb notes that "history has shown that Islam is unique in its ability to provide guidance for the entire range of human activity." Thus, Islam "does not separate spiritual and secular life, for what seems to belong to the citizen and to Caesar is in reality God's property." Proper religiosity "is comprehensive and covers all aspects of life just as capillaries and nerves direct themselves to all parts of the body."[2]

Clearly the approximately 6,200[3] verses of the Qur'an do not cover every possible human contingency. According to Ismail al-Faruqi[4] and Jalal-ud-din al-Suyuti (c. 1445-1505) in *Itqān fi 'Ulūm al-Qur'ān* ("Perfection in the Qur'anic Sciences"), only five hundred of its verses describe law, while Mutawalli puts the verse count at two hundred.[5] Bennett suggests a middle number of three hundred.[6] Whatever the actual tally, less than 10 percent of the Qur'an's verses have a legal connotation. The lacuna had to be covered by Muhammad's sayings and deeds.

The fact that Muhammad [lived] through all the major experiences to which a human being may be exposed in the course of his life gives the practice of the religion its specific character and lends this "imitation" a remarkable precision, even in the simplest acts of daily life.[7]

Muhammad's experiences cited include being orphaned at a young age, living in a city and in the desert, traveling to Syria as an adolescent, mixing with the rich, experiencing poverty, engaging in commerce, being involved in monogamous and polygamous marriages, having the joy of fatherhood, then the sadness of seeing all but one of his children die, facing persecution and rejection, and then becoming the successful religious, political, and military leader of a growing community. He is described as exhibiting "great moral character."[8] Having lived a full and varied life, he died at age sixty-three.[9]

(a) The Qur'anic basis for a sunnah focused on Muhammad

During his public ministry, Muhammad was recognized by other Muslims as the undisputed earthly ruler and sole legislator of Islam. According to the Qur'an, obedience to him must be unquestioning. Muhammad is presented to Muslims as a judge in all disputes. His decisions must not be resisted but accepted with full submission.[10] Those who obeyed him would be blessed[11] and triumphant,[12] but those who disobeyed would suffer the punishment of hell.[13] The implications of submission to Islam are presented as important. Muhammad said: "If you love God, follow me, and God will love you, and forgive you your sins."[14] The Qur'an formulates a one-to-one correspondence between divine and prophetic obedience: "He who obeys the Messenger has indeed obeyed Allah.[15] Making a pledge to the Prophet was the same as making a pledge to Allah.[16] Muhammad is therefore given a place of great honor: "God and His angels bless the Prophet. O believers, do you also bless him, and pray him peace."[17]

Muhammad's impact went far beyond his legal enactments. "For the original Muslim community . . . all authority was invested in the

Prophet. The figure of the Prophet dominated Islam . . . The unity of that community is not centred on the statements the Prophet makes but on the Prophet himself . . . because the message is manifested in the actions of the messenger. In other words, the Prophet reveals what Islam is, but Islam is also what the Prophet does."[18]

Muslims claim that Muhammad is the model for all people to follow. His actions were not simply descriptive of his own life, but also prescriptive for all Muslims. The Qur'anic bases for this are several: "You have had a good pattern in God's Messenger"[19] and "And whatsoever the Messenger gives you, take it, and whatsoever he forbids you, abstain (from it)."[20] According to Islam, this is the path of purity, freedom, and prosperity (see Sidebar *Muhammad's Authority*). Based on the frequent injunctions to "obey Allah and his messenger,"[21] as well as warnings against disobedience to Muhammad,[22] Brown comments: "The *imitatio Muhammadi* thus became the standard for ethical behavior among Muslims, forming the basis for Islamic law and setting the standard for even the most mundane activities—the order in which fingernails should be cut or the proper length of the beard."[23]

> ## MUHAMMAD'S AUTHORITY
>
> "Those who follow the messenger, the unlettered Prophet, whom they find mentioned in their own (scriptures)—in the Law and the Gospel—for he commands them what is just and forbids them what is evil; he allows them as lawful what is good (and pure) and prohibits them from what is bad (and impure); He releases them from their heavy burdens and from the yokes that are upon them. So it is those who believe in him, honour him, help him, and follow the light which is sent down with him—it is they who will prosper." (Q.7.157)

One scholar outlines the logic: "The underlying assumption was presumably that Muhammad's practice would be in accordance with his understanding of the revelation, and that, since he was the recipient of the revelation and so closest to it, his understanding of it would be better than most Muslims."[24] It was not the first time such an application had occurred: "This practice was no Islamic innovation, for the inclination to look towards a tribal leader's person and behavior for guidance was a common aspect of pre-Islamic culture."[25] However, there is more than the pragmatism of following established custom. Jews and Christians, as well as Muslims, are enjoined to follow the Prophet's teaching and example for their own welfare, because their eternal destiny is at stake: "Whoso obeys God and His Messenger, He will admit him to gardens underneath . . . dwelling forever . . . But whoso disobeys God and His Messenger . . . He will admit to a Fire, therein dwelling forever."[26]

(b) The Hadith's basis for a sunnah focused on Muhammad

Although Muhammad's sayings as collected in the Qur'an were seen to be absolutely requisite, "even when the Prophet did not claim his words to be divinely inspired, his utterances were generally held to bind the community."[27] He said: "If I forbid you to do something, then keep away from it. And if I order you to do something, then do of it as much as you can."[28]

In the Hadith, Muhammad presented himself as the best example to follow. He told his followers: "By Allah I fear Allah more than you do, and am more obedient to Him than you."[29] He encouraged others to follow his *sunnah*[30] and to leave "the ways and traditions of the Days of Ignorance."[31] He stated that "he who does not follow my tradition in religion, is not from me (not one of my followers)."[32] There was a special incentive for Jews and Christians. Those who left their former monotheistic religion and followed Islam would receive a double reward.[33] When a group of Muslims did not follow his example in a particular matter, he chided them in a sermon: "What is wrong with such people as refrain from doing a thing that I do? By Allah, I know Allah better than they, and I am more afraid of Him than they."[34] His followers extended this imitation to include behavior which Muhammad did not undertake himself, but did not prohibit when it occurred in his presence. For example, at a meal, Muhammad "left the *mastigar* [sand-lizard] because he disliked it. Muhammad's cousin Ibn 'Abbās said, 'The *mastigar* was eaten at the table of Allah's Apostle and, if it had been illegal to eat, it could not have been eaten at the table of Allah's Apostle.'"[35]

Throughout the Hadith, Muhammad's status is increasingly enhanced in comparison to the other prophets. On his ascent to heaven, he is greeted by all the other prophets.[36] Moses wept because more of Muhammad's followers would enter Paradise than his own followers.[37] On the day of Resurrection, Muhammad claimed he would be "the chief of all people" whose intercession would be accepted.[38]

The Hadith reiterate this, for Muhammad said: "He who obeys me, obeys Allah, and he who disobeys me, disobeys Allah."[39] He even made a claim to absolute geographical sovereignty: "The earth belongs to Allah and His apostle."[40] This gave him universal responsibility: "Allah has trusted all the people of the earth to me."[41]

(c) The legal schools' basis for a sunnah focused on Muhammad

Muhammad b. Idrīs al-Shāfi'i (d.204/820), the founder of one of the four orthodox Sunni schools, taught that the recurring phrase "the Book and the Wisdom"[42] referred to the Qur'an and the Hadith. The wisdom achieved by Muhammad is placed alongside the Qur'an itself. Muhammad retorted to a questioner: "Who would obey Allah if I disobeyed Him?"[43] Due to his apparently infallible perception, it is believed that all his acts were inspired and could be applied to situations for which the Qur'an supplied no answer. One hadith suggested this: "The best talk is Allah's Book (Qur'an), and the best guidance is the guidance of Muhammad."[44] It is little wonder that Muhammad's companions sought to imitate him in every way.[45] His wife Aisha saw no gap between the Prophet and his book. When asked about his character, she replied: "The character of the Apostle of Allah (peace be upon him) was the Qur'an."[46] Hassan al-Barbahāri (d.329/941) put it simply: "Islam is the Sunna, and the Sunna is Islam."[47] The four Sunni legal schools—Hanafi, Maliki, Shāfi'ī, and Hanbāli—all present Muhammad as the model of full humanity.

"If the Muslim is to tap that same source and become 'one who understands', he has no choice but to model himself upon this 'perfect exemplar', imitating Muhammad so far as he is able, both in his character and in his mode of action. Since the Prophet is 'closer to the believers than their [own] selves' (Q.33.6), it can be said that he is the believer's *alter ego* or—to take this a step further—more

truly 'oneself' than the collection of fragments and contrary impuls-
es which we commonly identify as the 'self'."[48] The polemicist
Ahmed Deedat goes further, declaring Muhammad to be "the
Greatest Saviour of humanity and Islam."[49]

Some decades earlier Sir George Bernard Shaw is alleged to have
said, "I have studied [Muhammad]—the wonderful man and in my
opinion far from being an anti-Christ, he must be called the Savior
of Humanity."[50]

Muhammad was presented as unique through his designation as
"the seal of the prophets."[51] When he claimed in his final sermon,
"To-day I have perfected for you your religion, and have completed My
favour upon you, and am well-pleased with Islam as your religion,"[52]
he closed the door to further revelation.[53] The possibility of later
prophets, as in Judaism, or the inspiring role of the Holy Spirit, as
in Christianity, was not envisaged.[54] Muhammad saw himself as the
final and necessary brick in an otherwise beautiful edifice.[55]

Following Muhammad's death, and as Islam spread to other
lands, new Muslims were curious about the life of the founder of
their religion. Stories about Muhammad were transmitted orally for
some generations and were eventually collected. For most Muslims,
the *sunnah* of the Prophet became a key foundation for both belief
and action.

2. THE FORM OF THE HADITH

The Hadith are written accounts of the actions and sayings of the
Prophet Muhammad and some of his "companions" (*sahāba*) and
"successors" (*tābi'un*). A companion was someone who knew
Muhammad personally, but who can be classed as a companion is a
matter of some dispute.[56] Muhammad's earliest biographer, Ibn
Ishāq, gives one list of the earliest companions,[57] and al-Bukhāri
cites 208 companions.[58] Others are more expansive, with numbers
varying from the 1,525 in the earliest census taken at the Treaty of
Hudaybiya to the 40,000 present at the Farewell Pilgrimage to Abū
Zar'a al-Rāzi's estimate of over 100,000 who ever saw or heard the
Prophet.[59] Successors (*tābi'un*) were those who had conversed with

one of the companions of the Prophet. Put together, these make an impressive pool of potential contributors to the Hadith.

Each hadith is recorded in a self-contained pericope or account, varying from only a sentence long, or they may extend to several pages. The text of the hadith is called the *matn* (lit. "letters") (see Sidebar *An Example of a* Hadith).

Every hadith is usually accompanied by an *isnād* (chain of transmitters) as a form of authentication. This describes the human links by which the tradition was passed from the Prophet (or companion or successor) to the eventual compiler. An example of an *isnād* is:

> **AN EXAMPLE OF A** *HADITH*
>
> "Allah's Apostle was the most generous of all the people, and he used to reach the peak in generosity in the month of Ramadan when Gabriel met him. Gabriel used to meet him every night of Ramadan to teach him the Qur'an. Allah's Apostle was the most generous person, even more generous than the strong uncontrollable wind (in readiness and haste to do charitable deeds)." (al-Bukhāri 1:5)

Humaidi Abdullah bin ul-Zubair narrated to us (that he) said that Sufyān narrated to us (that he) said that Yahya bin Sa'id al-Ansari narrated to us (that he) said that Muhammad bin Ibrahim al-Tayma informed us that he heard Alqama bin Waqas al-Laythi saying: I heard Umar bin al-Khattab (God be pleased with him) say: I heard the Prophet of God (God bless him and grant him salvation) say: . . .[60]

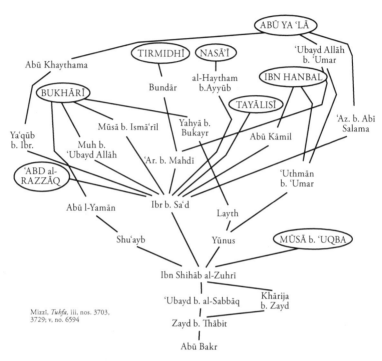

ILLUSTRATION 1: A network of isnāds for a single hadith from Abu Bakr. The eight collectors of this hadith are circled.

A single *matn* may have a variety of *isnāds* or routes by which the tradition was transmitted to the compiler. Illustration 1 shows the variant and complex paths by which a saying of the Companion Abū Bakr (in the square at the bottom) found its way to the various compilers (who are circled).[61] This particular hadith describes the process by which the Qur'an was compiled during the Caliphate of Abū Bakr (d.13/634).[62]

Not all transmitters were considered equally reliable. A hadith relayed by one *isnād* may be deemed stronger or weaker than another, even though they have identical *matns*. Most hadiths of the classical period, the second century after Muhammad, have between five and ten transmitters in their *isnāds*.

3. COLLECTIONS OF THE HADITH

As the "science of hadith" developed, six collections of hadith became generally accepted as "canonical." Information about these collections is outlined in Table 1.[63]

Of these six books (al-kutub al-sitta), the two approved versions (the sahīhayn) of al-Bukhāri and Muslim are seen as the pinnacle of reliability among the Sunni hadith. Some of the details of these are disputed, whether the total number of hadiths,[64] the number without repetition,[65] or the number of hadiths considered.[66]

COMMON NAME OF THE COLLECTION	NAME OF COMPILER	DATES OF COMPILER	NUMBER OF HADITHS	NUMBER WITHOUT REPETITION	NUMBER OF HADITHS CONSIDERED
Sahīh Al-Bukhāri	Muhammad b. Ismā'īl **al-Bukhāri**	d.256/870	7,275	2,602	300,000 or 600,000
Sahīh Muslim	**Muslim** b. al-Hajjāj	d.261/875	7,190	3,030	300,000
Sunan Abu Dāwūd	**Abu Dāwūd** Sulayman b. al-Ash'ath al-Sijistāni	d.275/889	5.274	4,800	500,000
Almujtaba ("the selected") from Kitāb al-sunan al-kubra	Ahmad b. Shu'ayb **al-Nasā'i**	d.303/915	5,270		
Al-Jāmi' al-Sahīh	Muhammad b. Isa **al-Tirmidhi**	d.279/892	3,956	3,873	
Sunan Ibn Mājah	**Ibn Mājah** al-Qazwīni	d.273/886	4,341	1,339	

TABLE 1: Details of the six books

4. THE AUTHORITY OF THE HADITH

The Hadith are generally seen as eclipsed in authority only by the Qur'an. Rahman refers to the Hadith as "the authoritative second source of the content of Islam besides the Qur'an."[67] Anderson speaks of the relationship between the Hadith and the Qur'an as "equally inspired in content though not in form."[68] However, al-Shāfiʻi placed the Hadith on equal footing with the Qur'an in authority with his statement, "The command of the Prophet is the command of God."[69] Al-Bukhari's collection holds a place of special eminence. Khan claims that it "is widely considered by many to be the most authentic book after the Qur'an."[70]

Rahman claims that the Hadith are a necessary support for the Qur'an. "For, if the Hadith *as a whole* is cast away, the basis for the historicity of the Qur'an is removed at one stroke."[71] The South African Council of Muslim Theologians finds an unbreakable link between the Qur'an and the Hadith:

> The Holy Qur'an without the Hadith or Sunnah of the Prophet remains unintelligible in certain instances and in view of that, the Holy Qur'an has, in several verses, ordered Muslims to follow the Prophet in all his deeds and sayings. Therefore, if one believes in the Holy Qur'an, there is no other alternative but to uphold the Hadith of the Prophet.[72]

NOTES

1.   Hakim, *Islamic Ideology,* xi.

2.   Qutb, *Islam and Universal Peace,* 3.

3.   "The total number of Qur'ān verses is variously given as 6204, 6214, 6219, 6225 or 6236." Juynboll, "hadith and the Qur'an," vol. 2, 386. Bennett counts 6,666. Bennett, *Search,* 20. Hughes, *Dictionary,* 489 details sources of the different numberings of the verses.

4.   Al-Faruqi, *Islam,* 35-44.

5. Source: http://www.islamic-world.net/islamic-state/consti_reading. htm (accessed October 14, 2015).

6. Bennett, *Search*, 20.

7. Eaton, "Man," 36.

8. Q.68:4. Many books have been written extolling the virtues of Muhammad, e.g., Al-Sheba, *Muhammad: The Messenger of Allah*.

9. B.5:243, 742. We will follow the generally held convention for references to al-Bukhāri's Hadith, using this format. "B" stands for "al Bukhari" and B.5:243, 742 means volume 5, accounts no. 243 and 742. There are nine volumes in al-Bukhāri's Hadith, based on the translation by Khan, *Translation*. Some references also or instead list the "Book" of the Hadith. See the appendix for a list of how the "Books" correlate with the "Volumes." The references can also be found on the websites www.sunnah.com and www.searchtruth.com using the Search facility.

10. Q.4:65.

11. Q.4:81.

12. Q.24:52.

13. Q.4:115; 72:23.

14. Q.3.28, 29.

15. Q.4:80.

16. Q.48:10.

17. Q.3.56.

18. Sayyid, *A Fundamental Fear*, 53.

19. Q.33.21.

20. Q.59.7.

21. This phrase occurs at least fifteen times throughout the Qur'an, e.g., Q.3:32,132; 4:59, 69; 5:92; 8:120, 46; 9:71; 24:52, 54; 33:31; 47:33; 49:14; 58:13; 64:12. Variants are found in Q.4:64, 66, 80.

22. E.g., Q.4:14; 8:13; 33:36; 59:4.

23. Brown, *Rethinking tradition*, 1.

24. Watt, *Islamic Revelation*, 72.

25. Firestone, *Jihad*, 93.

26. Q.17:18.

27. Wild, "Political interpretation," 273.

28. B.9:391.

29. B.3:683.

30. B.2:71, 82.

31. B.2:382, 384, 385.

32. B.7:1.

33. B.1:97.1; 4:655; 7:20.

34. B.8:123.

35. B.3:749; 7:301, 303, 312, 314 c.f. 9:453.

36. B.4:429.

37. B.5:227.

38. B.4:556.

39. B.4:204; 9:251, 384, 385.

40. B.4:392.

41. B.4:558.

42. Q.2:129, 151, 231; 3:48, 79, 81, 164; 4:54, 113; 62:2.

43. B.4:558.

44. B.8:120.

45. B.1:167.

46. Muslim 369 cited by Sa'd ibn Hisham ibn Amir. References from CD-ROM "The Islamic Scholar," Hadith/Muslim.

47. Brown, *Hadith*, 174.

48. Eaton, *Islam and the Destiny of Man*, 186.

49. Cited in Al-Kalby, *Prophet Muhammad*, 5. The term "Saviour of the world" had previously been applied to Jesus (John 4:42; 1 John 4:14).

50. George Bernard Shaw, "The Genuine Islam," vol. 1, no. 8, 1936. http://prophetofislam.com/what_do_others_say.php (accessed October 14, 2015). The reliability of this quote has been challenged by various writers who claim that this book never actually existed. See http://idlethink.wordpress.com/2008/12/03/being-an-unforgivably-protracted-debunking-of-george-bernard-shaws-views-of-islam/ (accessed October 14, 2015).

51. Q.33:40.

52. Q.5:3.

53. The door to *ijtihad* (independent interpretation of the legal sources) was seen as still open, at least until the time of al-Ghazāli (d.1111) writing his "The Incoherence of the Philosophers," when he deemed this door closed. Muhammad Iqbal (1875-1938) called for the reinstatement of ijtihad by a Muslim legislative assembly in order to restore an Islamic legal system that accorded with modern conditions.

54. References to the "Holy Spirit" *rūḥ alqudus* e.g., Q.2:87, are commonly believed by Muslims to refer to the angel Gabriel.

55. B.4:735, also 4:734.

56. Hughes, *Dictionary of Islam*, 25–26.

57. Ibn Ishaq, *Sira*, 115–117 (Guillaume's translation).

58. Siddiqui, *Hadith Literature*, 18.

59. Ibid., 14–15

60. B.1:1.

61. The source of this diagram is Juynboll, "Hadith and the Qur'an," vol. 2, 383, Diagram D.

62. B.6:201; 6:509; 6:551; 9:301.

63. These figures are obtained from various sources, including Khan, *The Translation of the Meanings of Sahih Al-Bukhāri*, vol. 1, xv, and Kutty, "The Six Authentic Books of Hadith," 20.

64. Guillaume, *The Traditions of Islam*, 28, recognizes that other authorities give figures of 7,295 and 7,397 (e.g., Brown, *Hadith*, 32).

65. Guillaume, *Traditions*, 28, citing Houdas. Brown, *Hadith*, 32, agrees with the number of 2,602. Kutty, "The Six Authentic Books of Hadith," 20, gives a figure of 2,762.

66. Guillaume, *Traditions*, 28, quoting Uwaydah, Khan, *Authentication*, 31, cites the larger figure.

67. Rahman, *Islam*, 43.

68. Anderson, *Islam in the Modern World*, 39.

69. Brown, *Rethinking tradition*, 8.

70. Khan, *Authentication*, 139.

71. Rahman, *Islam*, 66 (italics his).

72. Cited in Caner and Caner, *Unveiling Islam*, 96.

2

CLASSIFYING THE HADITH

1. THE CONTENT OF THE HADITH

It is difficult to collate and classify the Hadith. A single hadith may contain several points addressing a variety of topics. They may be unrelated in content, but were reported at the same time.[1] Nor is it easy to determine the context in which they occurred. Like the Qur'an, the Hadith accounts are not in chronological order. This makes it difficult to tell which hadith might have come earlier, indicating an initial reaction, or which came later, indicating perhaps a more mature and measured response.[2] Many of the hadith are repeated, some up to ten times in a single collection, because they have been transmitted by varying routes of *isnād* or chain of transmitters. In Arab culture, repetition is often a means of emphasizing a point, or it may simply be an aid to comprehension. "Whenever the Prophet spoke a sentence (said a thing), he used to repeat it thrice so that the people could understand it properly from him."[3]

Although the topics mentioned in the sidebar (*Headings in the Hadith*) are all found in each hadith in that type, any particular hadith may address a series of topics, so these categories are only a rough indication of content of the hadiths in each category. Many of the groupings contain common material—almost identical accounts of donkeys walking in front of a group of people being led in prayer by the Prophet.[4]

They fall under three different classifications of content, labeled as "Knowledge," "Virtues of the Prayer Hall," and "Characteristics of Prayer."

HEADINGS IN THE HADITH

The compilers of the Hadith have classified them according to content. "In the classical manuals and compilations Hadiths were organized by topics. In the *Sahih* of Bukhārī they are organized under such headings as faith, purification, prayer, alms, fasting, pilgrimage, commerce, inheritance, wills, vows and oaths, crimes, murders, judicial procedure, war, hunting, and wine."[a] The numbers of entries under each heading vary greatly from only six ("revelation" in Book 1:1-6) to over five hundred (prophetic *tafsīr* "commentary" in Book 6:1-501). A full compendium of topics in al-Bukhārī's collection, with the numbers of Hadith listed after them is found in the Appendix.

The broad categories conceal much detail in the Hadith narratives. One hadith,[5] for example, does contain some information about "Characteristics of Prayer," but it also relates the story of a man cursed with a long, difficult life for lying to others.

2. CATEGORIZING THE HADITH

The hadith may be categorized in a variety of ways, based on different criteria.[6]

(a) Based on their origin

There are two types of hadith based on their origin. In a *Hadīth nabawi* ("prophetic hadith"), the Prophet speaks on his own authority, whereas in a *Hadīth qudsi* ("sacred hadith"), God speaks through the mouth of the Prophet. The overwhelming number of hadiths are of the first kind, with only several hundred or so of the second type. The most comprehensive collection, *al-Ahādīth al-Qudsiyyah*, compiled by the Committee of the Qur'an and Hadith of the Higher Council for Islamic Affairs in Egypt in 1978, contains "four hundred Sacred Hadith with different variants where they occur."[7]

Despite this distinction, a claim for divine inspiration for all the Hadith is made by some scholars: "The teachings of Islam are based

a. Lapidus, *History*, 102.

primarily on the Quran and the Hadith and . . . both are based on divine inspiration."[8] One translator of al-Bukhāri's Hadith refers to it as "the Second Inspiration."[9]

(b) Based on their ultimate source

Hadiths may be categorized according to the ultimate source from which they originated (see Table 2).

TYPE	MEANING	DEFINITION	EXAMPLE
Qudsi	"sacred"	Traced back to God	B.4:415
marfū'	"elevated"	Traced back to Muhammad	B.1:1
mawqūf	"stopped"	Traced back to a "companion" i.e. who had met Muhammad	B.1:173
maqtū'	"severed"	Traced back to a "successor" i.e. who had met a 'companion'	B.6:352

TABLE 2: Hadiths categorized based on the ultimate source

These relationships can be depicted in a diagram (see Illustration 2):[10]

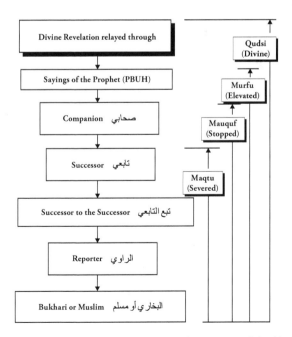

ILLUSTRATION 2: Relationships between the sources of the Hadith

(c) Based on links in the isnād

Hadith may have some gaps in the links between the transmitters (see Table 3).

TYPE	MEANING	DEFINITION	EXAMPLE
musnad	"supported"	No break in the chain back to Muhammad	Muslim Bk 10, no. 3780
muttasil	"continuous"	Uninterrupted chain going back only to a companion or successor	
mursal	"unattached" or "hurried"	The generation between Prophet and successor (i.e., companion) is missing	"No marriage is valid except by the consent of the guardian" (B.9:98).
munqatiʿ	"broken"	The generation between the successor and the compiler is missing	Muhammad prophesied that the Muslims would kill his grandson al-Hussein.[b]
muʿdal	"perplexing"	More than one consecurive reporter is missing	Adam was caught by the hair after he ate the fruit.[c]
muʿallaq or *balaghah*	"hanging" or "reaching"	No isnād, Muhammad is quoted directly	"The differing amongst my Ummah is a mercy."[d]

TABLE 3: Hadith categorized based on their isnāds

b. "Al-Hakim said, 'This is a sahih Hadith according to the conditions of the two Shaykhs (i.e. Bukhāri & Muslim), but they did not collect it.'" Source: http://www.muslimaccess.com/sunnah/hadeeth/scienceofhadith/aape.html (accessed October 14, 2015).

c. Source: http://www. muslimaccess.com/sunnah/hadeeth/scienceofhadith/asb2.html (accessed October 14, 2015).

d. According to al-Subki (d.756 AH), no *isnād* exists for this hadith. Source: http://www. muslimaccess.com/sunnah/hadeeth/scienceofhadith/aape.html#G16 (accessed October 14, 2015).

(d) Based on the number or reporters in each stage of the isnād

Each hadith may have only one or several reporters at each stage of its *isnād* (see Table 4).

TYPE	MEANING		DEFINITION	EXAMPLE
mutawātir	"consecutive"		Multiple reporters at every stage	B.1:109
ahād "single"	*mashūr*	"famous"	At least three reporters at every stage	B.1:239
	'azīz	"strong/ rare"	At least two reporters at every stage	B.1:14
	gharīb	"strange/ scarce"	Only one person at one stage	"Travel is a piece of punishment"[e]
	fard	"solitary"	Reported in only one locality	

TABLE 4: Hadith categorized by number of reporters

(e) Based on the manner or mode in which the Hadith was reported

Hadiths were reported in different ways, using an array of terminology in the *isnād* describing how this hadith was heard from its earlier source (see Table 5).

---

e. "With regard to its isnād, this Hadith is sahih, although most gharib aHadith are weak; Ahmad b. Hanbal said, 'Do not write these gharib aHadith because they are unacceptable, and most of them are weak.'" Source: http://www.muslimaccess.com/sunnah/hadeeth/scienceofhadith/aape.html (accessed October 14, 2015).

TYPE	MEANING	DEFINITION
haddathanī	"he narrated to me"	A recognized teacher recited the hadith to his student.
haddathanā	"he narrated to us"	The teacher recited the hadith to a group of his students.
akhbaranā	"he informed us"	The students repeated the hadith to their teacher and the teacher affirmed its veracity.
+ *'an*	"on the authority of"	There is no clear indication of how the tradition was received.
sami'tu	"I heard"	This indicates that the reporter personally heard the hadith from his own teacher.
qāla	"he said"	This is more vague and can signify either hearing from the teacher in person or through something else.
tadlīs	"concealing"	*tadlīs al-isnād* –narrator reports something from a contemporary whom he never met.
		tadlīs al-shuyūkh –a transmitter's name is concealed by a nickname or other name.
		tadlīs al-taswiyyah –an intermediate weak transmitter's name is omitted.
musalsal	"uniformly linked"	All reporters use the same mode of transmission.

TABLE 5: Hadith categorized by mode of reporting

(f) Based on the nature of the matn and its isnād

The reporters listed in the *isnāds* were not considered of equal reliability (see Table 6).

TYPE	MEANING	DEFINITION	EXAMPLE
Shadhdh	"irregular"	It is reported by a trustworthy person against the narration of a more reliable reporter.	Tirmidhi reported by Abu Huraira "lie on right side after prayer." cf. B.1:599
munkar	"denounced"	The narration of a weak reporter, particularly if it contradicts the general sayings of the Prophet.	'Asma bint Abu Bakr was ordered to treat her mother kindly. c.f. B.8:9
ziyadatu thiqa	"an addition by one trustworthy"	A reliable person reports additional material not found in other authentic sources.	Muslim bk 1 no. 152 Two reporters, Al-Hasan b. Makdam and Bindar, reported it with the addition, ". . .at the beginning of time."
mudraj	"interpolated"	The reporter adds something, e.g., explanation of a difficult word.	"Complete the ablution for the Abu 'l-Qasim . . . said: 'Woe to the heels from the Fire.'" c.f. B.1:57

TABLE 6: Hadith categorized by stringency of reporting

There is an element of subjectivity in these definitions, for hadith reporters and transmitters varied in their stringency.

It should be noted that even these rankings are not absolute. Some scholars of Hadith were stricter than others. The scholars of Hadith themselves are ranked as *"Mo'tadel"* (moderate) such as Al-Zhahabi, *"Motashaddid"* (strict) such as Ibn Al-Jawzi and Al-Daraqutani and *"Mutasahil"* (Lenient) such as Al-Hakim.[11]

(g) Based on defects in the isnād or matn

Some hadiths contained imperfections according to various commentators (see Table 7).

TYPE	MEANING	DEFINITION	EXAMPLE[f]
ma'lūl or *mu'allal*	"defective"	Wrong classification of a hadith or wrong attribution of the companion.	Muslim bk 39 no. 6707
mudtarib	"shaky"	Equally reliable reporters disagree about some points in an *isnād* or text.	B.3:386
maqlūb	"changed" or "reversed"	The name in an *isnād* or the order of a sentence in the text is reversed, or one text or *isnād* is replaced with another.	Muslim bk 5 no. 2248

TABLE 7: Hadith categorized by shortcomings in the text[g]

---

f.   http://www.usc.edu/dept/MSA/fundamentals/hadithsunnah/scienceofhadith/asb6.html (accessed October 14, 2015).

g.   Examples taken from http://www.muslimaccess.com/sunnah/hadeeth/scienceofhadith/aape.html (accessed October 14, 2015).

h.   According to http://mac.abc.se/home/onesr/d/wvmge.pdf (accessed October 14, 2015).

i.   This wording is *da'īf*, but a similar concept is presented by Ibn Majah and al-Nasai. Source: http://www. muslimaccess.com/sunnah/hadeeth/scienceofhadith/aape.html#G21 (accessed October 14, 2015).

j.   According to Al-Khatib al-Baghdadi, it is a statement of al-Hasan al-Basri. Source: http://www.muslimaccess.com/sunnah/hadeeth/scienceofhadith/aape.html (accessed October 14, 2015).

k.   Aly, *People Like Us*, 153, admits: "This famous 'greater jihad' report is of highly questionable historical authenticity. It does not occur in any of the most authoritative collections of narrations of the Prophet, and probably surfaced for the first time among ascetic movements just before al-Ghazzālī's time."

(h) Based on the quality of the reporters

Reporters of hadiths varied in their reliability. Not all were considered equal (see Table 8).

TYPE	MEANING		DEFINITION	EXAMPLE
sahīh 'sound'	*'ādil*	"just"	The reporter was a pious, honest and truthful Muslim.	
	thābit	"steadfast"	The reporter was known for his accuracy.	
	thiqa	"trustworthy"	The reporter was known for his reliability.	
	Hāfid	"memorizing"	The reporter was known for his powers of recollection.	
hasan	"fair		The reporter does not reach the high standards above, but he is not criticized.	"Whoever visits my grave, my intercession will be guaranteed for him."[h]
da'if	"weak"		The reporter was known to have a weak memory or was careless.	"Pardise is under the feet of mothers."[i]
mawdū' or *sakhīm*	"fabricated" or "forged""infirm"		The text goes against the Prophet's norm.	"The ink of the scholar is holier than the blood of the martyr."[j] "We have returned from the lesser Jihad to the greater Jihad (i.e. the struggle against the evil of one's soul.)"[k]
			The *isnād* contains a liar.	
			There is a discrepancy of times or dates.	

TABLE 8: Hadith categorized by trustworthiness of their reporters

These classifications can be depicted in a diagram (see Illustration 3).[12]

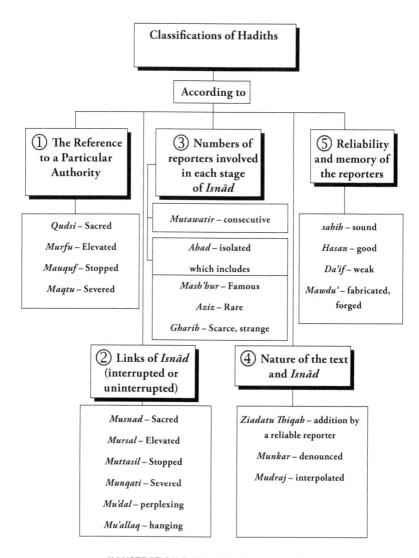

ILLUSTRATION 3: Classifications of hadiths

Besides these major classifications, there are at least sixty other ways of assessing the hadith. These incorporate the *rijāl* ("men") studies of the backgrounds and qualifications of the transmitters, including "the manners required in traditionists," "knowledge of brothers and sisters among reporters," and "knowledge of the dates of birth and death of reporters."[13]

(i) Meccan and Medinan Hadiths

There arises the question of how to identify the chronology in the Hadith. At times, the task appears simple: the conversation about the decision to embark on the "apostasy" *ridda* wars against the rebelling Arab tribes is presented as taking place in the early days of Abū Bakr's caliphate (AD 632–624).[14] Some statements by Muhammad, e.g., "Faith consists of more than sixty branches,"[15] could have been made at any time during his prophetic ministry.

Whether a particular verse or passage of the Qur'an was revealed in Mecca or Medina or earlier or later is often important for the science of *tafsīr* (interpretation). The law of abrogation determines that a later verse abrogates an earlier verse. Crucial in establishing the sequential order of verses is an understanding of the "occasion of revelation" (*asbāb al-nuzūl*). The Hadith collections can be helpful in determining this, for they often identify when and where a certain verse was revealed, allowing the verse's chronological priority to be established. It could be used to settle disputes.

> The people of Kufa disagreed (disputed) about the above Verse. So I went to Ibn Abbas and asked him about it. He said, "This Verse: 'And whoever kills a believer intentionally, his recompense is Hell,' was revealed last of all (concerning premeditated murder) and nothing abrogated it."[16]

Sometimes it is clear whether a particular hadith relates to Mecca or Medina. The hadith which begins, "I came to the Prophet while he was leaning against his sheet cloak in the shade of the Ka'ba. We were suffering greatly from the pagans in those days," is clearly early Meccan, from the period before the *Hijra*. The identity of the source can be an important clue. Aisha, for example, who is responsible for 18 percent of the hadiths, was only eight years old when she left Mecca, so she could hardly have been a reliable witness of the events in Mecca.

3. THE ROLE OF THE HADITH IN THE LIVES OF MUSLIMS

Significantly, the Hadith are preserved in narrative form, as stories. They are not simply ways of passing on historical accounts to be preserved for their own sake. "Stories frequently serve as a means of transmitting behavioural expectations of human relationships. Stories are tribal codes for establishing order in all societies."[17] The Hadith are required to be acted upon. Some would claim that not accepting the Hadith as authoritative deems one to be a *kāfir* (unbeliever).[18] Despite this, they are not seen only as prescribing rules of behavior.

The Hadith have impacted Muslim societies and individuals in at least four ways (see Illustration 4):

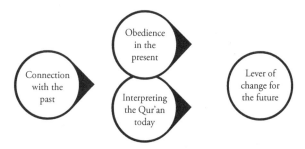

ILLUSTRATION 4: Ways of using the Hadith

(a) A spiritual connection to the past

From the earliest days, many Muslims yearned for a closer union with God. This was sought through spiritual disciplines, such as memorizing the Qur'an or the Hadith. The length of the *isnād* was seen to play a role in this. "The early ascetic Muhammad b. Aslam al-Tūsī (d.242/856) asserted: "Proximity in the *isnād* is proximity— or a means to gain proximity—to God." Ibn al-Salāh [al-Shahrazūrī d.643/1245], after quoting the words of al-Tūsī, continued: "He is right because proximity in the *isnād* is proximity to the Messenger of God and proximity to him is proximity to God."[19]

The eighteenth century saw great changes in the Muslim world. Western colonialism brought economic development and social turmoil. The Neo-Sufi movement arose partly in response to this. It differed from traditional Sufism, for it "restated the goal of the Sufi path in terms of the individual being in harmony with the spirit of the Prophet rather than losing individual identity by absorption into the absolute being."[20] The Hadith took on a new importance. Rejecting medieval scholasticism and classical *tafsīr* (commentaries), Neo-Sufis turned to the original sources, including the earlier collections of the Hadith, which were elevated to a higher status. "Elevation" meant discovering the hadiths with the shortest *isnāds*.

> But the significance of elevation lay in the realm of spirituality rather than the transmission of knowledge. [There were] . . . certain affinities between the circulation of hadīth and the circulation of Prophetic relics. Elevation turned hadīth into a special kind of relic. It allowed the believer to come into a closer contact with the spiritual power of the Prophet. Whereas the believer was stuck at his own historically (inferior) station in terms of years *(ta'rīkh)*, by a different view of time, shorter isnāds allowed him to be closer to the Prophet in terms of generations *(tabaqāt).*[21]

Even a modern Muslim may seek the deeper attachment to Muhammad that the Hadith offer.

> The intimate knowledge we have of Muhammad's life (much of which we owe to Aisha) is, from a practical point of view, just as important as his religious teaching and the example he set in affairs of greater consequence. The believer feels close to him in life and hopes to be closer still after death, loving him not only as master and as guide but also as brother-man. It is in the light of this relationship that we may understand parts of the record which often appear trivial to the occidental.[22]

(b) A code of behavior for daily life

The Hadith were taken seriously by devout Muslims. Ibn Hanbal, the revered founder of the Hanbalite school of Islamic jurisprudence, was reputed never to have eaten watermelon because of the lack of a prophetic hadith concerning it.[23] Many Muslims are comforted by the comprehensive and regulatory nature of the Prophet's *sunnah,* for it determines how they should behave in every situation. "Islam is a complete way of life. It is comprehensive guidance covering all areas of human activity."[24]

(c) An interpretative tool for the Qur'an in the present

Azami suggests that "if there is no other authentic source of knowledge than the Qur'an, and if the reports of the sayings and deeds of the Prophet are rejected as untrustworthy, then the meaning and significance of many of the verses of the Qur'an itself will remain unclear and incomplete." He cites the example of Zaid's divorce[25] and Muhammad's encounter with the blind man.[26] "It is almost impossible to understand or explain the meaning of a large number of Qur'anic verses if the Traditions are rejected as useless and inauthentic."[27]

(d) A lever for change for the future

Rather than simply being an anchor of conservatism within Islam, the Hadith can also operate as a means of renewal. "The use of myth and story is not value-neutral. [People] can use story and storytelling in organisations to describe and sustain the current power structure, or to nurture and fuel creativity and liberation and to develop new meaning."[28] Even old stories may be employed in this way. Brown says: "I would suggest that tradition is not an enemy of change, but the very stuff that is subject to change. Tradition both changes and may be used to justify change; it can, in fact, be revolutionary."[29] He cites ancient examples (Khārijites, 'Abbāsids and Ibn Taymiyya) and modern ones (Iran, Arab Sunni revivalism, and Islamic feminism) as movements that conscript tradition into the fight for change. Instead of looking at tradition as an ancient storehouse enshrouded in darkness and modernity as the source of light, we could see tradition as "a beam of light, refracted by the prism of modernity. A tradition emerges from the prism of modernity as a multi-coloured spectrum of responses."[30]

Despite pointing backwards to the seventh century, the Hadith have been enlisted as a tool by reformers at various stages of history. Shaykh 'Abd al-Haqq Dihlawī (d.1642) championed "a 'reformist' type of Islamic belief which stressed Hadith as the basis of Muslim learning and pious practice opposed to the excesses both of legal studies and of Sufi spirituality."[31] The Moroccan scholar Ahmad bin Idrīs (d.1837) was a proponent of Neo-Sufism on the Arabian peninsula. "When Ahmad's reformism brought him into conflict with the conservative establishment in Mecca, it was as a *muhaddith* [Hadith scholar] that he was publicly examined by a panel of 'ulama [and] . . . was able to confound his critics and emerge with an enhanced reputation."[32]

4. Attitude of this study toward the Hadith

Questions have been raised about the historicity and authenticity of the Hadith by both Muslims and non-Muslims. Not only is the jury still out, but it is vigorously debating these issues. Does this negate the use of the Hadith in such an undertaking as this? Not necessarily. Stories can have a significant impact on individuals and communities even if they are not historical recordings of events which actually occurred. Stories are socially constructed. They have been preserved because they refer to values and themes that are important to the members of an organization.[33] Fables, myths, and legends have a significant role in providing an identity for a community as well as affirming and strengthening its values. Later research may suggest or even prove that these early accounts have little or no basis in reality, or that they reflect the needs and thinking of a later period and are therefore not historically verifiable. Despite this, the teaching embedded in these narratives can continue to fashion and reinforce the tenets of the society because it attributes dependability and legitimacy to them.

Since the Hadith collections are deemed to be true and authoritative by most Muslims, they can be regarded as a *textus receptus*. A parallel can be found in the "canonical criticism" and "post-critical alternative" which is applied to the Old Testament.[34] Such an approach addresses the text as a document which forms and informs the community of faith, rather than simply "as a means to ascertain its genetic history."[35] Clark provides a pragmatic reminder:

> Ultimately the question of the historical validity of these traditions is less important than the fact that they have worked: they have proved able to bring a sacramental sense of the divine into the life of millions of Muslims over the centuries.[36]

This study will proceed on the basis that the Hadith are believed by most Muslims to be a reliable record of the sayings and actions of Muhammad and his companions, and hence have become a source of authority and inspiration for their thinking and actions even today.

NOTES

1. The Hadith read much like Martin Luther's "Table Talk," responding to particular questions asked by people or giving details of events which happened to him and interpreting them for their own situations.

2. Some hadith do record the events during the reigns of later Caliphs, e.g., B.4:326.

3. B.1:94, 95.

4. As found in B.1:76, 474, and 820. This was supposed to annul prayer according to B.1: 486, 490, 493, but Aisha, Muhammad's favorite wife, objected to this saying because it equated dogs and donkeys with women.

5. B.1:722.

6. This area of study is called *mustalah al-Hadīth* "classification of the Hadith." For more detail see http://www.scribd.com/doc/16764070/Mustalah-Al-Hadith. Much of the material from this section was adapted from Reem Azzam, "Modern Historical Methodology vs. Hadeeth Methodology." Source: http://www.muslimaccess.com/sunnah/hadeeth/historyandhadeeth/azzamcomparison.html (accessed October 14, 2015) and Robson, "Hadīth," vol. 3, 25-26.

7. According to Ibrahim and Johnson-Davies, *Forty Hadith Qudsi*, 16.

8. Hamidullah, *Introduction to Islam*, 23.

9. Khan, *The Translation of the Meaning of Sahih Al-Bukhāri*, xvii.

10. Source: http://www.muslimaccess.com/sunnah/hadeeth/scienceofhadith/brief1/introduction.htm (accessed October 14, 2015).

11. Source: http://ibnayyub.wordpress.com/2007/10/31/the-science-of-hadith-based-on-classic-primers (accessed October 14, 2015).

12. Source: http://www.muslimaccess.com/sunnah/hadeeth/scienceofhadith/brief1/introduction.htm (accessed October 14, 2015).Note that this diagram follows different transliteration conventions.

13. See Azami, *Studies.*

14. B.2:483.

15. B.1:8.

16. B.6:114.

17. Hansen and Kahnweiler, "Storytelling," 1391.

18. Source: http://islamicsystem.blogspot.com/2007/11/refutation-of-gadaffi-others-who-reject.html.

19. Dickinson, "Ibn al-Salāh al-Shahrazūrī and the isnād," 503.

20. Voll, *Islam,* 36.

21. Dickinson, "Ibn al-Salāh al-Shahrazūrī and the isnād," 481.

22. Eaton, *Destiny*, 186.

23. Robinson, *Christ in Islam and Christianity,* 75.

24. Sarwar, *Islam,* 13.

25. Q.33:37.

26. Q.80:1-3.

27. Azami, *The Sunnah in Islam,* 29-31.

28. Boyce, "Organisational story and storytelling," 10.

29. Brown, *Rethinking*, 2. This is reminiscent of Jeremiah's radical call to Israel to return to "the ancient paths . . . where the good way is, and walk in it, and you will find rest for your souls" (Jer 6:16).

30. Brown, *Rethinking tradition in modern Islamic thought*, 3.

31. Lapidus, *A History of Islamic Societies*, 450.

32. Voll, *Islam: Continuity and Change in the Modern World*, 78. By contrast, Moroccan Sultan Muhammad ibn Abdallah (r.1757-1790) used the Hadith to support his fundamentalist views. His son, Malway Suleyman (r.1792-1822), opposed Sufi tendencies and sent a delegation to Mecca for consultation with the Wahhabis, later accepting

many of their interpretations. Voll, *Islam: Continuity and Change in the Modern World*, 102.

33.   Polkinghorne, *Narrative Knowing and the Human Sciences.*

34.   This is the approach by Childs, *Introduction*, 109-135.

35.   LaSor et al, *Survey*, 13.

36.   Clark, *Islam*, 38.

3

CAN CHRISTIANS USE THE HADITH?

1. APPROACH OF THIS BOOK

The focus of this book will be an examination of the *matn* (contents) of the Al-Bukhāri's Hadith collection, accompanied by analysis and theological reflection. This study will seek to categorize the Hadith literature and assess how its various texts may serve as a diagnostic tool and resource for responses by Christians to *dār al-islām* (the house of Islam).

(a) Two lenses of assessment

The Hadith will be assessed through two lenses.

First, they will be evaluated positively from a comparative viewpoint. The goal of this method is to find the common ground between Muslims and Christians. There is shared truth which can be openly declared. "We will want to see how far we can walk along the same road with the Muslim before we come to the fork where our paths diverge."[1] This can occur without denying or betraying one's own faith commitment. There can be forward movement side by side, like a pair of railway tracks, without stepping in the other's footprints. Truth should be recognized even if it does not originate within one's own faith tradition. Yāqūb ibn Ishāq al-Kindy, "the Arab Philosopher" (d.259/873), states: "We should not shy away from welcoming and acquiring the truth regardless of where it came from, even if it came from distant races and nations that are different from us. Nothing is more important than seeking the truth, except the truth itself. We should not belittle the truth, or those who utter it or bring it."[2]

Christian apologists have long suggested that all truth comes from God, with Jesus as the *logos* of the universe through whom the world was created.[3] Justin Martyr rather boldly announced that "whatever things were rightly said among all men are the property of us Christians."[4] The Bible proclaims that in Christ "are hidden all the treasures of wisdom and knowledge."[5] St. Augustine of Hippo is reputed to have said, "Truth, wherever it is to be found, it is the Lord's. Even the gold of Egypt is still gold."[6] Echoing this, Parshall notes that "truth is truth wherever it is to be found."[7] The conservative theologian Benjamin Warfield (1851–1921) applied this approach broadly.

> We must not then, as Christians, assume an attitude of antagonism towards the truths of reason, or the truths of philosophy, or the truths of science, or the truths of history, or the truths of criticism. As children of the light, we must be careful to keep ourselves open to every ray of light. Let us, then, cultivate an attitude of courage as over against the investigations of the day. None should be more quick to discern truth in every field, more hospitable to receive it, more loyal to follow it, whithersoever it leads.[8]

Secondly, the Hadith will be assessed from the perspective of biblical teaching in order to find springboards to truth which will be helpful in the apostolate to Islam. Every religious system contains some links which can be starting points for connection to a biblical perspective, and Islam is no exception. Many historical examples of such cultural adaptation exist (see Sidebar *Cultural Adaptation*).

One of the goals of this study is to identify these links and determine ways in which they can be developed.

This approach taps into the stream of general revelation for Christians who "believe that God uses general revelation as a type of preparation for the special revelation of the Bible . . . [because] general revelation results in indirect components in a culture that provide bridges for understanding religious truths found in the Bible."[9]

Kraft suggests that "we should (1) take seriously those passages of Scripture (e.g. Acts 14:17; 17:22-31; Rom. 1, 2; Gen. 14:18-20) that indicate that God has been at work with every people at every time; (2) that, therefore, Christian witnesses need to be diligent in discovering such workings (e.g. in redemptive analogies)."[10]

CULTURAL ADAPTATION

Cultural adaptation was recommended by Francis Xavier and applied by sixteenth-century Jesuits to Chinese and Indian culture and religion.[a] The concept of "redemptive analogies," finding elements of non-Christian religion and traditions which illustrated Christian truths, was developed by Richardson.[b] Other examples could include the use of the Talmud[c] in witness by Messianic Jews. Some have found pointers within ancient Chinese characters to the truths of primeval history revealed in the book of Genesis. They claim that this is a verification of Paul's declaration about God: "He did not leave Himself without witness."[d]

---

a. Ronan and Oh, *East Meets West*. Robert de Nobili in India and Matteo Ricci in China used this approach.

b. Richardson, *Eternity* and *Peace Child*. Richardson's approach has been criticized, e.g., Glasser "Old Testament Contextualisation," 38. Remarkably, Richardson himself disavows the use of Islamic motifs in discovering bridges of truth. "I learned that Islam is unique among non-Christian religions. It stands alone as the only belief system that, due to its very design, *frustrates* anyone who seeks to use the redemptive-analogy approach . . . The more digging I did into the Koran the more I realised when it comes to Islam the redemptive-analogy approach cannot work" (italics his). Richardson, Secrets, 18–19.

c. Taylor, "Al-Bukhāri and the Aggada," 191–202, speculates on parallels between al-Bukhāri and the Talmud.

d. Acts 14:17. Kang and Nelson, *Discovery*, 10.

The identification and application of such material will constitute the major focus of this work. This need not lead to compromising the truth of the Bible.

> To proclaim relevantly therefore is not, as Helmut Thielicke observes, "To accommodate ourselves or ape those we would reach." Far from it. Paul actually contradicted the Greeks and Jews and showed them God was completely different to what they had expected. But it was in terms of *their* suppositions and notions that he searched them out. He met their questions on their level. That makes all the difference. He did not ape what they were saying just to make the Gospel palatable.[11]

As careful a scholar as Kenneth Cragg has advocated the use of Islamic texts in presenting the reality of Christ. He asks rhetorically:

> If Muslims are to understand new truth, or find fuller implications in admitted truth, will it not be as the Quran can be recruited to their help? . . . The Muslim's Scripture has too often been undervalued by Christians for what we may perhaps call its "Christian potential."[12]

This approach should be just as applicable to the Hadith.

(b) Why this approach is applied

Some may question the value of such an approach. Is it worthwhile to expend the time and effort to examine the traditions of others, such as the Hadith of the Muslim faith? Surely Christian history and theology is a rich enough lode to quarry without needing to access other religious systems. There are, however, pedogogical and missiological reasons for engaging with the texts of another faith.

First, this may be the best way to communicate. It is an axiom of teaching to proceed from the known to the unknown. "To be meaningful to people, the gospel and the church must be expressed in cultural forms they understand and trust. . . . The missionary must identify with another culture to communicate the gospel in ways those people understand. . . . Theology must answer the questions they face."[13]

Second, it helps Christians and others to understand Muslims. When William Carey produced a one thousand-page book on Sanskrit grammar and translated Hindu classics into English, he was criticized in England by friends of the Baptist Missionary Society which sent him.[14] He retorted: "Those who are to be employed in propagating the Gospel should be familiar with the doctrines he is to combat and the doctrines he is to teach, and acquire a complete knowledge both of the Sacred Scriptures, and of those philosophical and mythological dogmas which form the soul of the Buddhist and Hindoo Systems."[15]

Third, it says something significant to the hearers. Refusing to even consider the belief systems of others may be seen at best as condescending, but at worst as a scornful dismissal of what they hold precious. Christian workers have sometimes fallen into this trap. Some mid-nineteenth-century missionaries were positivists who believed that the gospel must be translated literally, expressed in identical words and symbols, or the meaning would be lost. "There was a widespread fear that the use of native symbol forms would introduce 'pagan' meanings that would lead to syncretism. Consequently, the use of local symbols was widely rejected. . . . Conversion involved not only following Christ, but also adopting Western cultural forms."[16]

Robinson suggests an alternative: "People do have different backgrounds, preferences, and tastes. Cultures vary. Communication of any form, including communication of the gospel, requires respect for the background and sensitivity of the hearers."[17]

(c) Christian missional responses to the Hadith

Christians involved with Muslims in missional contexts have taken a variety of approaches toward Islam in general and the Hadith in particular (see Illustration 5). Pfander (1803-1865) emphasized the differences between Islam and Christianity, resulting in a more confrontational stance. The Hadith were often cited to highlight shortcomings in the behavior of Muhammad.[18] Zwemer (1867-1952), initially adversarial but later more irenic, sought ways to declare Christian truth, with Islamic teaching as the backdrop.[19] Cragg (b.1913) looked for similarities that could enhance dialogue.[20] The development of these different stances may reflect political changes from a colonial and imperialistic past evolving to the more modern multicultural and inclusive attitudes.

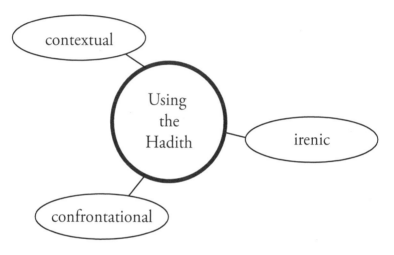

ILLUSTRATION 5: Christian responses to the Hadith

Another approach has been one of contextualization. Contemporary writer Phil Parshall searched for dynamic equivalents in Islamic doctrine, practice, and culture,[21] and he has written on the Hadith.[22] His analysis of the Hadith is not confrontational[23] and is appreciative of the good in Islam.[24] He does not ignore the shortcomings of Islam and Muslims[25] and is equally willing to criticize Christianity and the West.[26] He seeks for ways to share Christ appropriately.[27] However, the book shows little evidence of extensive research[28] and is clearly written to appeal to a popular audience. Ultimately Parshall's approach is more informational than missional. Gudel's short article gives a justification for a missional approach using the Qur'an and the Hadith. Yet he only provides general encouragement and gives no methodology or specific examples from the Hadith.[29] Clearly, little work has been done in this area.

2. THE USE OF ONE RELIGIOUS SYSTEM TO SUPPORT OR PROMOTE A DIFFERENT ONE

It will be suggested in this study that the Hadith offer links to biblical truth, but the question needs to be asked: How fair or honest is it to appropriate aspects of one religious tradition to support or promote a different approach?

(a) Examples from history

The use of elements from another culture or religion took place at a material level at the Exodus from Egypt. The gold, silver, and cloth despoiled from the Egyptians[30] were most likely used to provide the lavish furnishings of the tabernacle.[31] Gifts, tribute, and plunder from foreign nations were dedicated to divine service by the early kings of Israel.[32] In Isaiah's eschatological vision, the tribute of the pagan nations pours into Jerusalem, providing acceptable sacrifices for Yahweh's temple.[33]

The objection may be raised that these were simply physical objects, which can be religiously neutral, and are significantly less central than ideas.[34] Moses was, however, willing to heed the wisdom of his father-in-law, Jethro, the Midianite priest.[35] Later Moses, as he led the people of God through the wilderness, sought the guidance of Hobab, his pagan brother-in-law, to "know where we should camp in the wilderness." "You can be our eyes,"[36] Moses told him. Borrowing from or relying on objects and concepts which were not direct divine revelation was clearly acceptable.

One famous missionary suggested other non-material appropriation. Thomas Valpy French (1825-1890) was the first bishop of Lahore in Pakistan. He appreciated the wide range and the richness of Indian literature. He queried, "Is it more profitable to Christianity . . . that this store should be thrown away as valueless for the purpose of Gospel extension?" Citing Micah 4:13, "I will consecrate their gain unto the Lord, and their substance unto the Lord of the whole earth" (KJV), he asks: "Is the wealth of India's literary treasures less available, less capable of consecration to the highest and holiest purposes than the merchant spoil of Tyre? . . . Is not the attempt to use it for the Lord's service worth making?"[37]

The idea of using tenets of another religion to present one's own religion is well established in the Bible. Whereas critical approaches find the contrasts between various belief systems, contextualization searches for the similarities.

The Bible was not revealed in a vacuum. Many nations existed nearby as Holy Scripture was being revealed to the Jewish nation, and evidence of the ideas and cultural forms of these communities is found in the Bible. Biblical examples of borrowing and adaptation of ideas from other religions and traditions abound.

(b) Contextualization in the Old Testament

Although warned against mimicking the idolatry of the nations around them, the Israelites adopted and adapted pagan forms. In some cases this led to apostasy or syncretism, but in other cases it led to a broader and deeper expression of Judaistic religion. The new form became a perfectly adequate way of operating faithfully. The anthropological distinction between "form" and "meaning" is helpful here, for a particular cultural object or activity ("form" or denotation) may have a different association ("meaning" or connotation) in another context.[38]

The name of the Canaanite high god, *El,* is applied to *Yahweh*, the God of the Hebrews.[39] The Babylonian high god *'Elahh* is similarly adopted. This Chaldean word for "God" occurs as an appellation for Yahweh ninety-five times.[40] Abraham followed Nuzi inheritance laws in working out his family bequests.[41] Hittite Suzerainty treaties may have provided a template for the Mosaic law,[42] the Elamite Code of Hammurabi had similar content,[43] and close parallels existed between Jewish and Hittite sacrifice laws.[44] Solomon's temple appears to be based on Phoenician architecture of the same era.[45]

There is also evidence of literary dependence and borrowing. The Old Testament writers were operating in a context of other documents to which they referred (see Table 9).

The Book of the Wars of the Lord	Numbers 21:14,15
The Book of Jasher	Joshua 10:13; 2 Samuel 1:18
The Records of Nathan the prophet	2 Chronicles 9:29
The Prophecy of Ahijah the Shilonite	
The Visions of Iddo the Seer	
The Book of the Annals of King David	1 Chronicles 27:24
The Book of the Annals of Solomon	1 Kings 11:41
The Book of the Annals of the Kings of Judah	1 Kings 14:29; 15:7,23; 22:45; 2 Kings 8:23; 12:19; 14:18; 15:6, 36; 16:19; 20:20; 21:17,25; 23:28; 24:5
The Book of the Annals of the Kings of Israel	1 Kings 11:41; 14:19; 15:31; 16:5,14,20,27; 22:39; 2 Kings 1:18; 10:34; 13:8,12; 14:15,28; 15:11,15,21,26,31; 2 Chronicles 20:34; 33:18
The Book of the Annals	Nehemiah 12:23; Esther 2:23
The Book of the Annals of the Kings of Media and Persia	Esther 10:2

TABLE 9: List of books referred to in the Old Testament

Unnamed poets are also quoted.[46] In a number of situations, there seems to be direct literary accession. The Wisdom literature of Israel shows a remarkable likeness to the teaching of nearby nations. These include the Egyptian *Teaching of Amenemope*,[47] Babylonian *Counsels of Wisdom* from the Kassite period (1500-1100 B.C.),[48] Egyptian *Instructions of Vizier Ptah-hotep*,[49] Mesopotamian literature in Sumerian and Akkadian,[50] and some quotes comparable to the book of Job in a Babylonian theodicy from the period c.1000 B.C.[51] Akhenaten's hymn to Aten[52] "is quite similar to Psalm 104, and some direct borrowing is possible."[53]

Old Testament scholar William LaSor sees the divine hand in all this. He speaks of "the condescension of God in utilising literary forms and legal customs as the most suitable vehicles for revealing his purposes to his children in the most easily understandable and clearly comprehensible manner."[54]

(c) Contextualization in the New Testament

This approach continues in the New Testament. Jesus quoted well-known proverbs[55] and even nursery rhymes,[56] although He clearly did not accept all popular wisdom.[57] Every item in the Lord's Prayer has parallels in the Old Testament or Jewish literature (e.g., Ben Sirach, Pirke Aboth). Paul quoted pagan philosophers,[58] even calling one of them "a prophet."[59]

There are many books quoted from or alluded to in the New Testament (see Tables 10 and 11).

i) Jewish non-biblical books

NAME OF BOOK	REFERENCES	NEW TESTAMENT REFERENCE
Judith	8:4-6	Luke 2:37
	8:24,25	1 Corinthians 10:9,10
Book of Wisdom	3:5,6	1 Peter 1:6,7
	3:7	Matthew 13:43
	7:26,27	Hebrews 1:3
Tobit	12:12,15	1 Corinthians 15:29; Revelation 5:8; 8:3,4
Ben Sirach	5:11	James 1:19
Baruch	3:29	John 1:14;3:13,38;4:7; 1 Corinthians 10:20
	4:9	Luke 13:29
2 Maccabeus	7:1-29	Hebrews 11.35b
	12:44	1 Corinthians 15:29
Psalms of Solomon	2:6	Romans 16:7
Ascension of Isaiah	1:9; 5:2; 5:14	Hebrews 11:37
Assumption of Moses		Jude 9,14
Apocalypse of Isaiah : Martyrdom of Isaiah		Hebrews 11:37
Apocalypse of Elijah		1 Corinthians 2:9; Ephesians 5:14
Enoch	1:9	Jude 4,6,13, 14-16
Book of Jannes and Jambres		2 Timothy 3:8
Ecclesiasticus	36:20	1 Corinthians 6:13

TABLE 10: Jewish non-biblical books

ii) Greek books

AUTHOR	NAME OF WORK	NEW TESTAMENT REFERENCE
Aratus	*Phaenomena*	Acts 17:28b
Epimenidas	*Cretica*	Titus 1:12; Acts 17:28a
Menander	*Thais*	1 Corinthians 15:33
Euripides	*Bacchus*	Acts 26:14

TABLE 11: Greek books

iii) Unknown book:

Book of the Wisdom of God–Luke 11:49

According to Accad, there are at least 133 references or quotes from other books in the New Testament.[60]

A Lausanne paper concludes:

> Biblical writers were familiar with the religious and secular writings of their neighbours. Biblical writers borrowed certain expressions and concepts from other sources. So did Jesus. Borrowing did not imply total agreement with the original, which was sometimes adapted even to the extent of teaching a totally different point from the original. Paul contextualised his message to suit Greek or Jewish audiences. This would suggest a similar freedom in the use of the Qur'an.[61]

By analogy, we could apply a similar approach to use of the Hadith.

Some scholars have noted that the borrowing has not been only in the direction of the Bible. The Qur'an appears to have borrowed from others. Al-Suyūti, in *Itqān fī 'Ulūm al- Qur'an,* found 275 non-Arabic words in the Qur'an, and Jeffery has identified 118 words which were appropriated from languages other than Arabic.[62] Woodberry states: "What have come to be known as the 'pillars' of Islam are all adaptations of previous Jewish and Christian forms."[63]

Hughes, writing a century earlier, claimed that only Judaism was accessed in this way:

> Muhammad took little of his religious system from Christianity. He was vastly indebted to Judaism both for his historical narratives and his doctrines and precepts. Islam is nothing more or less than Judaism plus the Apostleship of Muhammad. The teachings of Jesus form no part of his religious system.[64]

O'Leary refuses to come down on one side or another, but recognizes that extensive borrowing did occur: "It has been disputed whether Muhammad owed most to Jewish or Christian predecessors, apparently he owed a great deal to both."[65] As we shall see, there is also a significant amount of common material in the Bible and the Hadith.[66] Firestone suggests that similar material in two sources need not require the supposition of direct borrowing of one from the other.

> The existence of parallels can . . . be explained simply by the fact that they both derive from the same original revelation. . . . The traditions found in the Islamic sources . . . cannot be simply reduced to inaccurate reproductions of biblical sources. Like all human creations, they are indebted to an infinite series of associations with earlier and contemporaneous creations. . . . The historical and literary evidence is consistent in supporting the existence of biblicist legends in the Arabian peninsula before the birth of Muhammad. . . . Part of the sublimity of the Qur'an was its success in rendering biblicist traditions that had found their way into Arabia meaningful to the indigenous non-biblicist Arab population—to provide the framework for successful diffusion. . . . The qur'anic stories, references, and allusions to characters found in the Bible were not made up or adapted from biblical texts. The revelation rather drew heavily upon the corpus of monotheistic traditions extant in the Arabian

hijaz in the late sixth century, which was at least recognised if not well known by most of its inhabitants. Much of it was derived from a Biblicist milieu, although some was derivative of other sources as well. . . . The mass of extant Biblicist and hybrid Biblicist-Arabian material represented a pool of monotheistic lore that was recognizable and available as the basis for the sacred history of a newly-evolving monotheism, Islam. It was a natural source of monotheistic wisdom in relation to which the revelations of the Qur'an would be meaningful.[67]

Historians holding such a view would be looking for the common source material which both biblical and Islamic literature accessed.

(d) Does utilization imply dependence?

This study attempts to reverse the order chronologically by beginning with the content of the Hadith and working backwards to the ideas of the Bible. Would this methodology make biblical teaching subject to or dependent upon the teaching of the Qur'an and Hadith? Not necessarily. A properly built edifice stands independently of the scaffolding used in its construction. Scaffolding is a temporary device used only while the structure is being erected.

It is not intended to have any role beyond that. The Hadith may serve as "mental scaffolding" for Muslims as they seek to understand the Bible. Some scholars have used both a physical and a literary metaphor to express a relationship between the Qur'an and the Bible. "There are 'stepping stones' in the Qur'an that can lead Muslims to Christ, notably the references to Jesus himself. It is like a palimpsest written over an imperfectly

ILLUSTRATION 6: Early Qur'anic palimpsest with original text underneath.[e]

---

e.   Source: http://historyofinformation.com/expanded.php?id=217 (accessed January 20, 2016).

erased biblical text. Our calling is to help Muslims 'see the biblical text underneath'"[68] (see Illustration 6).

In a like manner, the glimpses of truth found in the Hadith may point Muslims to the full-orbed revelation found in Holy Scripture.

The concept of using a source that the speaker does not necessarily rely on or need as confirmation for what they are saying is found in the statement of Jesus to the Jews about John the Baptist. Jesus said: "You have sent to John and he has testified to the truth. Not that I accept human testimony; but I mention it that you may be saved."[69] Morris comments on these verses: "The whole emphasis of this passage is on the divine attestation of Jesus. His purpose in referring to John, then, is not to adduce further confirmation of what He already knows from God. It is to direct the attention of His hearers to that which might bring them to salvation. John's witness, if heeded, could start them out on the path that leads to salvation."[70]

Jesus was clear that his credentials relied on the testimony of his Father,[71] of Jesus himself,[72] his own works (miracles),[73] and the previous Scriptures.[74] Consequently he did not need any further human testimony. However, some Jews may have needed more than this, and so John the Baptist was sent to them.

Likewise there is more than sufficient revelation in the Bible for salvation.[75] However, some Muslims, like the Jews of Jesus' day, may need more than this to begin to understand the gospel. The Hadith could be one of the stepping-stones in this process. But it would not be expected that the Hadith would be needed beyond that for their faith. As Paul wrote in another context, "When perfection comes, the imperfect disappears."[76]

This topic is revisited briefly later.[77]

NOTES

1.   Chapman, *Cross and Crescent*, 324.

2.   *Arab Development Report*, 32. A frequently quoted hadith is "Seek knowledge, even if you have to go to China." According to an important Islamic website on the Hadith, this account is spurious. "This additional statement is found in a few of the (weak) narrations of the previous hadith, and is declared as maudu' by Ibn Hibban,

Ibn al- Jauzi, al-Sakhawi and al-Albani. (Al-Da'ifah, no. 416; Da'if al-Jami' al- Saghir, nos. 1005-6)." Source: http://www. muslimac-cess.com/sunnah/hadeeth/scienceofhadith/afor.html#F2 (accessed October 14, 2015).

3.   John 1:1-3.

4.   Justin Martyr, *Second Apology,* xiii, http://www.earlychristianwritings. com/text/justinmartyr-secondapology.html (accessed October 14, 2015).

5.   Col 2:3.

6.   Bell, *Grace for Muslims?*, 68.

7.   Parshall, *Bridges*, 19.

8.   Cited in Collins, *Language*, 178-179.

9.   Moreau, *Contextualization*, 66-67.

10.   Kraft, "Distaste for the Combative Approach," 140.

11.   Michael Cassidy, "Third Way," quoted in John Harrower, *What is Contextualisation?* Source: http://bushchurchaid.com.au/pdf/What_is_Contextualisation_Bishop_John_Harrower.pdf (accessed October 14, 2015).

12.   Cragg, "Islamic Theology," 197.

13.   Hiebert, *Cultural Anthropology*, xxi.

14.   Neill, *History*, 264.

15.   Walker, *Carey*, 237.

16.   Hiebert, "Form and Meaning," 103.

17.   Robinson, *Transforming*, 45.

18.   Pfander, *Mizanu'l Haqq.*

19.   E.g., Zwemer, *Moslem Christ.*

20.   E.g., Cragg, *Muhammad and the Christian.*

21.   E.g., Parshall, *Muslim Evangelism.*

22.   Parshall, *Inside the Community* (1994), reprinted as *Understanding Muslim Teachings and Traditions* (2002).

23.   Ibid., 14, 211.

24.   Ibid., 68.

25.   Ibid., 63, 85.

26.   Ibid., 98-99, 180.

27.   Ibid., 98-99, 180.

28.   He cites only ten books in his bibliography, seven of which are of his own authorship.

29. Joseph P. Gudel, "Using the Qur'an and the Hadith as a bridge for sharing the gospel," in *Christian Research Journal*, vol. 27, no. 1 (2004). Source: http://www.equip.org (accessed October 14, 2015).

30. Ex 3:21–22; 11:2–3; 12:35–36.

31. Ex 25:1–9. It was probably used in building the golden calf as well, providing an object lesson about the dangers of syncretism.

32. 2 Sam 8:7–12; 1 Chr 18:7–11.

33. Isa 60:7; 66:19–21.

34. Polkinghorne (*Narrative,* 3) argues that the "material" realm is the most basic and lowest in the hierarchy of reality, and is exceeded by the "organic" when life emerges, with the highest being the "meaning" structures where consciousness resides. According to Qutb (*The Islamic Concept,* 60), Plato would have agreed with this schema, as would Georg Hegel (1770-1831), who taught that Mind is real and Matter is its reflection.

35. Ex 18:12–24.

36. Num 10:29–34.

37. Stacey, "Attitudes," 31.

38. Kraft, *Anthropology,* chapter 9, "Forms and meanings," 132 ff.

39. Gen 14:18–22.

40. Between Ezra 4:24 and 7:26, and Dan 2:11 and 6:26. It also occurs once in Jer 10:11 in Aramaic, where it refers to the pagan gods who will perish. Strong's concordance ref. H.426. Source: http://www.blueletterbible.org/lang/lexicon/lexicon.cfm?Strongs=H426&t=KJV (accessed October 14, 2015).

41. Pritchard, *Ancient Near Eastern Texts,* 219 H (2) = Gen 15:2-3; p. 543 (4) = Gen 16:1-4; p. 220 (3) = Gen 17:19-22.

42. Thompson, "Covenant (OT)," vol. 1, 791.

43. Youngblood, *Heart,* 71.

44. Rogerson and Davies, *Old Testament World,* 96.

45. La Sor, *Survey,* 194, and Meyers, "Temple, Jerusalem", vol .6, 330–369. This is not surprising, since the builders were Phoenician (1 Kgs 5:1).

46. Num 21:27–30.

47. Eliade, *From Primitives to Zen,* 553–554.

48. La Sor, *Survey,* 449.

49. Ibid., 448.

50. Ibid., 450.

51. Ibid., 452-453.

52. Pritchard, *Ancient Near Eastern Texts*, 369-370. This was the work of Pharaoh Amenhotep IV, who ruled c.1370-1360 BC.

53. Rogerson and Davies, *Old Testament World*, 94.

54. Youngblood, *Heart*, 71.

55. Luke 12:54; 4:23.

56. Luke 7:32.

57. Cf. John 9:2.

58. Acts 17:28.

59. Epimenedes in Titus 1:12.

60. Accad, *Bridges*, 26.

61. Association of Evangelicals in Africa, et al., *Ministry in Islamic contexts*, 32.

62. Jeffery, *Foreign Vocabulary*.

63. Woodberry, "Contextualisation among Muslims," 254.

64. Hughes, *Dictionary*, 236.

65. O'Leary, *Greek Science*, 46.

66. See especially chapter 7, part 3.

67. Firestone, *Journeys*, 8, 156-157.

68. Lausanne, *Ministry*, 32.

69. John 5:33-34.

70. Morris, *John*, 326.

71. John 5:32, 37; 8:18.

72. John 8:12-18.

73. John 5:36; 10:25, 38; 14:11.

74. John 5:39, 46; Luke 24:27.

75. See John 20:30-31.

76. 1 Cor 13:10.

77. See Chapter 17 Parts 11 & 12

II

FINDING CONCORD

BEGINNING WITH THE POSITIVE

It is possible, from a Christian perspective, to affirm some of what Islam teaches. Zwemer noted: "To help our Moslem brethren to answer this question ["What think ye of Christ?"] we must . . . lead them up to higher truth by admitting all of the truth which they possess."[1] Some themes in the Hadith resonate clearly with biblical teaching. Several significant Christian scholars of Islam are optimistic about uncovering helpful links between Islam and Christianity. According to Kraft, Islam, despite coming later than Christianity, conformed to some pre-Christian ideals. He believed that Islam could be considered chronologically AD, but informationally BC.[2] Chapman challenges his readers to look at New Testament Judaism, which was the context into which Christianity was born. He then asks about Islam, "Can it sometimes be a genuine preparation for the gospel?"[3] William Temple Gairdner (AD 1873–1924), CMS missionary in Cairo, believed so, referring to Islam as a *preparatio evangelica*.[4] This study will consider ways in which the teaching of the Hadith may prepare Muslims for a deeper understanding about Christian belief.

In the next chapters, we will consider two potential models: concord and connection.

NOTES

1.   Zwemer, *Moslem Christ,* 8.

2.   Kraft, *Christianity in Culture,* 402.

3.   Chapman, *Cross and Crescent,* 275.

4.   Kerr, "Christian Mission," 12. This concept of *preparation evangelica* merits further study. It has been applied to other religions as well as elements of culture. However, its applicability and limits should be explored, along with the issue of discontinuity. See Figure 4 for some examples and several references.

4

POSITIVE ASPECTS OF
MUHAMMAD'S LIFE

1. HIS CHARACTER—A COMPARISON WITH MOSES

Muhammad has many similarities with the biblical Moses.[1] Both gave leadership in political, military, social, and religious arenas. They brought their followers from a position of disarray and subjugation to a place of victory, freedom, and development. Both had suffered opposition and rejection in their earlier years, but died as successful leaders. Both had more than one wife. According to the Hadith, they met in heaven during Muhammad's lifetime. Accounts of the *mi'rāj* (Muhammad's ascent to heaven) have Moses welcoming Muhammad as "a pious Prophet and a pious brother."[2]

In character, there were also some likenesses.

(a) Obedience and application of the law

The Hadith reveal Muhammad as epitomizing *murūwa* (Arab manhood). His bravery was notable,[3] a characteristic evident in Moses.[4] Muhammad was referred to as "the best of all the people in character."[5] His rigorous application of the *hudūd* (prescribed punishments) included ordering the tooth of a girl to be pulled out in *Qisās* (retaliation) after she slapped another girl whose tooth broke.[6] He claimed that he would have commanded amputating the hand of his own daughter Fātima if she had stolen.[7] The context was a legal ruling.

"A woman from the tribe of Makhzum committed theft. She was brought to [Muhammad] and she sought refuge (intercession) from Umm Salamah, the wife of [the Prophet]. Thereupon Allah's Apostle (peace be upon him) said: 'By Allah, even if she were Fatimah [his daughter], I would have her hand cut off.' And thus her hand was cut off."[8] In a similar way, Moses called the Levites to strap on their swords and kill those, including their own brothers, friends, and neighbors, who were involved in the incident of the golden calf.[9] Both Israel's lawgiver[10] and Islam's prophet gave the command and oversaw the execution of lawbreakers by stoning.[11] Like Jeremiah,[12] Muhammad was commanded by God not to pray for certain people.[13]

According to one of his enemies, Muhammad did not lie, but kept his promises.[14] Concerning the faithful God who spoke to Moses "face to face,"[15] it is asserted that "not one word has failed of all the good promises he gave through his servant Moses."[16]

MUHAMMAD AND MATERIALISM

He refused to wear a silk cloak to impress others.[a] He removed a silk shirt after wearing it once, saying, "It is not the dress of Allah-fearing pious people." He announced, "A well-dressed (soul) in this world may be naked in the Hereafter."[b] Yet he allowed two men to wear silk due to skin diseases.[c] Clothing, household furnishings, and wealth that distracted him from prayer were discarded.[d] His lifestyle was simple, at times verging on poverty. When he died, his suit of iron armor was still mortgaged to a Jew in exchange for barley grains that Muhammad had bought on credit.[e] He left behind few possessions.[f]

---

a.   B.2:11, 69; 4:289.

b.   B.1:372; B.1:115.

c.   B.4:168, 170, 171, 172; 7:730.

d.   B.1:369, 370, 719; B.1:371; B.1:810; 2:511.

e.   B.3:282, 283, 309, 404, 453, 454, 571, 685, 686, 690; 4:165; 5:743.

f.   B.4:2, 125, 160, 330; 5:738.

Muhammad was scrupulous about material possessions (see Sidebar *Muhammad and Materialism*).
Similarly Moses

> refused to be known as the son of Pharaoh's daughter. He chose to be mistreated along with the people of God rather than to enjoy the pleasures of sin for a short time. He regarded disgrace for the sake of Christ as of greater value than the treasures of Egypt, because he was looking ahead to his reward.[17]

Like Moses, Muhammad claimed access to the divine voice which gave him an advantage in judging the secret actions and motives of people,[18] but later leaders were able to judge only external actions.[19] Muhammad asserted that judging justly between two people was a source of *sadaqa* (charity).[20] However, on one occasion, he gave the responsibility to Sa'd bin Mu'ādh to judge the treatment of the Jewish tribe Bani Quraiza, accused of betrayal, and commended him on his judgment.[21]

At times Muhammad proposed his own greatness, encouraging his followers to name themselves after him, but not to call themselves by his *kunya* (nickname, i.e., *abū l-Qāsim* "father of al-Qāsim").[22] At other times he disclosed a humbler assessment of himself. "None of you should say that I am better than Yūnus (i.e. Jonah)," he told his followers.[23] Muhammad's contemporaries occasionally compared him with Moses. When a Muslim and a Jew argued over which prophet was greater, Muhammad stated: "Don't give me superiority over Moses, for the people will fall unconscious on the Day of Resurrection and I will be the first to gain consciousness, and behold! Moses will be there holding the side of Allah's Throne."[24]

(b) Generosity and care for others

Muhammad was "the most generous of all people," even in debt settlements to his disadvantage.[25] Food received as a gift was quickly given away.[26] Like the Bible's picture of the noble wife,[27] an idealized description of a certain "Abu Zar" is applied by Muhammad to himself. This "Abu Zar" is generous and considerate of his wife.[28] Islam's prophet also encouraged a friend to reduce a debt claim, in a passage suggestive of the Parable of the Unforgiving Servant.[29] Like Moses, Muhammad was known for never turning down a request, even when it applied to military strategy.[30] Both were willing to take the advice of others in the application of their laws.[31]

People's needs were placed above ritual requirements. Muhammad's preaching and public prayer times were shortened to prevent boredom and stress in the congregation.[32] His example was cited by others.[33] He was perceptive of the feelings of others and criticized those who were less sensitive to their listeners' time demands.[34] The sense is of a shepherd concerned for the welfare of his flock, a depiction also applied to Moses.[35]

Just as Moses ascended the mountain to speak to God face to face and receive the divine law, Muhammad likewise undertook an epic upward journey. On his ascension to heaven, he negotiated with Allah the number of obligatory diurnal prayers at the advice of Moses: "Go back to your Lord (and appeal for reduction) for your followers will not be able to bear it." Consequently they were reduced from fifty, in decrements of five, to the current five daily prayers.[36] He ceased his lengthy night prayers lest they be considered compulsory for others.[37]

In contrast to the exacting demands of Islamic ritual, it is interesting to see glimpses of freedom and spontaneity. Muhammad, for example, offered his *du'ā* (petitions or non-compulsory prayer) while riding his camel.[38] Both Moses and Muhammad interceded for their people before God,[39] spoke of God's mercy,[40] and invoked blessings on those under their care,[41] extending even to their household utensils.[42] When a man confessed to adultery, Muhammad tried to avoid passing sentence, initially by ignoring him and then by trying to minimize the offense.[43] Similarly a woman who confessed to adultery was given several chances to avoid the sentence of stoning.[44] Another man was forgiven a legally punishable sin without it being named or investigated.[45] Muhammad's wise action in replacing the Black Stone in the Ka'ba was another example (see Illustration 7).

ILLUSTRATION 7: Replacing the Black Stone: To settle the dispute about who should have the honor of placing the Black Stone in the Ka'ba, Muhammad put it on a cloak and called the tribal leaders to carry it together.[g]

(c) Humanity and humility

Muhammad is depicted as very human. He wore a ring,[46] snored at night,[47] fainted when he worked too hard,[48] and was unable to sleep at night due to security worries.[49] He openly expressed his emotions, including joy,[50] dislike,[51] disgust,[52] anger,[53] fury,[54] and hatred.[55] He smiled more than laughed.[56]

Muhammad served his own household with domestic duties.[57] He covered up for a servant who dropped a dish full of food.[58] When a baby urinated on him, he simply washed the place with water.[59] After a man was killed by an unknown assailant, Muhammad paid the *diya* (blood money or compensation) himself to avoid a bloody feud between Arab and Jewish tribes.[60]

He was not a mystic recluse, for he organized a horse race,[61] listened to singing with instruments[62] and without them,[63] and joined in spear play in the mosque.[64] He invited others to his wedding banquet,[65] and he had a penchant for sweet food.[66]

He was found lying flat on his back relaxing in the mosque, with his legs crossed,[67] and at another time he prayed carrying his small

---

g.   A 1315 illustration by Jami al-Tawarikh. Source: https://commons.wiki-media.org/wiki/File:Mohammed_kaaba_1315a.jpg (accessed January 20, 2015).

granddaughter on his shoulders.[68] There was a lump on his back which is referred to as *al-khātim* (the seal) of Prophethood.[69] A girl, despite her father's protestations, was allowed to play with this lump. It was about the size of a partridge's egg, possibly a sebaceous cyst, a mole, or a birthmark.[70]

He was not above normal human afflictions. He was struck with severe illness, for Aisha reported: "I never saw anybody suffering so much from sickness as Allah's Apostle."[71] He allowed a married female acquaintance to check his hair for head lice when he visited her, falling asleep as she did so.[72]

Moses was acutely aware of his own limitations. He recognized his lack of eloquence, so his brother Aaron was sent with him as his spokesperson.[73] When challenged by the people in open revolt, Moses and Aaron fell on their faces in front of the assembly.[74] Aged and tired, Moses needed a stone to sit on and supporters to hold up his arms in order for Israel to win a battle.[75] When he came down from the mountain, Moses covered his face so the Israelites might not see the fading glory of his shining face. This may have been so that they were not distracted from his divine message, or they turned away due to his dazzling visage. Moses was clearly more concerned with his people's welfare and growth in knowledge than his own appearance and reputation.[76]

Muhammad likewise was humble enough to consult others about divorcing Aisha over her contact with the young soldier Safwān ibn al Muʿattal.[77] He also asked advice about how to deal with those who were slandering her.[78]

The impression of Muhammad given in some accounts of the Hadith is of a man who was unassuming, without pride or arrogance, claiming he would accept a simple invitation to eat animal trotters.[79] He was described as "more shy than a virgin in her separate room,"[80] much like Moses' legendary humility.[81] When tempted to magnify himself by showing that he had defeated a "jinn,"[82] Muhammad reminded himself of Solomon's modesty.[83] He warned his follow-ers: "Do not exaggerate in praising me as the Christians praised the son of Mary, for I am only a slave. So, call me the Slave of Allah and His Apostle."[84] Clearly some descriptions were simply legends.

One follower, for example, claimed that their prophet "does not touch his bed at night, being busy in worshipping Allah."[85]

(d) Forgiveness and tolerance

Muhammad refused to take revenge for his own sake, but only when Allah's laws were broken.[86] A known troublemaker,[87] a Bedouin who crept up on him and grabbed his sword in a threatening way,[88] and those who stole his camels [89] were forgiven. He excused the troublemaker 'Abdullah bin Ubayy bin Salūl who opposed him because Abdullah had been deprived of kingship in Medina by Muhammad's arrival.[90] He stopped his followers from killing the Jewish woman who roasted a poisoned sheep for him to eat.[91]

A tribe refused to follow him, and he was urged to invoke divine retribution on them. Instead he prayed: "O Allah! Give guidance to the people of Daus, and let them embrace Islam."[92] When the angel Gabriel offered to make two mountains fall on the people who rejected Muhammad on the day of 'Aqaba, Muhammad's response was: "No, but I hope that Allah will let them beget children who will worship Allah Alone, and will worship none besides Him."[93]

Muhammad made allowances for others when they were under stress or not being their normal selves (see Sidebar *Muhammad and His Drunk Uncle*).

MUHAMMAD AND HIS DRUNK UNCLE

His uncle Hamza became intoxicated and had mutilated two camels which Ali intended as the wedding gift for his marriage to Fātima, the daughter of the Prophet. Ali complained to Muhammad, who went to confront Hamza.

"The Prophet started blaming Hamza for what he had done. Hamza was drunk and his eyes were red. He looked at the Prophet then raised his eyes to look at his knees and raised his eyes more to look at his face and then said, 'You are not but my father's slaves.' When the Prophet understood that Hamza was drunk, he retreated, walking backwards went out and we left with him."[h]

---

h. B.5:340; also 4:324.

Abdullah b. Ubayy b. Salūl was negotiating on behalf of his client, the Jewish tribe of Bani Qaynuqaʼ.

> The apostle turned away from him, whereupon he [Abdullah] thrust his hand into the collar of the apostle's robe; the apostle was so angry that his face became almost black. He said, "Confound you, let me go." He answered, "No, by God, I will not let you go until you deal kindly with my clients." . . . The apostle said, "You can have them."[94]

Another time a rough Bedouin grabbed a blanket that Muhammad was wearing because he wanted a share in the recent booty. The violence of the pull left a mark on the Prophet's shoulder. "The bedouin said, 'O Muhammad! Order for me some of Allah's property which you have.' The Prophet turned towards him, (smiled) and ordered that he be given something."[95]

An ecumenical and tolerant spirit was displayed several times. Muhammad stood for a passing Jewish funeral procession,[96] which some scholars claim was a sign of respect,[97] and he prayed on hearing of the death of the Christian king of Ethiopia.[98] He gave one of his two shirts as an interment shroud for the "hypocrite" leader Abdullah bin Ubayy at the request of the dead man's son,[99] and then prayed at the hypocrite's funeral,[100] putting his own saliva on the corpse.[101] Both Moses and Muhammad employed pagan guides to lead them through the desert.[102] Just like the motley group of slave and free, rich and poor, male and female, young and old, involved in the *hijra* (immigration) from Mecca to Medina,[103] "many other people" accompanied Moses in the escape from Egypt.[104] Davis calls this a "mixed multitude" of ethnic peoples including other Semites and native Egyptians.[105] There was an openness to other cultures and races, and an acceptance of what they had to offer.

2. MUHAMMAD'S PROPHETHOOD

(a) Revelatory parallels with biblical prophets

Some descriptions of Muhammad's episodes of inspiration appear to resonate with the experiences of biblical personalities.

Yahweh had told Aaron and Miriam: "When a prophet of the LORD is among you, I reveal myself to him in visions; I speak to him in dreams."[106] God spoke in dreams to many people, including Abraham,[107] Jacob,[108] Daniel,[109] and Joseph.[110]

Muhammad experienced his first revelation as a dream in the cave in Mount Hirā.[111] "The dreams of the Prophets are Divine Inspirations,"[112] and a good dream is one of the forty-six parts of prophethood.[113] His biographer, Ibn Ishaq, reported the Prophet saying, "I awoke from my sleep, and it was as though these words were written on my heart."[114] There was a clear link between sleep and revelation.[115] Observers noted that Muhammad snored like a camel during some inspiration incidents,[116] and at other times he was silent.[117] Just as Gabriel brought the revelation to Muhammad,[118] the law of Moses was said to be delivered by angels.[119] Zechariah likewise reported that the revelation and its explanation were brought to him by an angel.[120] To prepare him for the prophetic role, an angel purified Isaiah's lips with a live coal,[121] just as two angels opened Muhammad's chest and cleansed the inside of his body with Zam-Zam water.[122]

The initial divine inspiration was an intensely physical experience. "The angel caught me (forcefully) and pressed me so hard that I could not bear it any more."[123] At other times it came "like the ringing of a bell," a form which is "the hardest of all."[124] The bodily manifestations could be transmitted to others. One companion reported: "Allah sent down revelation to His Apostle while his thigh was on mine and it became so heavy for me that I feared that my thigh would be broken."[125]

Inspiration was a frightening event for Muhammad: he described "his heart beating severely. Then he went to [his wife] Khadīja bint Khuwailid and said, 'Cover me! Cover me!' They covered him till his fear was over."[126] His lips quivered during revelation,[127] he suffered from excessive perspiration,[128] his face turned red,[129] and he breathed heavily.[130] His neck muscles were twitching with terror.[131] Biblical prophets relate similar psychosomatic responses (see Sidebar *Biblical Prophetic Manifestations*). Behavior seen as spiritual may be described in psychological or physical terms without prejudicing its etiology.

BIBLICAL PROPHETIC MANIFESTATIONS

Uncontrollable trembling afflicted Daniel, Jeremiah, and perhaps Ezekiel.[i] Jeremiah implored God: "Do not be a terror to me."[j] Daniel's experience of revelation drained him: "I had no strength left, my face turned deathly pale and I was helpless. . . . overcome with anguish. . . . I can hardly breathe."[k] Habakkuk describes what might be the bodily impact of an event of divine disclosure: "I heard and my heart pounded, my lips quivered at the sound; decay crept into my bones, and my legs trembled."[l] Jeremiah recounts a febrile exhaustion associated with his calling: "his word is in my heart like a fire, a fire shut up in my bones. I am weary of holding it in; indeed, I cannot."[m]

Muhammad's swoonlike condition parallels the common response to a theophany or angelic visitation. Falling facedown was reported by Balaam, Ezekiel, Daniel, Paul, and John,[132] among others. But at other times, Muhammad remained standing during a revelation.[133]

(b) Accusations of demon possession and insanity followed by public rejection

Demon possession was attributed to John the Baptist,[134] Jesus,[135] and Muhammad.[136] Just as the jinn announced that Muhammad was a prophet[137] and some even believed in his message,[138] demons acknowledged that Jesus was "the Holy One of God," "Son of God," "the Christ," and "Son of the Most High God."[139] Along with

i. Dan 10:10,11, Jer 23:9, Ezek 12:8.

j. Jer 17.17.

k. Dan 10:9, 16, 17.

l. Hab 3:16.

m. Jer 20:9.

Jesus, Paul, and the unnamed prophet of Jehu's era,[140] Muhammad was sometimes considered insane.[141] Muhammad was warned that he would be treated with hostility by his own people,[142] as were the earlier prophets. Rejection by the public and by those in power was a common experience of Old Testament prophets, such as Isaiah, Jeremiah, Amos, and Ezekiel, and was asserted by Jesus ("a prophet has no honor in his own country").[143]

(c) Waiting for revelation

A cycle of dumbness and renewal of speech had been reported by Ezekiel,[144] perhaps mirroring the departure and return of the divine afflatus described by Islam's Prophet. Revelation did not come at Muhammad's beck and call,[145] for it ceased for some long periods.[146] The answer to a request for information or personal need could be delayed for weeks or a month, causing public embarrassment for Muhammad and marital discord with Aisha.[147] Sometimes when he was asked "his opinion" about a matter, Muhammad simply gave an answer (e.g., about *coitus interruptus* with captured women)[148] or refused to answer the question (about a woman who wanted to marry him),[149] but at other times a divine revelation came upon him (e.g., about wearing perfume while performing the lesser pilgrimage).[150]

Moses, when asked by some ceremonially unclean Israelites if they could celebrate the Passover, replied: "Wait until I find out what the Lord commands concerning you."[151] Jeremiah's "word from the Lord" came ten days after a request from Johanan and the soldiers.[152] Another prophet was told to wait for the revelation to come.[153]

NOTES

1. This comparison is also developed in Phipps, *Muhammad and Jesus*, 87–89. The frequent Muslim claim that Moses' statement in Deut 18:15 was a prophecy about Muhammad does not accurately reflect the biblical term "a prophet like me from among your brothers." In Deuteronomy "from among your brothers" refers to fellow Israelites, e.g., Deut 17:15 (choose a king "from among your brothers") and Deut 18:1–2 (Levites would have no inheritance "among their brothers"). Moreover, Deuteronomy 18:15 is applied to Jesus in Acts

3:19–23. Jesus noted that "Moses wrote about me" (John 5:46), but Muhammad made no such claim.

2. B.1:345; 4:429; 5:227.

3. B.4:279.

4. Ex 2:17.

5. B.8:222.

6. B.6:27, 135; 9:32. However, the offended family forgave her so her tooth was spared.

7. B.4:681; 5:79; 8:778, 779.

8. B.5:597; 4:681; 8:778, 799.

9. Ex 32:26, 27. The parallel passage to this event is found in the Qur'an: Q.2:54

10. Num 15:32-36.

11. B.2:413; 3:421, 860, 885; 4:829; 6:79; 7:195, 196; 8:629, 805, 806, 809, 810, 813, 814, 815, 821, 825, 826, 842; 9:303, 365, 432, 633.

12. Jer 7:16; 11:14; 14:11.

13. B.2:359; 6:193, 194; 7:688, which refer to the revelation of Q.9:84.

14. B.1:6; 4:191, 221; 6:75; 8:277.

15. Ex 33:11.

16. 1 Kgs 8:56.

17. Heb 11:24–26.

18. B.5:702.

19. B.3:809.

20. B.4:232.

21. B.4:280; 5:148, 447; 8:278.

22. B.1:110; 3:331,332; 4:435,737; 8:205, 206, 207, 208, 216, 217.

23. B.4:624, 608, 625, 627; 6:127, 128.

24. B. 8:524, 525; 6:162; 4:626, 610, 620; 3:594; 9:52, 524, 564.

25. B.1:5; B.1:434; 8:448.

26. B.7:281.

27. Prov 31:10–31.

28. B.7:117. Even though Abū Zar later divorced her for another woman, the first wife still saw him as better than her second husband.

29. B.1:447, 460; Matt 18:23–35.

30. Ex 18:13–16; B.2:367; B.8:109.

31. Ex 18:13–26 and B.1:148.

32.   B.1:68, 70; 8:420; B.1:675–678, 827; 8:420.

33.   B.8:349.

34.   B.4:764; 1:90,669, 670; 8:131; 9:273.

35.   Isa 63:11.

36.   B.1:345; 5:227; 4:429; 9:608. This may be a confusion with the story of Abraham bargaining with God for the people of Sodom. Abraham also started with the number fifty, and arrived decrementally at ten (Gen 18:22–33).

37.   B.1:696–698; 2:46; 9:393.

38.   B.1:393; 2:114, 202, 203.

39.   Ex 32:7–14; Ps 106:23; B.5:227, 612.

40.   Deut 13:17; B.7:559.

41.   Lev 9:23; B.8:366.

42.   Deut 28:5; B.3:113, 339, 340; 4:139, 143, 7:336, 558; 8:374, 383, 705.

43.   B.8:813, 814.

44.   B.8:806, 810.

45.   B.8:812.

46.   B.1:630; 7:756, 765; 8:646.

47.   B.1:117; 665, 666.

48.   B.1:360; also 5:170.

49.   B.9:337.

50.   Fifty passages in al-Bukhāri's collection mention Muhammad smiling.

51.   B.4:763; 8:124.

52.   B.8:132.

53.   B.1:19; 8:669, 671; 9:273.

54.   B.8:131.

55.   B.7:844.

56.   B.6:353; 8:114.

57.   B.1:644; 7:276; 8:65.

58.   B.7:152.

59.   B1:222, 223; 7:377; 8:31, 366.

60.   B.4:398; 9:36, 302.

61.   B.1:412; 4:120, 121, 122; 9:436.

62.   B.2:70,72; 4:155; 5:336.

63. B.9:29.
64. B.1:445; 4:155; 7:118.
65. B.3:437.
66. B.7:193, 342, 504, 514, 586.
67. B.1:464; 8:302.
68. B.1:495; 8:25.
69. B.4:305; 7:574; 8:363. Muhammad is referred to as "the seal of the Prophets" (Q.33:40). Cf. Jesus' self-reference to the Son of Man on whom "God the Father has placed his seal of approval" (John 6:27).
70. B.4:305; B.1:189. Redha, *Mohammad*, 38.
71. B.7:549 also 7:550, 551.
72. B.4:47; 9:130.
73. Ex 4:10–16.
74. Num 14:5.
75. Ex 17:8–13.
76. Ex 34:33–35; 2 Cor 2:13.
77. B.3:805; 5:462; 6:274; 9:462. Eventually a revelation came vindicating her.
78. B.9:463.
79. B.7:107
80. B.8:124, 140; 4:762.
81. Num 12:3.
82. A spirit made from smokeless fire.
83. B.1:450.2; 2:301; 4:634; 6:332.
84. B.4:654.
85. B.8:172.
86. B.4:760; 8:777, 836.
87. B.4:720.
88. B.4:158.
89. B.4:278; 5:507.
90. B.6:89; 8:226, 271.
91. B.3:786. There was a wider communal complicity in this event (B.4:394; 5:551; 7:669). The poison may have been responsible for Muhammad's eventual death (B.5:713). Hughes, *Dictionary of Islam*, 380 claims that the woman, named Zainab, was immediately put to death.

92. B.4:188; 8:406.
93. B.4:454.
94. Ibn Ishaq, *Sirat*, 363.
95. B.8:111.
96. B.2:398, 399.
97. E.g. Ramadhan, *Messenger,* 90.
98. B.2:412, 417, 418.
99. B.2:433.
100. B.2:359; 6:194.
101. B.2:360.
102. Num 10:29–31 and B.3:464.
103. Ibn Ishaq, *Sīra,* 213–218.
104. Ex 12:38.
105. Davis, *Moses*, 156.
106. Num 12:6.
107. Gen 15:12ff.
108. Gen 28:12ff.
109. Dan 7:1; 10:9.
110. Matt 1:20.
111. B.1:3, 140; 6:478, 479, 480; 9:111.
112. B.1:818.
113. B.9:112, 116, 117, 118, 144.
114. Ibn Ishaq, *Sirat,* 106.
115. B.4:47, 144.
116. B.3:17.
117. B.2:544; 4:95; 5:462.
118. B.1:2,3; 9:111.
119. Gal 3:19; Heb 2:2.
120. Zech 1:9; 2:3; 4:1; 5:5; 6:4.
121. Isa 6:6.
122. B.9:608.
123. B.1:3; 6:478, 479, 480; 9:111.
124. B.1:2.
125. B.4:85.
126. B.1:3; 6:478, 479, 480; 9:111.

127. B.1:4.

128. B.1:2; 2:544; 4:95; 5:462.

129. B.5:618.

130. B.6:508.

131. B.9:111.

132. Num 24:4; Ezek 1:28; Dan 8:17, 18; 10:9; Acts 9:4; Rev 1:17.

133. B.9:400; 6:245.

134. Matt 11:18.

135. John 7:20; 8:48; 10:20.

136. Q.17:47; 25:8. The Qur'anic term is *mashūr* "bewitched."

137. B.5:206.

138. B.1:740; 6:239, 443; Ibn Ishaq, *Sirat,* 193–194.

139. Luke 4:34, 41/Matt 8:32/Mark 1:24; Mark 5:7.

140. John 10:20; Acts 26:24; 2 Kgs 9:11.

141. Q.7:184; 37:36; 68:2; 81:22.

142. B.1:3.

143. John 4:44.

144. Ezek 3:22–27; 24:25–27; 33:21–22.

145. B.2:225; 5:494.

146. B.9:111; 4:461. See also Ibn Ishaq, *Sirat,* 136–137.

147. B.3:805; 5:462; 6:274; 9:462.

148. B.3:432.

149. B.7:79.

150. B.3:17; 5:618; 6:508.

151. Num 9:8.

152. Jer 42:7.

153. Hab 2:3.

5

POSITIVE TREATMENT AND
DEPICTION OF WOMEN

WOMEN ARE MENTIONED FREQUENTLY in the Hadith. "Woman" or "women" are mentioned in 572 and "Aisha" in 368 out of the 7,275 hadiths in al-Bukhāri. This is about 13 percent. Lapidus proposes that Islam "enhanced the status of women and children, who were no longer to be considered merely chattels or potential warriors, but individuals with rights and needs of their own."[1] Muhammad had many dealings with women, as did Jesus. In this section, we will compare the positive ways in which Muhammad and Jesus interacted with females.

1. KEY WOMEN IN THE LIVES OF
MUHAMMAD AND JESUS

One of the most important women in Muhammad's life was his first wife, Khadija. For Jesus a significant female was his mother, Mary. There are several parallels in these relationships. Prior to Muhammad's preaching of Islam, some women in the Meccan community exercised considerable freedom and influence. Khadīja bint Khuwalid ibn Asad, a widow and a divorcee, was operating a trading company in which she employed the young Muhammad. Many Quraishis envied her riches and noble lineage.[2]

Mary came from a royal lineage, even though she was obviously poor. Both women entered into these relationships by choice. Mary was invited by the angel Gabriel to bear Jesus and accepted this role.[3] At age forty, Khadija proposed marriage to her twenty-five-year-old employee. Khadija had been widowed twice so Muhammad became her third husband.[4] (See Illustration 8.)

When he reached the age of 25, Mohammed married a wealthy widow named Khadija (right). She relieved him of financial worries, bore him children, and eventually became the first convert to the Prophet's new religion.

ILLUSTRATION 8:
Muhammad's marriage
to Khadīja[a]

The loss of his own mother when he was six years old, and the fifteen-year age difference between Khadija and Muhammad, may have made this more like a mother-son relationship. This age difference may have been approximately the same for Mary and Jesus, since first-century Jewish women often married young.

Both Mary and Khadija faced opposition and possible danger due to their connections with Jesus and Muhammad. Mary's pregnancy outside of marriage opened her to the risk of death under Jewish law.[5] "A sword will pierce your own soul too," the insightful Simeon warned her after the birth.[6] Khadija suffered under the boycott of the early Muslims by the Quraish for two or three years before her death.[7] Both women faced violent threats and discrimination. Mary was forced to flee from Israel to Egypt with Joseph and the infant Jesus, and Khadija suffered for two or three years under the boycott of Bani Hāshim.[8] The Muslims migrated from Mecca to Medina not long after Khadīja's death.

Both women were important in helping launch and sustain the public ministry of their respective men. Mary cared assiduously for the young Jesus after accepting the great responsibility of bearing him. When the boy Jesus was lost in Jerusalem, Mary and Joseph spent three days anxiously searching for him.[9] Khadija cared for Muhammad by

---

a.   Desmond Stewart, *Early Islam*, 23 [taken from Ms. Hazine 1222, folios 30, 158, courtesy of Topkapi Museum (Ara Guler)].

providing for his needs. Her business acumen and wealth allowed him the leisure of long periods of meditation in the cave at Mount Hirā, outside Mecca, where his revelations began. It was Mary's request to Jesus at the wedding at Cana that brought him to public attention through his first miracle. Khadija likewise quickly devised a method to ascertain if the spirit visiting Muhammad was good or evil.[10] She also took him to her cousin Waraqa bin Naufal, a Christian, who assured him that he was a prophet.[11] Mary stood with Jesus at the foot of the cross as he died. Khadija accepted Muhammad's teaching, becoming the first Muslim.[12] Mary was praying with the first disciples in the upper room after the ascension of Jesus.[13]

Both women were rewarded for their devotion. The angel Gabriel described Mary as "highly favored" for God was with her.[14] In his dying moments, Jesus gave Mary into the care of his friend John.[15] The angel Gabriel promised Khadija a palace made of pearl as a reward.[16] Muhammad called her "the best amongst the women (of this nation)."[17]

2. RELIGIOUSLY OBSERVANT WOMEN

Mary and Khadija were not the only women who were significant, valued, and honored. Women were allowed to take an almost full part in the religious life of the new Muslim society. They were expected to participate in public prayers[18] and even woken to do so.[19] Their men were told to give them permission to attend the mosque at night.[20] The women apparently prayed behind the men: they were ordered to remain facedown while men prostrated. As the males bowed with their waist-cloths tied around their necks, they exposed their private parts to those behind them. The women were ordered by Muhammad to keep their faces on the ground to spare them this unedifying sight.[21] "Gentleness to women" is sometimes listed as one of Muhammad's virtues.[22]

At one time, the women felt they were being neglected in favor of the men, and asked the Prophet to set aside time just for them. He did so, giving them "religious lessons and commandments."[23] There was a spirit of inquiry: "Whenever 'Aisha heard anything which she did not understand, she used to ask again till she understood it completely."[24]

Many women were not intimidated by Muhammad. "Some Quraishi women were sitting with him and they were asking him to give them more financial support while raising their voices over the voice of the Prophet."[25] Aisha even challenged Muhammad by quoting his Qur'anic verses back at him to justify her actions.[26]

Jesus also taught women.[27] His conversations with the woman of Samaria and the Canaanite woman showed that he was willing to discuss theological matters with women.[28] He openly chatted about practical[29] issues, and responded positively to their urgent physical needs.[30]

3. WOMEN AS MATERIAL PROVIDERS

Women contributed to the material, financial, and military life of the early Islamic community. One had her slave carpenter build a pulpit for Muhammad, either at her suggestion[31] or his request.[32] Female believers were required to give alms.[33] In battles, they brought water to the troops,[34] treated casualties,[35] and transported the wounded and killed.[36]

Jesus also accepted women's contributions. Among Jesus' group traveling from village to village were women including the formerly demon-possessed Mary Magdalene, the well-connected wife of the manager of Herod's household, and "many others [who] were helping to support them out of their own means."[37] This included accepting the hospitality offered by women.[38]

4. RESPONDING TO WOMEN'S SOCIAL AND EMOTIONAL NEEDS

Muhammad was sensitive to women's needs. He said, "When I stand for prayer, I intend to prolong it but on hearing the cries of a child, I cut it short, as I dislike to trouble the child's mother."[39] He forbade the Arab practice of burying unwanted infant girls alive.[40] In an attempt to treat all his wives fairly, he cast lots to determine which wife would accompany him on each journey.[41] On his deathbed, he asked the permission of all his wives to allow him to be moved to and remain in the house of Aisha.[42] He was free in his relationships with women, for "any of the female slaves of Medina could take hold of the hand of Allah's Apostle and take him wherever she wished."[43]

Jesus likewise showed a similar concern for those with children and a freedom in relating to women. He blessed the children brought to him, even though his disciples wanted to send them away.[44] Of the three people reported in the Gospels as raised from the dead by Christ, two of them were children, and the only child of their parents.[45] Jesus broke with social convention when he conversed alone with a woman in an open place[46] and allowed women to wash and anoint his feet on public occasions.[47] He chose to heal a crippled woman on the Sabbath, even though it brought him into conflict with the religious authorities.[48]

5. RELIGIOUS NEEDS AND UNCLEANNESS

Muhammad catered for the religious needs of women around him. He prayed the funeral prayer for a black woman sweeper at her graveside.[49] Women were told that they would be shielded from the hell-fire if two or three of their children died before puberty.[50]

Jesus made a point of highlighting women performing religious duties. He drew attention to a poor widow who gave only two copper pennies as an example of true generosity.[51] Another widow is made the heroine in a story about persistent prayer.[52] Female figures are used as examples of God's care. A woman sweeping her house to find a lost coin represents God's assiduous concern for those who have gone astray.[53] Jesus compared himself to a mother hen wanting to shelter her chicks under her wing.[54] Clearly Jesus was comfortable with women as heroes and with employing feminine images.

Regarding menstrual discharges, Muslim women were in quite a different legal position to Old Testament Israelite women (see Sidebar *Menstrual Matters*).

A Jewish female with a vaginal blood emission was unclean for as long as the bleeding continued.[55] This was a problem for a woman in the New Testament.[56] Hyssop served a cleansing role in the Old Testament.[57] For an Israelite man to touch a woman in an unclean state or to handle anything she had been in contact with made him ritually unclean until the evening, even after washing.[58] Such a person would be barred from the temple.[59]

Islamic practice was not as strict. Although Muhammad was careful not to touch any woman while she was making her pledge of allegiance after her migration to Medina,[60] he often fondled his wives during their menstrual periods[61] and was touched by them,[62] even sleeping in the same bed.[63] He also prayed beside them in bed, sometimes making physical contact during his prayers.[64]

MENSTRUAL MATTERS

During her monthly period, a Muslim woman was not permitted to go to the mosque or prayer place,[b] nor could she pray,[c] yet she was not required to make up for the missed prayers.[d] A bath scented with musk sufficed to make her fit to pray again.[e]

A woman with vaginal bleeding asked Muhammad: "Shall I give up my prayers?" Allah's Apostle replied: "No, because it is from a blood vessel and not the menses. So when the real menses begins give up your prayers and when it (the period) has finished wash the blood off your body (take a bath) and offer your prayers."[f] The same rule applied to other vaginal discharges.[g] Despite being unable to pray, menstruating women could attend the annual pilgrimage, the *Hajj*, although without participating in the full rite.[h]

6. THE ROLE OF WOMEN IN DEVELOPMENT OF THE RELIGION

Aisha played a key part in the development of early Islam. "Muhammed had authorized Aisha, in his absence, to give religious advice, allegedly telling Muslims to 'take half of your religion from this woman.'"[65] One female commentator notes the significant role the nineteen-year-old widow held after her husband's death. "Because she had spent

---

b.   B.1:321; 2:714.

c.   B.1:327.

d.   B.1:318.

e.   B.1:311-312.

so much time at Muhammad's side, she became a leading religious authority." However, Brooks incorrectly reads the motives (and the figures) behind the discounting of many hadiths sourced from Aisha: "Originally, 2,210 hadith were attributed to her: ninth century scholars, *dismissing the word of a mere woman*, threw out all but 174."[66] This is 8 percent of those accredited to Aisha, a far higher representation than al-Bukhāri's normal acceptance rate of 2.5 percent of all the hadith he gathered. In fact, Aisha contributed more accounts to al-Bukhāri's collection than any other person, responsible for 1,250 or nearly 18 percent of the hadiths.[67]

Likewise women were important at the key events in Jesus' ministry—his death and resurrection. It was the women who wept and wailed for him on the road to Calvary[68] and stayed at the cross when most of the men had deserted Jesus.[69] Women observed where he was buried,[70] and women were the first witnesses of the resurrection.[71]

Much about women in the Bible and the Hadith can be basis for futher discussion between Christians and Muslims.

---

f.   B.1:303, 322, 324. This, incidentally, could be a significant discovery affecting women's health issues. The author's wife worked as a doctor in female clinics on the Arabian peninsula. Many women refused to use certain cheap and effective methods of birth control due to concern about the extra-menstrual blood spotting which sometimes occurred, claiming it disqualified them from praying and fasting. This hadith discriminates between menstrual and non-menstrual bleeding, with the latter no disqualification from religious duties. For sexually active, married women, a further issue was their husbands' fear of defilement through contact with menstrual blood during copulation.

g.   B.1:306-309, 323.

h.   B.1: 293, 302, 321, 325, 326.

NOTES

1. Lapidus, *History*, 30.
2. Ibn Ishaq, *Sirat*, 82.
3. Luke 1:38.
4. Ibn Ishaq, *Sirat,*83, 711, 792
5. Lev 20:10–12.
6. Luke 2:35.
7. Ibn Ishaq, *Sirat*, 159–160. Armstrong suggests that Khadija's death was hastened by the economic boycott of the Muslims by the Quraish, as a response to Muhammad's preaching. Armstrong, *Muhammad*, 87.
8. B.2:659; 5:221; 5:580. See also Ibn Ishaq, *Sirat*, 159–162.
9. Luke 2:48.
10. "She disclosed her form and cast aside her veil while the apostle was sitting in her lap. Then she said, 'Can you see him?' And he replied, 'No.' She said, 'O son of my uncle, rejoice and be of good heart, by God he is an angel and not a satan.'" Ibn Ishaq, *Sirat*, 107.
11. B.1:3.
12. Ibn Ishaq, *Sirat*, 111. His ten-year-old nephew, Ali b. Abū Talib, accepted Muhammad's message after her, becoming the first male believer. Ibn Ishaq, *Sirat*, 114.
13. Acts 1:14.
14. Luke 1:28.
15. John 19:26–27.
16. B.3:19; 5:164, 165, 167, 168; 7:156; 8:33; 9:588.
17. B.4:642; 5:163. Despite this, she is not mentioned at all in the Qur'an and only 21 times in al-Bukhāri's Hadith.
18. B.1:321.
19. B.1:115; 8:237. Public prayer contrasts with modern practice, where Muslim women usually pray at home. The initial requirement to pray at home (Q.33:33) applied only to Muhammad's wives, because "you are not like other women" (Q.33:32).
20. B.1:824.
21. B.1:358, 778.
22. Armstrong, *Muhammad: A Western Attempt to Understand Islam*, 79.
23. B.1:101; 7:176; 9:413.

24. B.1:103.
25. B.8:108.
26. B.4:602; 5:464; 6:213, 281.
27. Luke 10:39.
28. John 4:7–26; Matt 15:21–28.
29. Luke 10:40–43.
30. Luke 7:11–17; 8:43–48.
31. B.1:440.
32. B.1:439.
33. B.1: 97.2, 301, 822; 2:81, 92, 94, 511, 529, 541, 545; 6:418; 7:176, 768, 769, 771; 9:426.
34. B.4:131, 132; 5:393, 398; 7:583.
35. B.1:321; 2:714; 7:583.
36. B.4:133-134; 7:583.
37. Luke 8:3; Mark 15:41.
38. Luke 10:38; John 12:2.
39. B.1:675; 1:827.
40. B.8:480; 9:395.
41. B.3:766; 4:130; 6:274.
42. B.1:197; 1:634; 3:761; 5:727; 7:612.
43. B.8:97.
44. Mark 10:13–16.
45. Luke 8:42; Luke 7:12.
46. John 4:4–42.
47. Luke 7:36–50; Mark 14:3–9.
48. Luke 13:10–17.
49. B.1:328, 448, 450.1, 816.
50. B.1:101, 102; 2:340, 341, 342, 463. This may also reflect Muhammad's family situation. Khadija bore him two or three sons, who died in infancy. Of his four daughters, only Fatima outlived Muhammad. His Egyptian concubine, Mary the Copt, bore Ibrahim, who also died as a baby. This hadith suggests an interesting parallel to the puzzling verse in 1 Tim 2:15.
51. Mark 12:42,43/Luke 21:2–4.
52. Luke 18:1–5.
53. Luke 15:8–10.

54. Matt 23:37/Luke 13:34.

55. Lev 15:25.

56. Matt 9:20–22/Mark 5:25–34/Luke 8:43–48.

57. Lev 19:17.

58. Lev 15:19–23

59. 2 Chr 23:19.

60. B.6:414.

61. B.1:298, 299, 300. This appears to contradict the edict of the Qur'an: "They ask thee concerning women's courses. Say: they are a hurt and a pollution: so *keep away from women in their courses*, and do not approach them until they are clean" (2:222 Yusuf Ali translation, italics mine). The Arabic word for the underlined term is *a'tazilū*, defined as "keep away, stand aloof, leave, withdraw, retire, seclude, segregate, . . . dissociate, separate, isolate [oneself]." Wehr, *Dictionary*, 610. The word *taqrabūn* "approach" is commonly used in a sexual sense in the Qur'an, e.g., Q.2:187, 223; 26:165; 27:55; 29:29.

62. B.1:294, 295, 296; 7:808, 809.

63. B.1:297, 319, 320.

64. B.1:329, 376, 497.

65. Brooks, *Nine Parts*, 85. Although widely quoted, the source of this tradition is difficult to locate. The earliest occurrence seems to be in the writing of Imam Zarkashi (Muhammad ibn Bahadur ibn Abdullah, Abu-Abdullah Badr al-Din al-Zarkashi), a Turkish scholar of the Shafi' school. He was born in 745/1324. This quote is found in his *Al-Ijaba li 'irad ma Istadrakatu A'isha ala al-Sahaba* "Collection of Aisha's Corrections to the Statements of the Companions," 37–38, cited by Bennett, *Muslims and Modernity*, 141. Bennett makes no comment on the statement's veracity, but a Shia website declares: "This tradition is fabricated and had no basis in truth." Source: http://www.al-islam.org/ENCYCLOPEDIA/Shia1a.txt. This is not surprising, since Shi'a Muslims often denigrate Aisha due to her opposition to Ali.

66. Brooks, *Nine Parts*, 87 (emphasis mine).

67. Source: http://islamicsystem.blogspot.com/2007/11/refutation-of-gadaffi-others-who-reject.html (accessed October 14, 2015).

68. Luke 23:27.

69. Matt 27:55–56/Mark 15:40.

70. Matt 27:61/Mark 15:47/Luke 23:55.

71. Matt 28:1–10/Mark 16:1–10/Luke 24:1–10.

THEOLOGICAL ASPECTS

THERE ARE THEOLOGICAL AND DEVOTIONAL aspects found in the Hadith which strike a familiar chord with Christian teaching.

1. THE NATURE OF GOD

(a) Divine omniscience

The Hadith present God's prior knowledge of many significant events. "Keys of the unseen knowledge are five which nobody knows but Allah. . . . Nobody knows what will happen tomorrow; nobody knows what is in the womb; nobody knows what he will gain tomorrow; nobody knows at what place he will die; and nobody knows when it will rain."[1]

The Bible states that "the Lord is a God who knows."[2] This knowledge encompasses human hearts,[3] human needs,[4] things done in secret,[5] and the events of the future.[6] There are "secret things" which belong to Yahweh alone.[7]

(b) God and emotion

The Qur'an presents Allah as being *rādi* (pleased) with certain people: those in Paradise and the early Muslims.[8] The Hadith extend these categories. Divine satisfaction is expressed toward a man who removed a thorny branch on the path,[9] a couple who deprived themselves and their children of food in order to feed guests,[10] "the repentance of his slave,"[11] and a man who told the truth about his past.[12] However, a Qur'anic verse expressing God's pleasure with the seventy martyrs of Bani Salim was later canceled.[13] Allah also laughs.[14] At other times, the divine wrath is portrayed. Allah will be angry with those who grab land by false oaths[15] and those who tell lies.[16] His anger will be strongest on the day of Judgment,[17] but Muhammad's anger against something also invokes Allah's anger.[18]

The Bible similarly reveals a rich tableau of emotions. At various times God is angry,[19] repents[20] (implying feelings of regret), and is grieved,[21] but also laughs[22] and is pleased.[23]

It is difficult to determine whether such descriptions are simply anthropopathic or if they reflect the true emotional life of God. Both Qur'an and Bible assert the unchangeability of God, but the passages listed here suggest that God is not totally impassive in response to different situations.[24]

(c) Desire for repentance

It is said that "there is none who likes that the people should repent to Him and beg His pardon than Allah" [sic].[25] Isaiah records the long-suffering God who proclaims: "I revealed myself to those who did not ask for me; I was found by those who did not seek me. To a nation that did not call on my name, I said, 'Here am I, here am I.' All day long I have held out my hands to an obstinate people, who walk in ways not good, pursuing their own imaginations."[26] God's forbearance is due to his "not wanting anyone to perish, but everyone to come to repentance."[27]

2. PRAYERS OF MUHAMMAD

(a) Prayers of worship and submission

The Hadith record several prayers by Muhammad. Some, with minor omissions, could easily be found in Jewish or Christian worship. They often display similar connections and progressions (see Illustration 9). The following tahajjud (optional evening prayer) was prayed by Muhammad:

O Allah! All the praises are for you. You are the Holder of the Heavens and the Earth, and whatever is in them. All the praises are for You. You have the possession of the Heavens and the Earth and whatever is in them. All the praises are for You; You are the Light of the Heavens and the Earth and all the praises are for You. You are the King of the Heavens and the Earth and all the praises are for You. You are the Truth and Your Promise is the truth, and to meet You is true. Your Word is the truth and Paradise is true and Hell is true and all the Prophets (Peace be upon them) are true and Muhammad is true and the Day of Resurrection is true. O Allah! I surrender (my will) to You; I believe in You and depend on You and repent to You. With Your help I argue (with my opponents, the non-believers) and I take You as a judge (to judge between us). Please forgive me my previous and future sins and whatever I concealed or revealed. You are the One who makes (some people) forward and (some) backward. There is none to be worshipped but you.[28]

ILLUSTRATION 9: Connections and progressions in prayer

(b) Recognition of needs

As the Muslims dug the ditch around Medina in the face of the advancing Meccans, Muhammad called upon his God, reciting poetic verses composed by 'Abdullah Ibn Rawāha:

> O Allah. Were it not for You, we would not have been guided, nor would we have given in charity, nor prayed. So, bestow on us calmness, and when we meet the enemy, then make our feet firm, for indeed, yet if they want to put us in affliction, (i.e. want to fight against us) we would not (flee but withstand them).[29]

The Old Testament contains similar expressions of dependence on God for His guidance, for generous giving by His people, for encouraging prayer, and for the ability to withstand enemies.[30]

While on a military expedition, the Prophet prayed: "O Allah, the Revealer of the Holy Book, and the Mover of the clouds and the Defeater of the clans, defeat them, and grant us victory over them."[31] Likewise Yahweh is presented as the One who reveals his commands in a book,[32] moves the clouds,[33] defeats Israel's opponents,[34] and gives His people victory.[35]

(c) Prayers for forgiveness and guidance

When Muhammad's best friend Abū Bakr asked to be taught a prayer, the Prophet recited the following: "O Allah! I have done great injustice to myself and none except You forgives sins, so please forgive me and be Merciful to me as You are the Forgiver, the Merciful."[36] There is a recognition that sin is both a discredit to oneself as well as an offense against God. Wisdom, personified in the Old Testament, proclaims to her listeners: "But if you wrong me, you damage your very soul,"[37] while the repentant King David says to God, "Against you, you only, have I sinned and done what is evil in your sight."[38] The Pharisees and teachers of the law, doubting Jesus' claim to be able to pardon wrongdoing, rightly asked the question, "Who can forgive sins except God alone?"[39]

Muhammad was deeply aware of his own failings. He spoke of "my sins that I did in the past or will do in the future, and also the sins I did in secret or in public."[40] Consequently he prayed for forgiveness for himself: "O Allah! Wash away my sins with the water of snow and hail, and cleanse my heart from all the sins as a white garment is cleansed from the filth, and let there be a long distance between me and my sins, as You made East and West far from each other."[41] David begged God for cleansing using similar terms: "Wash me and I will be whiter than snow."[42] The removal of sins in the Bible is declared as an accomplished action—"as far as the east is from the west, so far has he removed our transgressions from us"—rather than as an aspiration or unrealized hope.[43]

ILLUSTRATION 10:
Muhammad
praying at
the Ka'ba[a]

Other prayers reveal a very human desire not to be overcome by potential problems of earthly existence. "O Allah! I seek refuge with You from having worries, sadness, helplessness, laziness, miserliness, cowardice, from being heavily in debt and from being overpowered by other persons unjustly." Similar prayers included deliverance from "reaching a degraded geriatric old age. . . the afflictions of the world and from the punishment in the grave."[44]

A prayer for divine direction, called *istikhāra*, is outlined, to be used when about to embark on a new venture.

O Allah! I ask guidance from Your knowledge, and Power from Your Might and I ask for Your great blessings. You are capable and I am not. You know and I do not and You know the unseen. O Allah! If You know that this job is good for my religion and my subsistence and in my Hereafter—(or said: If it is better for my present and later needs)—then You ordain it for me and make it easy for me to get, and then bless

a.   Source: Desmond Stewart, *Early Islam*, 21 [taken from Ms. Hazine 1222, folio 151, courtesy of Topkapi Museum (Ara Guler)].

me in it, and if You know that this job is harmful to me in
my religion and subsistence and in the Hereafter—(or said:
If it is worse for my present and later needs)—then keep it
away from me and let me be away from it. And ordain for
me whatever is good for me, and make me satisfied with it).[45]

Identical themes are found in the Bible: the request for guidance
from God;[46] a recognition of God's knowledge,[47] power,[48] and
might;[49] a desire for his blessings;[50] human inability in the face of
God's capability;[51] God's knowledge of the invisible[52] and of what is
best for his people;[53] and satisfaction with what God has provided.[54]

(d) Prayers of thanksgiving

Following a victory, Muhammad prayed: "None has the right
to be worshipped but Allah Alone, Who has no partner. All the
Kingdom belongs to Him and all the praises are for Him and
He is Omnipotent. We are returning with repentance, worshipping, prostrating ourselves and praising our Lord. Allah fulfilled
His Promise, granted victory to His slave and He Alone defeated all
the clans."[55] Similar expressions of thanksgiving are found throughout the Hadith.[56]

These accord with themes found in the Jewish and Christian
Scriptures. The incomparable God[57] is the only One worthy of
worship[58] and has no partners or equals.[59] He is the great King,[60]
omnipotent,[61] receiving praises.[62] His people respond with repentance,[63] worship,[64] and prostration.[65] God fulfills His promises,[66]
gives victory to those who serve Him,[67] and defeats those who
oppose His people.[68] The proper response to God's mighty acts of
mercy and deliverance is a life of praise and obedience.

GODWARD	Recognition of Allah's power	8:612; 1:805
	Praise	2:221, 253; 8:342
	Dependence and forgiveness	6:490, 491, 492; 9:534, 482, 590
	Forgiveness (for himself and for others)	1:760, 796; 2:221; 8:318, 319, 335, 379, 386, 388, 407, 408; 9:485
DAILY SITUATIONS	Before going to toilet	1:144; 8:334
	After meals	7:368, 369
	Before bed	9:490
	Before and after sleeping	8:324; 9:491, 492
	Before sleep	1:247; 8:323, 324, 325, 326, 327, 336, 337
	Protection while sleeping	9:580
	Evening prayer	9:482, 483
SPECIAL SITUATIONS	Before sex	1:143; 4:493, 503; 8:397; 9:493
	Guidance (*istikhara*)	2:263; 8:391; 9:523
	If in difficulty	9:523, 526
	For rain	2:126, 253
	Greeting in mosque	2:294
	Haircuts and shaving	2:785, 786
	To save friends and harm enemies	2:120, 121
	For life or death	7:575
	Healing	7:638, 639, 640, 646
	Prosperity and salvation	3:203; 8:398
	Victory before battle	4:266.1, 272, 317, 430, 8:617; 9:581
	Returning from battle	3:23; 5:442; 8:394

TABLE 12: List of Muhammad's prayers in al-Bukhari

(e) List of prayers

The Hadith record the contents of Muhammad's prayers for a variety of occasions (see Table 12).[69]

3. ESCHATOLOGY

(a) Events of the end times

Descriptions of the end times outlined in the Hadith bear some similarities to biblical depictions of the end times. There are many parallels in the events preceding the last day (see Table 13).

Interestingly, famines forecast in the Bible are not mentioned in the Last Day scenarios in the Hadith. Perhaps they were a relatively common occurrence in Arab experience.[70]

The same major personalities are involved, including false prophets,[71] Christ, and the Antichrist. The actions of *Masih ad-Dajjal* (the false Christ) mirror those of the false prophet of Revelation.[72] Like the biblical "beast," whose fatal wound was healed, *ad-Dajjāl* was impervious to normal physical attack.[73] Just as unfaithful people would accept the mark of the beast on their foreheads, the false Christ will have the word *kāfir* (unbeliever) written between his eyes.[74] He will perform miraculous signs involving fire and water[75] and bring the dead to life.[76] The return of Christ is seen as inculcating a period of justice and prosperity, paralleling the millennial reign of Christ. Jesus "will descend as a just ruler and . . . there will be abundance of money and nobody will accept charitable gifts."[77] Muhammad believed that the period between his era and the end times would be very short,[78] occurring within the lifetime of his companions.[79] In both the Bible and the Hadith, God expresses His sovereign rule over creation by rolling up the heavens in His hand.[80]

(b) Heaven and hell

Both the Bible and Hadith describe degrees of punishment in hell. The Hadith speak of those who will receive the "minimum punishment."[81] The biblical revelation suggests that it will be more bearable for some than others.[82] Some will be beaten with many blows, and some with few,[83] but others will be punished most severely.[84]

Wars	B.4:787,788,789,790; 9:237	Matthew 24:6; Mark 13:7,8; Luke 21:10
Earthquakes	B.2:146; 9:137,237	Matthew 24:7; Luke 21:11
Celestial signs	B.6:159, 160; 8:513; 9:237	Matthew 24:29; Acts 2:20 Luke 21:11,25; Joel 2:31
False prophets and deceivers appear among the believers	B.6:577; 9:64,65,66,237	Matthew 24:11; 2 Peter 3:3,17; Mark 13:6,21,22
Idol worship will reappear	B.9:232	Revelation 9:20
Affliction will result in apostasy	B.4:799	Matthew 24:8–13
Declining moral standards	B.1:56; 4:808; 6:577; 7:158; 8:503,504; 9:64	Matthew 24:12; 2 Thessalonians 2:10
Believers will flee to the mountains and remote places to preserve their faith	B. B.4:798; 9:210	Matthew 24:16–21; Mark 13:14-16; Luke 21:21
People will seek shelter among the rocks	B.4:176, 177, 791	Revelation 6:15,16 c.f. Isaiah 2:10
Gog and Magog will arise	B.2:663; 4:565,566,797; 6:265; 7:215; 8:537; 9:181,249,250	Ezekiel 38,39; Revelation 20:8
The end will come quickly and unexpectedly. People unable to complete normal household tasks	B.9:237; 8:513	Matthew 24:40–44; 1 Thessalonians 5:2; 2 Peter 3:10
The perseverance of righteous people could be in jeopardy	B.4:565,797; 9:181,249	Matthew 24:22; Mark 13:20
People will desire death	B.9:231,237	Revelation 9:6

TABLE 13: Eschatological parallels between the Hadith and the Bible

The symbol of a seed is used to describe the new life enjoyed in heaven or paradise. Following the teaching of Jesus,[85] Paul wrote of the seed which must die before it can come to life. Although it is sown natural and perishable, in dishonor and weakness, it will be raised spiritual and imperishable, in honor and power.[86] Likewise Muhammad spoke of those who had been rescued from the fire. They had been "burnt and became like coal, and then they will be thrown into the river of *Al-Hayyāt* (life) and they will spring up just as a seed grows on the bank of a rainwater stream." The Prophet said, "Don't you see that the germinating seed comes out yellow and twisted?"[87]

The Islamic paradise is portrayed as a place with gold and silver[88]and pearl,[89] similar to heaven with its crystal glass, gold, and precious stones.[90] There is a portrayal of unity and love, centered on the praise of God,[91] much as the biblical heaven is depicted.[92]

NOTES

1.   B.2:149; 6:151, 219, 301; 9:476.
2.   1 Sam 2:3.
3.   Acts 1:24.
4.   Matt 6:32.
5.   Matt 6:4, 18.
6.   Matt 24:36.
7.   Deut 29:29.
8.   Q.5:119; 8:557; 9:88, 609; Q.9:100.
9.   B.1:624.
10.   B.6:411.
11.   B.8:320, 321.
12.   B.4:670.
13.   B.4:57, 69; 5:416, 417, 421.
14.   B.1:770; 9:532.1.
15.   Based on Q.3:77, B.3:546, 599, 692, 839; 4:416; 8:653; 9:294, 537.
16.   B.4:670; 6:72.
17.   B.4:556; 6:236.
18.   B.3:648.
19.   Deut 1:34; Num 10:11.
20.   Ex 32:14, KJV; 1 Sam 15:35.
21.   Gen 6:6; 1 Sam 15:10.
22.   Ps 2:4; 37:13.
23.   Ex 33:17; 1 Kgs 3:10.
24.   E.g., Q.35:43; Ps 110:4; Jas 1:17.
25.   B.9:512.

26. Isa 65:1–2.
27. 2 Pet 3:9.
28. B.2:221; 9:482, 483, 534.
29. B.5:432, 430, 509; B.4:272, 89, 90; 8:617; 9:342.
30. Ps 73:24; 1 Chr 29:17–18; 2 Chr 7:14; Ps 18:29.
31. B.4:266.1.
32. Deut 30:10.
33. Job 37:12.
34. Judges 20:35.
35. Judges 12:3.
36. B.1:796; 9:485.
37. Prov 8:36, The Message.
38. Ps 51:4.
39. Mark 2:7; Luke 5:21.
40. B.9:482, 534, 590.
41. B.8:379; also 8:386, 388.
42. Ps 51:1–10.
43. Ps 103:12.
44. B.4:76, 77, 143; 7:336; 8:374, 376, 378, 380, 381, 382, 385, 399.
45. B.2:263; 9:487; 8:391.
46. Ps 143:10; Eph 5:17.
47. Job 37:16; Rom 11:3.
48. Ex 9:16; Rom 1:20.
49. 2 Chr 20:6; Phil 1:19.
50. Ps 119:41; 1 Cor 9:23.
51. 1 Kgs 8:27; Luke 18:27.
52. Deut 29:29; Matt 6:6.
53. Prov 30:8; Matt 7:11.
54. Prov 19:23; Phil 4:12.
55. B.4:238.
56. E.g., B.1:805; 2:253; 3:23; 4:514; 5:442.
57. Ex 8:10; Rev 19:16.
58. Deut 6:13.
59. Isa 46:5.
60. Ps 93:5; 1 Tim 1:17.

61. Isa 40:26; Eph 1:19.

62. Ps 18:49; 1 Pet 2:9.

63. 2 Chr 32.26; Mt 2:3.

64. Gen 24:26; Acts 13:2.

65. Deut 9:18; Rom 14:11.

66. Gen 28:15; Rom 15:8.

67. Deut 20:4; 1 Cor 15:57.

68. Deut 4:46; Luke 1:74.

69. Some of these themes are picked up in the prayers of the Qur'an, e.g., Q.1:1–7; 2:286; 3:8, 9, 191–194.

70. Matt 24:7; Mark 13:8; Luke 21:11; B.2:55, 121, 133, 143; 3:472, 635, 670; 6:215.

71. B.4:806 cf. Matt 24:5, 11.

72. B.1:86, 184, 795; 2:162; Rev 16:13; 19:20; 20:10.

73. Rev 13:3, 12; B.2:437; 4:290.1; 8:194. Al-Bukhāri's Hadith do not mention that Christ will kill ad-Dajjal, but this is described in Muslim bk 41 no. 7015 narrated by al-Nawwās ibn Samʿān and Muslim bk 41 no. 7023 narrated by ʿAbdullah Ibn ʾAmr.

74. Rev 13:16, 17; 14:9; 16:2; 19:20; 20:4; B.2:626; 4:754; 7:795; 9:245, 505.

75. B.4:659, 684, 685, 688; 8:488; 9:597, 599, cf. Rev 13:13; 2 Thess 2:9.

76. B.3:106; 9:246 cf. Rev 13:15.

77. Rev 20:1-6; B.3:425; also 3:656; 4:567.

78. B.7:221.

79. B.8:188. Some end times prophecies seem rather strange. An example is, "Allah's Apostle said, 'The Hour will not be established till the buttocks of the women of the tribe of Daus move while going round Dhi-al-Khalasa.' Dhi-al-Khalasa was the idol which the Daus tribe worshipped in the Pre-Islamic Period of ignorance" (B.9:232).

80. B.6:336; 8:526; and Heb 1:10–12.

81. B.8:562, 566.

82. Matt 11:22, 24.

83. Luke 12:47, 48.

84. Luke 20:47.

85. John 12:24.

86. 1 Cor 15:36, 37, 42–44.

87.   B.8:565.

88.   B4:468, 469; 9:171, 536.

89.   B.6:402.

90.   Rev 4:3–6; 21:10–21.

91.   B.4:468, 469.

92.   Rev 4:6–5:14; 7:9–12.

7

ETHICAL ISSUES

SOME MORAL INSTRUCTION in the Hadith also reveals a congru-
ence with biblical teaching. One commentator sees little disjunction
between Islam and Christianity. Renard postulates: "Non-Muslims
are often surprised, even shocked, to hear that Islam's central spiritual and ethical presuppositions are virtually identical to those of
Judaism and Christianity."[1]

1. ORIENTATION TOWARD OTHERS

Muslims are called to consider the well-being and benefit of others. "None of you will have faith till he wishes for his (Muslim)
brother what he likes for himself."[2] This has a parallel in the Golden
Rule: "Do to others what you would have them do to you."[3] In the
Hadith, however, positive speech and action is directed only toward
other Muslims rather than to humanity in general.[4] Sincerity and
truth and the love that reveals faith have their object only in those
who follow the path of Islam.[5]

Biblical altruism is generally less discriminatory: "Do everything
in love,"[6] although sometimes it is more focused: "Do good to all
men, especially to those who belong to the family of believers."[7] Just
as Jesus taught that "it is more blessed to give than to receive"[8] and

to "give to everyone who asks of you,"[9] Muhammad held that "the upper (i.e. giving) hand is better than the lower (i.e. taking) hand."[10]

Such acts of benevolence must not be carried out with a begrudging heart, for Islam's prophet stated that "he who is not merciful to others, will not be treated mercifully,"[11] a sentiment previously expressed in the Sermon on the Mount.[12] Such mercy extended to the forgiveness of debt: "If the debtor is poor, forgive him, so that Allah may forgive us."[13] The Lord's Prayer, taught by Jesus, suggests a connection between divine and human forgiveness.[14]

In a repetition of an Old Testament instruction,[15] runaway slaves who came to Medina were not to be returned to their masters, but allowed to remain free.[16] Caring for other believers resembles the parts of one body being affected by each other,[17] similar to the Pauline teaching.[18]

2. MORAL REQUIREMENTS

A list of directives attributed to Muhammad bears a remarkable similarity to the Ten Commandments:

Swear allegiance to me for

1. Not to join anything in worship along with Allah.

2. Not to steal.

3. Not to commit illegal sexual intercourse.

4. Not to kill your children.

5. Not to accuse an innocent person (to spread such an accusation among people).

6. Not to be disobedient (when ordered) to do good deed.[19]

Lying, dishonesty, breaking promises, betrayal of trust, and quarreling in an insulting manner were seen as the signs of a hypocrite.[20] One man's lies resulted in a long life of poverty.[21] Seven types of people will be protected at judgment: the just ruler, the pious youth, those who pray constantly, two people who love each other for Allah's sake, a man refusing illicit sex, a generous person, and those who weep for Allah.[22] Muhammad said: "The most beloved to me amongst you is the one who has the best character and manners."[23]

Other significant ways of developing and maintaining social adhesion were enjoined (see Sidebar *Maintaining Social Cohesion*).

Relationships were important. Blood, property, and honor were described as sacred to each other, just as the ritual slaughter day was sacred to the whole community.[24] Leaders were to be obeyed unless they had gone seriously astray.[25] Taking the initiative in mending fractured relationships was commanded by Jesus[26] and commended by Muhammad.[27]

Beyond these outward conformities, there was a recognition that the key to personal change was the heart: "Beware! There is a piece of flesh in the body if it

MAINTAINING SOCIAL COHESION

Muslims are told to feed the poor and to greet others, whether known or not.[a] Helping widows and the poor was equivalent to jihad, prayer, and fasting.[b] Similarly Jesus criticized those who prayed publicly while devouring widows' houses[c] and those who tithed meticulously while ignoring justice and mercy.[d]

The oppressed were to be aided by Muslims, and people should be helped to fulfill their oaths.[e] Muslims were required to return lost things to their owners,[f] and wedding invitations must be accepted.[g]

becomes good (reformed) the whole body becomes good but if it gets spoilt the whole body gets spoilt and that is the heart."[28] Jesus said: "The good man brings good things out of the good stored up in his heart,

---

a.   B.1:11, 27; 253.2.

b.   B.7:265; 8:253.1.

c.   Mark 12:40/Luke 20:47.

d.   Matt 23:23; Luke 11:42.

e.   B.7:104.

f.   B.1:91; 5:603. This was similar to the Mosaic law (Ex 23:4).

g.   B.2:331; 3:625; 7:104, 539, 753; 9:285.

and the evil man brings evil things out of the evil stored up in his heart. For out of the overflow of his heart his mouth speaks."[29]

Reward was connected with intention—people are to be recompensed in accordance with their motives, not simply their actions.[30] A man intending to kill another man, although prevented from doing so, would be sent to the hell-fire.[31] Even positive actions with ulterior motives are to be judged. Muhammad spoke of people who performed the *Hajj* "with the intention of seeking Allah's pleasure only and not to show off."[32] Those who did good things publicly to win human praise would be humiliated by Allah.[33] After describing such people in another context, Jesus said, "They have already received their reward."[34]

The Old Testament addresses this theme when Yahweh asks the people of Israel: "When you fasted and mourned in the fifth and seventh months for the past seventy years, *was it really for me* that you fasted? And when you were eating and drinking, were you not just feasting for yourselves?"[35] Just as Jesus identified adultery of the heart through lustful looks,[36] the Hadith recognize that "the adultery of the eye is the looking (at something which is sinful to look at), and the adultery of the tongue is to utter (what it is unlawful to utter), and the inner self wishes and longs for (adultery)."[37]

3. PARALLEL TEACHING

Some Hadith narratives and statements closely resemble Jesus' instruction (see Table 14).

TEACHING	JESUS' TEACHING	HADITH
The parable of the workers in the vineyard	Matthew 20:1–6	B.1:532; 3:468, 469; 4:665; 6:539; 9:559–Muslims receive double pay. B.3:471; 1:533–Muslims receive all the wages when Jews and Christians give up early.
Treasure hidden in the field	Matthew 13:44	B.4:678–has a different ending

"A good tree cannot bear bad fruit, and a bad tree cannot bear good fruit."	Matthew 7:18	B.2:544; 8:435 "Good never brings forth evil." Comparison with vegetation
Parable of the great banquet	Luke 14:16-25	B.9:385
Faith equal to a mustard seed	Matthew 17:20; Luke 17:6	B.1:21; 8:504,565; 9:208,600, 601
"He who exalts himself will be humbled."	Luke 14:11; 18:14	Allah "brings down whatever rises high in the world." B.4:124; 8:508
"Free the captives, feed the hungry and visit the sick."	Matthew 25:35,36	B.4:282; 7:103,104, 286, 552
Servant Songs applied to Muhammad who "shouts not in the markets,"	Isaiah 42:2 and Matthew 12:15-19	Q.48:8; B.6:362
... "does not return evil for evil"	Isaiah 53:7; 1 Peter 3:9 cf. Luke 6:29	
... "guides a crooked nation on the right path"	Isaiah 42:16; 45:2; Luke 3:5	
... will "cause to open blind eyes, deaf ears and hardened hearts."	Isaiah 35:5; Matthew 11:5/ Luke 7:22; Mark 7:37	
Oaths of any kind were forbidden.	Matt 5:34–37, particularly if based on physical objects (Matt 23:16–22); Isa 65:16	"If anybody has to take an oath, he should swear only by Allah." B.5:177; 8:129
"Give to anyone who asks you."	Luke 6:30	Muhammad gave a blanket to a man who asked for it B.2:367; 3:306
God sends sun and rain on the good and the evil; gives good things even to the evil.	Matt 5:45; 7:11	Allah is patient and sends health and provision even to those who ascribe children to him B.9:475

TABLE 14: Parallels between Hadith teaching and Jesus' teaching

The "otherworldly" teaching of Jesus, encouraging His followers to store up treasures in heaven,[38] resonates with a passage in the Hadith[39] where certain luxury goods "are for the unbelievers in this worldly life and for us in the Hereafter." The "Hereafter" is mentioned many times—wearing silk is for those with no share in the Hereafter, for a well-dressed soul may be naked in the Hereafter.[40] Muhammad describes those escaping the hell-fire as like "camels without a shepherd,"[41] similar to Jesus' portrayal of the harassed and helpless crowds of His day as "sheep without a shepherd."[42]

WEALTH, WEDDINGS, AND WEEPING

Islam's prophet stated that "a person who practices charity so secretly that his left hand does not know what his right hand has given will be shaded by Allah,"[h] a clear replica of Jesus' saying.[i] Wedding banquets should not include the rich only, but the poor should also be invited,[j] echoing Jesus' call.[k] Just as Christ proclaimed, "Blessed are you who weep now, for you will laugh" and "woe to you who laugh now for you will mourn and weep,"[l] Muhammad announced to his followers: "If you but knew what I know, you would laugh less and weep more!"[m]

Jesus, according to one Hadith account, refused to see the worst in people. One hadith reports that "Jesus, seeing a man stealing, asked him, 'Did you steal?' He said, 'No, by Allah, except Whom there is none who has the right to be worshipped.' Jesus said, 'I believe in Allah and suspect my eyes.'"[43] The gospels contain many accounts of Jesus' gracious responses to people who might not normally be considered worthy of such. These include the tax collectors Matthew[44] and Zaccheus,[45] the adulterous Samaritan woman,[46] the complaining and ungrateful man lying paralyzed beside the pool at Bethsaida,[47] and the criminal crucified alongside Jesus at Calvary.[48] Jesus had a reputation as "the friend . . . of sinners."[49] When challenged about mixing with such people, Jesus threw down the gauntlet to his detractors: "Go and learn what this means: 'I desire mercy and not sacrifice.'"[50]

---

h.   B.2:504, also 1:629; 8:799.

i.   Matt 6:3.

j.   B.7:106.

k.   Luke 14:13-14.

l.   Luke 6:21, 25.

m.   B.7:148; 8:492, 493, 627; 2:154; 6:145; 8:627, 632.

According to the Hadith, the real life is that of the Hereafter. There is no life except the life of the Hereafter. "There is no goodness except that of the Hereafter—it is 'the real goodness.'"[51] "Allah has given one of His slaves the choice of receiving the splendor and luxury of the worldly life whatever he likes or to accept the good (of the Hereafter) which is with Allah."[52] Muhammad's followers bemoaned their good fortune: "Worldly wealth was bestowed upon us and we were given thereof too much. We are afraid that the reward of our deeds have [sic] been given to us in this life,"[53] reflecting Jesus' warning: "they have received their reward in full."[54] Echoing John the Baptist,[55] Paul,[56] and the writer to the Hebrews,[57] Muhammad counsels satisfaction with one's financial situation: "Riches does not mean, having a great amount of property, but riches is self-contentment."[58]

Paul's words of the glory of heaven[59] are reprised in Allah's promise: "I have prepared for My pious slaves things which have never been seen by an eye, or heard by an ear, or imagined by a human being."[60] Muhammad's statement, "Be in this world as if you were a stranger or a traveler,"[61] is reminiscent of the writer to the Hebrews' description of those who "admitted that they were aliens and strangers on earth . . . they were longing for a better country—a heavenly one,"[62] and Peter's portrayal of fellow Christians as "aliens and strangers in the world."[63] Statements cautioning wealthy people, such as, "Those who are rich in this world would have little reward in the Hereafter except those who spend their money here and there (in Allah's cause), and they are few in number,"[64] find a parallel in Jesus' warnings against riches.[65]

Just as Jesus said it would be hard for a rich man to enter heaven,[66] Muhammad observed, "I stood at the gate of Paradise and saw that the majority of the people who entered it were the poor, while the wealthy were stopped at the gate."[67] Muhammad feared that wealth would destroy his people.[68] Comparing a poor and a rich passerby, he said: "This (poor man) is better than such a large number of the first type (i.e. rich men) as to fill the earth."[69] The antidote to wealth's poison was generosity (see Sidebar *Wealth, Weddings, and Weeping*).

At other times, there is a balance expressed between this world and the next: "O Allah! Our Lord! Give us in this world that, which is good and in the Hereafter that, which is good and save us from the torment of the Fire."[70] Likewise Jesus promised that those who gave up "home or brothers or sisters or mother or father or children or fields for me and the gospel" would receive a hundredfold in this life, and in the world to come, eternal life.[71] However, the number experiencing this will be comparatively small. Jesus said: "But small is the gate and narrow the road that leads to life, and only a few find it."[72] The Hadith puts a number on it. Apparently only 0.1 percent of the human race will escape the fire of hell.[73]

4. CONNECTION WITH GOD

Muhammad is portrayed as God's unique representative on earth. The angels claimed about him: "Whoever obeys Muhammad, obeys Allah; and whoever disobeys Muhammad, disobeys Allah."[74] In the Qur'an, Muhammad is told to inform the people, "If you love Allah, then follow me. Allah will love you and forgive you your sins."[75]

Remarkably this bold claim does not appear to be made by anyone in the Bible, apart from Jesus who used similar words to describe his relationship with God, His heavenly Father. One is reminded of statements by Jesus describing this close relationship (see Table 15).

"When he looks at me, he sees the One who sent me"	John 12:45
"He who receives me receives the One who sent me"	Matt 10:40
"Whoever welcomes me does not welcome me but the One who sent me"	Mark 9:37
"Whoever accepts me accepts the One who sent me"	John 13:20
"When a man believes in me, he does not believe in me only, but in the One who sent me"	John 12:44
"Anyone who has seen me has seen the Father"	John 14:9
"If you really knew me you would know my Father as well"	John 14:7
"He who does not honor the Son does not honor the Father, who sent him"	John 5:23
"He who hates me hates my Father as well"	John 15:23

| "He who rejects me rejects Him who sent me" | Luke 10:16 |
| "Whoever has my commands and obeys them, he is the one who loves me. He who loves me will be loved by my Father, and I too will love him and show myself to him." | John 14:21 |

TABLE 15: Jesus' descriptions of his relationship with his heavenly Father

5. REFLECTIONS

In the topics mentioned above, we find elements in the Hadith and the biblical revelation which strike a parallel chord. There are two possible errors that could result from identifying such similarities. The first is attributing a simple one-to-one correspondence. It would be easy, for example, to conclude that Muslims mean the same thing by "commandments" as Jews and Christians do. A similar form does not mean that it will have the same connotation or function in different religious communities. Anderson notes: "The law of Moses was in fact given to a redeemed people as a way of life not to an unredeemed people as the means of redemption."[76] Any notion must be interpreted within its cultural and religious metanarrative.

The opposite error would be to dismiss all such similarities as arbitrary accidents bearing only a superficial relationship to each other. This could result in overlooking some valuable connections that could be made. Law, for example, operated in a variety of ways in the Old Testament. It lay down ritual, social, and moral requirements for the community. The coming of Christ did not do away with all of these, since a variety of religious rituals, legal regulations, and ethical values are still practiced in every Christian community.

NOTES

1.   Renard, *In the footsteps*, 21. He does not go quite as far as a Victorian
     (Aust.) judge who claimed: "Islam and Christianity are basically the
     same." Islamic Council of Victoria v Catch the Fire Ministries Inc
     (Final) [2004], VCAT 2510 (December 22, 2004), http://www.
     austlii.edu.au/cgi-bin/sinodisp/au/cases/vic/VCAT/2004/2510.html?
     stem=0&synonyms=0&query=racial%20tolerance%20scotl (accessed
     October 14, 2015).

2.   B.1:12. Also in Hadith Muslim *Kitab al-Iman* no. 45.

3.   Matt 7:12. A similar concept is found in many other religions and
     philosophies. "The Hindus said: 'Utter not a word by which anyone
     could be wounded.' The ancient Chinese urged: 'Never do to others
     what you would not like them to do to you.' Cicero of Rome said:
     'Men were brought into existence for the sake of men that they might
     do one another good.'" Miller, *Discipling Nations*, 130.

4.   B.1:9, 10.

5.   B.1:54; B.1:16.

6.   1 Cor 16:14.

7.   Gal 6:10.

8.   Acts 20:35.

9.   Matt 5:42.

10. B.4:13, 371; 8:448.

11. B.8:42; 2:373; 9:473, 474, 540.

12. Matt 5:7.

13. B.4:687.

14. Matt 6:12.

15. Deut 23:15–16.

16. B.7:210.

17. B.8:40.

18. 1 Cor 12:12–26 esp. v. 26.

19. B.1:17.

20. B.1:32; B.1:33.

21. B.1:722.

22. B.1:629.

23. B.5:104.

24. B.1:67, 105.

25. B.4:203; 1:100.
26. Matt 5:23–24; 18:15.
27. B.8:254.
28. B.1:49.
29. Luke 6:45.
30. B.1:1,51; 3:706; 7:8; 8:680; 9:85.
31. B.1:30.
32. B.1:25.
33. B.8:506; 9:266.
34. Matt 6:2.
35. Zech 7:5–6, italics mine.
36. Matt 5:28.
37. B.8:609; 260. This may have been canceled by another hadith stating: "Allah has accepted my invocation to forgive what whispers in the hearts of my followers unless they act on it or utter it" (B.3:705). Yet this hadith may simply be stating that temptation by Satan (who whispers into human hearts Q.7:20; 20:120) is not the same as giving in to the sinful impulse.
38. Matt 6:19–20.
39. B.7:334.
40. B.2:11,69; B.1:115; 2:226; 3:317, 782, 788; 4:289; 8:237.
41. B.8:587.
42. Matt 9:36.
43. B.4:653.
44. Matt 9:9–13.
45. Luke 19:1–10.
46. John 4:4–26.
47. John 5:1–15.
48. Luke 23:32–43.
49. Matt 11:19.
50. Matt 9:12–13.
51. B.4:87; 5:425; B.4:209; 5:139, 140, 141; 8:422, 423; B.1:420; 4:88; 5:269, 424, 426; B.9:308.
52. B.5:244, 719.
53. B.5:376.
54. Matt 6:2, 5, 16.

55. Luke 3:14.

56. Phil 4:11; 1 Tim 6:8.

57. Heb 13:8.

58. B.8:453.

59. 1 Cor 2:9 quoted from Isa 64:4. This quotation is also used by Sufis, e.g., see Chittick, *Sufi Path of Love,* 205.

60. B.4:467; 6:302, 303; 9:589. These words were included in the Mahdi's letter inviting Queen Victoria in 1887 to come to Khartoum and submit to Islam following his defeat of British troops after General Gordon's death. Moorehead, *The White Nile,* 316. In doing this, the Mahdi was following Muhammad's example of calling world leaders to accept Islam, e.g., Heraclius of Byzantine, B.1:6; 4:191, 221; 6:75; 8:277, and Chosroes of Persia B.1:64; 4:190; 5:708; 9:369.

61. B.8:425.

62. Heb 11:13–16.

63. 1 Pet 2:11.

64. B.3:573; 8:285.

65. E.g., Luke 6:24.

66. Matt 19:23.

67. B.7:124.

68. B.5:351; 8:434, 435, 456.

69. B.8:454.

70. B.6:47; 8:398.

71. Mark 10:29–30.

72. Matt 7:14.

73. B.4:567; 6:265; 8:537.

74. B.9:385, 251.

75. Q.3:31.

76. Anderson, *Christianity,* 45.

III

SEEKING CONNECTIONS

DEVELOPING THE CONSTRUCTIVE

There are some teachings found in the Hadith which may inform and enrich the discussion of the biblical teaching with Muslims. They move beyond the realm of simple agreement. Those aspects described as "concord" in Section 2 reveal facets that have arrived at the *same destination* as biblical teaching, with an almost complete concurrence. However, the elements in this section could be described as moving in the *same or a similar direction* as a Christian understanding of the gospel without yet having arrived at the same conclusions. They contain within them the seeds of something more, for they can open doors to further discussion and development. These can be springboards to biblical teaching which might not be otherwise recognized by Islam. They begin a trajectory which can find its end point in the person and work of Christ, thus becoming a key in the Christian apostolic mission to Islam. The term "springboards" is preferred over "bridges," since the latter implies a definite destination and end point. Springboards require a "leap of faith," which may or may not result in the desired destination. Some room must be left for those Muslims and others who consider the same material and arrive at different conclusions.

A series of propositional statements from Christian theology may help us compare biblical teaching with some of the ideas found in the Hadith. They are as follows:

- Divine beneficence—God's basic attitude toward humanity is kind and generous.
- Divine holiness—in His essence, God is sacred and pure, separated from sin.
- Human worth—people are in the image of God and capable of relationship with Him.
- Human obduracy—all people are sinners, unable to earn God's pleasure by their own efforts.
- Human incapacity—no amount of good works will earn enough merit.
- The necessity of God's grace—humans cannot be saved without a divine intervention.
- Proximity and incarnation—God is near to us and able to enter into human existence.
- Christ's roles—as a sinless human, Jesus is eminently qualified as the mediator between God and humanity.
- Expiation—the principle of exchange of actions, rewards, and punishments is established.
- Salvation—the cross of Christ displays aspects of sacrifice, martyrdom, atonement, redemption, and victory over Satan in the context of betrayed hospitality.
- Intercession—Jesus stands as a mediator between God and humanity.
- Faith and love—these are the means of applying salvation to ourselves.
- Results of salvation—these include a new birth, cleansing, forgiveness, and eternal assurance.

These will be used as benchmarks for discovering the springboards that may be found in the Hadith. There are other vital elements of Christian doctrine, such as the inspiration of Scripture, the triune nature of God, the deity of Christ, and the work of the Holy Spirit which are not addressed in the Hadith.[1]

Clearly neither the Hadith, nor any other Islamic documents, outline a full and complete exposition of Christian teaching, otherwise they would not be Islamic. It would be naive in the utmost to suppose that a completely Christian worldview could be constructed using only Islamic sources. However, we do find some elements of the

Hadith which may become springboards for Muslims to approach the truth as it has been revealed in the Bible. These elements will be described. In the subsection labeled "Connections with biblical themes" at the end of each chapter, the lacuna between the Hadith's concepts and biblical teaching on the topic will be identified and some ways of connecting the two will be suggested.

NOTES

1. Norman Geisler suggests the following as essential doctrines of the Christian faith: (1) human depravity, (2) Christ's virgin birth, (3) Christ's sinlessness, (4) Christ's deity, (5) Christ's humanity, (6) God's unity, (7) God's triunity, (8) the necessity of God's grace, (9) the necessity of faith, (10) Christ's atoning death, (11) Christ's bodily resurrection, (12) Christ's bodily ascension, (13) Christ's present high priestly service, and (14) Christ's second coming, final judgment (heaven and hell), and reign. Source: http://www.equip.org/articles/the-essential-doctrines-of-the-christian-faith-part-two-. (accessed October 14, 2015)

8

THE CHARACTER AND ACTIONS OF GOD

1. DIVINE BENEFICENCE

God is described in the Hadith as the One who generates benefit out of mishap. Someone commented to Aisha when she recovered a lost necklace: "By Allah, whenever anything happened which you did not like, Allah brought good for you and for the Muslims in that."[1] The Christian concept is analogous: "The benevolence of God is manifested in his concern for the welfare of the creature and is suited to the creature's needs and capacities."[2] The Bible declares that "we know that in all things God works for the good of those who love him, who have been called according to his purpose."[3]

Yet God's desire for the welfare of His people is not necessarily reciprocated. Muhammad said: "None is more patient than Allah against the harmful saying.[4] He hears from the people they ascribe children to Him, yet He gives them health and (supplies them with) provision."[5] It is reminiscent of Jesus' description of the heavenly Father who "makes his sun rise on the evil and on the good, and sends rain on the just and on the unjust" and "is kind to the ungrateful and wicked."[6]

2. DIVINE HOLINESS

Both the Bible and the Qur'an refer to God's holiness.[7] Hannah declares, "There is no one holy like the Lord," and the redeemed in heaven sing, "For you alone are holy . . . for your righteous acts have been revealed."[8] God takes no pleasure in evil[9] and cannot even bear to look at it, let alone tolerate it.[10] Likewise in the Hadith Allah is not neutral about sin—he takes great interest. "Sins are Allah's *Hima* (i.e. private pasture) and whoever pastures (his sheep) near it, is likely to get in it at any moment. . . . The *Hima* of Allah on the earth is His illegal (forbidden) things. Beware!"[11] People are warned against trespassing on this pasture, for its owner is strict. Interestingly, a Greek word for "sin" *paraptoma* used in the New Testament is sometimes translated as "trespass."[12] The Prophet said, "There is none having a greater sense of *Ghīra* than Allah, and for that reason He has forbidden shameful deeds and sins (illegal sexual intercourse etc.)."[13] *Ghīra* is defined as "a feeling of great fury and anger when one's honour and prestige are injured or challenged."[14] The Bible many times describes the Lord as "a jealous God."[15]

3. DIVINE INITIATIVE

The Qur'an seems to limit Allah's activity to giving signs for humanity to see and sending prophets for humanity to hear. In the Hadith, we find an expansion of the divine role: Allah himself actively seeks fellowship with humankind. In a passage reminiscent of Yahweh coming down to the earth in the book of Genesis,[16] Allah descends from his throne toward the earth.

> Our Lord, the Blessed, the Superior, comes every night down on the nearest Heaven to us when the last third of the night remains, saying: "Is there anyone to invoke Me, so that I may respond to invocation? Is there anyone to ask Me, so that I may grant him his request? Is there anyone seeking My forgiveness, so that I may forgive him?"[17]

Similarities are found in the teaching of Jesus about "the true wor-shipers (who) worship the Father in spirit and truth, for they are the kind of worshipers the Father seeks."[18] Jesus described Himself as one who "came to seek and save what was lost."[19] Paul quotes God's patient anguish: "All day long I held out my hands to a disobedient and obstinate people."[20]

When people respond to this heavenly initiative, there is divine joy. "Allah is more pleased with the repentance of His slave than anyone of you is pleased with finding his camel which he had lost in the desert."[21] This echoes the parables of the lost sheep, the lost coin, the lost son, and the rejoicing in heaven over one sinner who repents.[22]

In a bold image evocative of the same chapter of Luke, a description in the Hadith pushes the analogy further (see Sidebar *The Running Father*).

As with the story of the prodigal son, the paternal-filial relationship was not based on works, but on deep affection. One day a man met Muhammad outside a mosque. "The man said, 'O Allah's Apostle! When will be the hour?' The Prophet asked him, 'What have you prepared for it?' The man became afraid and ashamed and then said, 'O Allah's Apostle!

THE RUNNING FATHER

The Prophet said, "Allah says: 'I am just as My slave thinks I am, (i.e. I am able to do for him what he thinks I can do for him) . . . and if he comes one span nearer to Me, I go one cubit nearer to him; and if he comes one cubit nearer to Me, I go a distance of two outstretched arms nearer to him; and if he comes to Me walking, I go to him running.'"[a] The parallel with the father's response to the returning prodigal son could hardly be stronger. "But while he was still a long way off, his father saw him and was filled with compassion for him; he ran to his son, threw his arms around him and kissed him."[b] This is the same Lord, described in the Old Testament, who "longs to be gracious to you; he rises to show you compassion."[c]

---

a.   B.9:502, 627, 628.

b.   Luke 15:20.

c.   Isa 30:18.

I haven't prepared for it much of fasts, prayers or charitable gifts but I love Allah and His Apostle.' The Prophet said, 'You will be with the one whom you love.'"[23]

The promise of Jesus concerning each one who follows Him is likewise reassuring. "My Father will love him, and we will come to him and make our home with him."[24]

4. DIVINE PROXIMITY

Islam has sometimes struggled to balance the transcendence and immanence of God. The Qur'an hints at God's immanence through physical images, e.g., he is "closer than your jugular vein,"[25] and "God stands between a man and his heart."[26] Allah says, "I am indeed near. I respond to the invocations of the supplicant when he calls on me"[27] for "He is with you wheresoever you may be."[28] However, Islam's greatest scholar, al-Ghazāli, is quick to point out that "His nearness is not like the nearness of bodies."[29]

The general trend of the Qur'an is to assert God's transcendence, emphasizing distance and difference (see Table 16).

His creatures "will never compass anything of His knowledge except that which He wills."	Q.2:255
He is "above what they attribute to Him."	Q.6:100
"No vision can grasp Him but His grasp is over all vision: He is above all comprehension yet is acquainted with all things."	Q.6:103
"There is nothing like Him."	Q.42:11
"There is none co-equal or comparable unto Him."	Q.112:4

TABLE 16: Qur'anic descriptions of the transcendence of Allah

Muhammad did not see God in a physical form during his ascension to Paradise, despite coming within two bow-lengths,[30] for Gabriel obscured the whole horizon.[31] "Whoever tells you that

Muhammad saw his Lord is a liar," stated Aisha.[32] One Muslim scholar notes: "However close a man may approach God in his journeying towards him, even in his highest ascension, man remains man and very much remote from God."[33]

Yet the Hadith enlarge the idea of the nearness of God. Muhammad told his followers: "Allah is not hidden from you."[34] Whilst hiding in the cave from the searching Quraish during their escape from Mecca to Medina, Muhammad admonishes his fearful, whispering companion: "O Abu Bakr, be quiet! (For we are) two and Allah is the Third of us."[35] Prayer facilitates a special proximity: "Whenever anyone of you is in prayer, he is speaking in private to his Lord,"[36] and "During the prayer, Allah is in front of every one of you."[37] When asked, "What is *Ihsan* (perfection)?" Allah's Apostle replied, "To worship Allah as if you see Him, and if you cannot achieve this state of devotion then you must consider that He is looking at you."[38]

The Qur'an speaks of a pure apparition of God in Paradise.[39] One reference notes: "This is the Islamic version of the Christian hope one day to hear the words 'Well done good and faithful servant,' and acts as the seal upon the many and varied blessings of Paradise, the ultimate proof that Islam is true, as the lowly slave of Allah gazes upon the face of the Almighty Himself."[40] The sight of the full moon at night or the sun on a cloudless day provided an object lesson regarding the Muslim vision of God in paradise.[41] Muhammad commented to his companions: "Certainly you will see your Lord as you see this moon and you will have no trouble in seeing Him."[42] Evidently Muhammad expected a clear view of God, for he described his own actions at the judgment: "When I see Him, I will fall down in prostration before Him."[43]

5. DIVINE ENFLESHMENT

Although most Muslims would react strongly against the doctrine of the incarnation, the Hadith present some strong links between the divine and the human. Clearly, spiritual beings can take on human flesh. The Qur'an speaks of Mary seeing the angel who "appeared before her as a man in all respects."[44] Likewise three angels visited Abraham, who set food before them.[45] The Hadith report similar angelophanies. "One day a man approached Muhammad and a group of Muslims. When the man left after a series of questions and answers, Muhammad said, 'That was Gabriel who came to teach the people their religion.'"[46]

Satan is classified as one of the jinn[47] and they are said to be made from smokeless fire.[48] However, when Satan was stealing food from the *Zakat* store, he was caught by Abū Huraira, who extracted some advice from Satan before letting him go.[49] Muhammad also told his companions that "I caught [a jinn] and intended to tie him to one of the pillars of the mosque so that all of you might see him."[50] In another version, it is Satan who was caught and choked by Muhammad.[51]

Likewise Allah is presented as having or taking on some kind of physical form. When Moses approached a fire in the desert, a voice from the flames said, "I am your Lord."[52] Nazir-Ali asks, "God can show himself to Moses in the burning bush, can he not show himself to us in the man Jesus?"[53]

An interesting image arises from a creation narrative in the Hadith. The Prophet said, "Allah created His creation, and when He had finished it, the womb got up and caught hold of Allah whereupon Allah said, 'What is the matter?' On that, it said, 'I seek refuge with you from those who sever the ties of kith and kin.'"[54] It is difficult to envisage how a woman's womb could catch hold of Allah or even how to understand this event as a metaphor.

God ...	Old Testament	New Testament	Qur'an
has a hand	Ex 7:4	Mark 16:19	Q.3:26
sees (eyes)	Gen 16:13	Matt 6:4	Q.3:163
hears (ears)	Ex 3:7	1 John 5:14	Q.34:50
speaks (mouth)	Ex 20:1	Heb :1	Q.2:253
sits on the throne	Ps 47:8	Rev 6:16	Q.7:54
has a face	2 Chr 7:14	Matt 18:10	Q.18:28

TABLE 17: Examples of anthropomorphic language in the Bible and Qur'an

In accord with Bible and the Qur'an (see Table 17), the Hadith mention several parts of the body attributed to God. His right hand is described as "full . . . not affected by the continuous spending night and day"[55] and his other hand as holding "the balance of justice."[56] He holds the heavens and the earth between His hands. He is also depicted as writing in "His Book which is with Him on His Throne."[57] The throne of Allah is also mentioned over thirty times, implying a sitting action.[58] After the judgment, Allah will put his foot on hell to make it smaller.[59] Allah is said to "turn his face" from those who turn their faces from him.[60] He is one who "sees and hears."[61]

At the judgment, the part of Allah's body which Muslims recognize will be his "shin" sāq, which he will uncover at their request.[62] Muslims are almost encouraged to speculate or visualize how Allah may appear, for Allah's form will be "a shape nearest to the picture they had in their minds about Him."[63]

These have been differently interpreted throughout the ages, by Jews, Christians, and Muslims.

6. CONNECTIONS WITH BIBLICAL THEMES

This topic of the nature of God contains promising material for discussion between Muslims and Christians.

(a) Beneficence

Reactively providing life's necessities for those in need, beneficence may be the material equivalent of a "tolerance" which accepts the existence of the other. An aloof philanthropist who gives anonymously

---

MARXIST VIEW OF GOD

The Marxist Maxime Rodinson contrasts the Muslim and Christian views of God. He describes Allah as "kind, merciful and close to man, whom he warned, loved and forgave like an indulgent father. But a great gulf divided him from his creature, a gulf which nothing could fill—not even unfailing care for a people lovingly chosen; nor the Redeemer, born of himself, so sensitive to human suffering that he came to share it. His paternal love for mankind was somewhat abstract and universal, expressed in a general goodness towards humanity as a whole or towards groups of men. It was . . . the busy, organizing but not particularly affectionate goodness of the head of a family."[d]

---

d. Rodinson, *Muhammad*, 235.

without personal contact may be seen as "beneficent" (see Sidebar *Marxist View of God*).

The biblical view seems more proactive, presenting a God who understands the deeper desires of the human heart, beyond mere physical provision, and responds to those needs.[64] The Old Testament contains "fifteen references to God as Father, while the NT speaks of God as Father on 245 occasions, most of which are on the lips of Jesus."[65]

(b) Divine holiness

Divine holiness is important when considering the concept of forgiveness. If sin is seen as a personal affront to God, then no amount of good works by the offender in an unrelated area will repair this relationship. There must be a change of attitude and an offer of forgiveness by the one offended before the relationship can be restored. The endowment of forgiveness remains with the one offended, not with the offender.[66] Paul points out the anomaly of the Gentiles and the Jews who sought for God's favor in different ways. "The Gentiles, who did not pursue righteousness, have obtained it, a righteousness that is by faith; but Israel, who pursued a law of righteousness, has not attained it. Why not? Because they pursued it not by faith but as if it were by works. They tripped over the 'stumbling stone.'"[67] That stumbling stone was Christ Himself, who became the cornerstone.[68] The Jews who tried to win divine goodwill by their own efforts incurred God's wrath because they rejected His gift[69] of "a righteous son"[70] or "a holy child."[71]

(c) Divine initiative

The Bible is much clearer about humanity's inability to save itself. "For it is by grace you have been saved, through faith—and this not from yourselves, it is the gift of God—not by works, so that no one can boast."[72] One is reminded of the Qur'anic account of Noah's other son who refused to enter the Ark. The son told Noah, "I will betake myself to a mountain, it will save me from the water." Noah replied: "This day there is no saviour from the Decree of Allah except him on whom He has mercy." The Qur'an reports that "a wave came in between them, so he (the son) was among the drowned."[73] Likewise, replacing the divine provision for deliverance with self-effort will have disastrous eternal consequences. "How shall we escape if we ignore such a great salvation?"[74]

(d) Divine proximity

Although the Hadith suggests that God can come close to people, the mystic Pope Shenouda III proposed that the beatific vision is not only an eschatological promise for Christians but a present possibility.

> Sit alone, consider and meditate, go deep into yourself and seek God. You will find Him there, in your inmost depths. You will see Him face to face and feel Him as a pouring and overflowing fount of love. Only then you will be greatly astonished and cry out in silent joy, "I have seen God!"[75]

In the Bible, the clear vision of God in heaven is proffered. Although Paul writes of "the invisible God,"[76] declaring that no one has seen or can see Him,[77] "certain scriptures . . . indicate that the redeemed will some day see him."[78] There is the promise, "We shall see Him as He is."[79] Knowing God through personal relationship is a consistent biblical theme. "The Bible from beginning to end is the story of God wanting to share his life and his love with people."[80]

(e) Divine enfleshment

The Bible seems a lot less circumspect in its use of terms about God's physicality. The mere hints of a theophany in Muslim teaching become a full-blown epiphany in the New Testament. Parsons' helpful distinction describes a "theophany" as "any visible appearance of God to people, whether in the form of a vision or an actual appearance on earth,"[81] whereas an actual appearance is designated an "epiphany," which is "a conceptual building block for understanding NT christology."[82] He notes that for Islam "at least in eschatological terms theophanic vision is much more strongly affirmed than epiphany."[83] What Islam pronounces as uncertain mystery is openly proclaimed in the Christian gospel. "Beyond all question, the mystery of godliness is great: He appeared in a body, was vindicated by the Spirit, was seen by angels, was preached among the nations, was believed on in the world, was taken up in glory."[84]

The Hadith hint that God may be more accessible than the Qur'an proposes. Since God may be seen, even "caught hold of" by a womb in some way, as the Hadith declares, new possibilities are opened up. There is the potential of God condescending to limit Himself enough to be apprehended by mere human beings (see Sidebar *Muslims Ponder the Incarnation*).

The Christian theologian P. T. Forsyth wrote that God "could not put more into humanity than humanity will hold."[85] As Paul articulated it, "The mystery that has been kept hidden for ages and generations . . . is now disclosed to the saints."[86]

The incarnation, like the Trinity, is impossible to accept as true only if people require God to conform to their expectations of truth, rather than allowing themselves to acknowledge

MUSLIMS PONDER THE INCARNATION

Akhtar begrudgingly admits the potential value of "God-becoming-man": *"if* the doctrine of the Incarnation were free from certain apparently fatal logical infirmities, *then* it could provide useful theological resources, lacking in Judaism and Islam" (italics his).[e] Another Muslim scholar recognizes the superiority of the means of revelation proposed by the Bible. Hamidullah concedes: "There are several ways of establishing contact or communication between man and God. *The best would have been incarnation*" (italics mine).[f] Christians believe that God chose what Hamidullah describes as "the best" way, and that this took place through the *kenosis* or "emptying" of the divine Son of God when He became man.[g]

---

e. Shabbir Akhtar, *The Final Imperative,* 80, cited in Zebiri, *Muslims and Christians,* 156.

f. Hamidullah, *Introduction*, 47. He goes on to say, "Islam has rejected it. It would have been too degrading for a transcendent God to become man, to eat, drink, be tortured by His own creatures, and even be put to death."

g. Phil 2:6-7.

His truth. C. S. Lewis expressed it well: "If Christianity were something we were making up, of course, we could make it easier. But it is not. We cannot compete, in simplicity, with people who are inventing religions. How could we? We are dealing with Fact. Of course anyone can be simple if he has no facts to bother about."[87]

NOTES

1.   B.1:332; 5:117; 7:93.
2.   E.g., Job 38:41; Ps 104:21: Matt 6:26. Thiessen, *Lectures in Systematic Theology*, 86.
3.   Rom 8:28.
4.   This means "those who speak harmfully [about Him]."
5.   B.8:121.
6.   Matt 5:45; Luke 6:35.
7.   Ps 77:13; 99:9; Isa 5:16; Luke 1:49, Acts 3:14; Q.62.1.
8.   1 Sam 2:2; Rev 15:4.
9.   Ps 5:4.
10.   Hab 1:13.
11.   B.3:267; 1:49.
12.   E.g., Rom 5:14, NIV. This term is found 23 times in the Greek New Testament. Vine, *Comprehensive Dictionary*, 1177.
13.   B.9:500; also 7:147, 148, 149, 150; 8:829.
14.   Al-Hilali and Khan, *Translation of the meanings of the Noble Qur'an*, 71.
15.   Deut 4:24; 5:9; 6:15; 32:21; Josh 24:19; Nah 1:2.
16.   Gen 3:8; 11:5; 18:21.
17.   B.2:246; 8:333; 9:586.
18.   John 4:23.
19.   Luke 19:10.
20.   Rom 10:21, citing Isa 65:2.
21.   B.8:321.
22.   Luke 15:7, 10, 32.
23.   B.9:267.
24.   John 14:23.

25. Q.50:16.
26. Q.8:24. It may be significant that both of these verses outlining God's intimate knowledge of a person's inner thoughts are found in the context of judgment (i.e., Q.50:12-19 and Q.8:21-25), not love, grace, and mercy.
27. Q.2:186.
28. Q.57:4.
29. Quoted in Zwemer, *The Moslem Doctrine of God*, 31.
30. Q.53:8–10.
31. B.4:457, 458.
32. B.6:378.
33. Hamidullah, *Introduction*, 47.
34. B.9:504.
35. B.5:5, 259; 6:185.
36. B.2:305.
37. B.2:304; 8:132.
38. B.1:47.
39. Q.9:72–73; 10:26; 75:22–23.
40. From the CD "World of Islam."
41. B.1:770; 9:532.1, 532.2. The inability to see God on the Day of Judgment is part of the lot of the evildoers (Q.83:15). Interestingly, an early Muslim theologian, Ahmad Ibn Hā'it (d.230/845), used the "full moon" hadith described above to propose the divinity of the Messiah. Thomas, *Anti-Christian polemic,* 5–6. Although it is not possible to argue an Islamic position from the thoughts of a Muslim who was considered unorthodox (ibn Hā'it died while under investigation for heresy), it is fascinating to see where one scholar's quest for knowledge led him.
42. B.1: 529, 547, 770; 6:105, 374; 8:577; 9:529, 531. Despite this, the Mutazila rejected this theme, based on Q.6:103. Twelver Shi'ites deny the beatific vision because it may imply that God has a bodily form.
43. B.9:532.3.
44. Q.19:17.
45. Q.51:25-28; 11:69, 70.
46. B.6:300; 1:47.
47. Q.18:50.
48. Q.38:76; 7:12; 15:26-27; 55:15.

49. B.6:530.

50. B.4:634; 6:332. Chiragh Ali (d.1895) asserted that "jinn" does not describe a spiritual being but was the name of a Semitic tribe. Brown, *Hadith*, 244.

51. B.2:301; 4:504.

52. Q.20:11, 12.

53. Nazir-Ali, *Frontiers in Muslim-Christian Encounter*, 127.

54. B.6:354; 8:16, 17, 18.

55. B.6:206; 9:508, 515.

56. B.9:509.

57. B.4:416; 9:501, 514, 518, 545, 643.

58. E.g., B.3:594, 595; 4:48, 413, 414.

59. B.9:481, 541; 6:371, 372, 373; 8:654.

60. B.1:66, 463.

61. B.9:484.

62. B.9:532.2 cf. Q.68:42, "the day when the *sāq* (shin) will be laid bare."

63. B.6:105; 8:246.

64. Ps 103:1-14. The term "Father" is never used of Allah in the Qur'an or the Hadith, and most Muslims would reject it totally, based on Qur'anic passages, e.g., Q.112:3.

65. Parsons, *Unveiling God*, 95.

66. Matt 5:23–25.

67. Rom 9:30–32.

68. Eph 2:20.

69. 1 Pet 2:7–8.

70. Q.19.19 *ghulaman zakiyyan*

71. Acts 4:30.

72. Eph 2:8–9.

73. Q.11:43.

74. Heb 2:3.

75. Shenouda, *The Release of the Spirit*, 92.

76. Col 1:15, cf. Rom 1:20.

77. 1 Tim 6:16.

78. Ps 17:15; Matt 5:8; Heb 12:14; Rev 22:4. Thiessen, *Systematic Theology*, 76. The nineteenth-century apologist William St. Clair

Tisdall claimed that any observable appearance of God must be Christ, since the Father is invisible. St. Clair Tisdall's Persian work *Miftah al-Asrar* ['Key of the Secrets'] (Agra: no publisher, 1850), 107-108, cited in Parsons, *Unveiling God*, 12.

79. 1 John 3:2.
80. Wilson, *Christianity alongside Islam*, 81.
81. Parsons, *Unveiling God*, xxxvii.
82. Ibid., xxix.
83. Ibid., xxxvii.
84. 1 Tim 3:16.
85. Quoted by Jones, *Christianity Explained*, 74.
86. Col 1:26.
87. Lewis, *Mere Christianity*, 145.

9

THE NATURE OF HUMANKIND

WHEN GOD CONNECTS with humanity, what does He find? What is the nature of humankind based on the various religious texts?

1. POSITIVE ASCRIPTIONS OF HUMANITY

According to the Bible, humans are created in God's image[1] and are thus capable of being partakers of the divine nature[2] as well as coworkers with God.[3] The psalmist wonders at God's provision and care for man, and at human power and dignity.[4] Humanity clearly has a noble status.

Islam likewise presents a positive assessment of humankind. Sarwar states: "The Islamic view [is] that man has always been fundamentally good."[5] The Qur'an says, "We created man in the best stature (mould)."[6] "We conferred on them special favors above a great part of Our Creation."[7] Consequently the first human being was worthy of worship by the angels.[8] Humans were made according to the *fitra* (nature or constitution) which God designed for them.[9] Man has become bearer of the Divine trust, which the earth and the heavens and the mountains did not have the power to bear.[10]

One Hadith passage matches the biblical account: "The Prophet said, 'Allah created Adam in His picture (image).'"[11] Kamali suggests an application: "Being created in the image of God, man seeks to emulate the divine qualities of the Creator. To be objective is, in a sense, to emulate God. Man is capable of objectivity because of the endowment in his nature of the divine qualities of impartiality and justice."[12] Another Muslim scholar, Kateregga, notes: "The Christian witness, that man is created in the 'image and likeness of God,' is not the same as the Muslim witness. . . . For Islam, the only Divine quality that was entrusted to man as a result of God's breath was the faculty of knowledge, will, and power of action."[13] Although he disagrees with their conclusions, he recognizes that "God breathing into man His (God's) spirit is believed by some scholars to be the faculty of God—like knowledge and will, which if rightly used gives man superiority over all creation." Moreover, "some modern Muslim scholars believe that the Qur'anic evidence suggests that man has a certain Godlikeness."[14]

The acknowledgement of this possibility is remarkable indeed. It may be this capacity which allows every person, regardless of gender or status in life, to operate within a sphere of influence with some authority. Muhammad stated: "Everyone of you is a guardian and everyone of you is responsible (for his wards). A ruler is a guardian and is responsible (for his subjects); a man is a guardian of his family and responsible (for them); a wife is a guardian of her husband's house and she is responsible (for it), a slave is a guardian of his master's property and is responsible (for that). Beware! All of you are guardians and are responsible (for your wards)."[15] This accords with the ascription of vicegerency to humans in both the Qur'an[16] and the Bible.[17]

2. NEGATIVE ASCRIPTIONS OF HUMANITY

Creation in the image of God is not the only word about humanity in the Qur'an, Hadith, or the Bible. People live out their lives in a tension between extreme glory and utter depravity. According to orthodox Christian belief, people are also sinners from birth, deceitful of heart, and lacking in self-understanding.[18]

Some Qur'anic verses suggest that evil originates from humanity. The following twenty-eight attributes are applied to people in general (see Table 18). The Qur'an presents these: "Indeed humanity is . . . *inna al'insāna*" or "he is . . . *innahu*," referring to humankind as a whole, without discrimination.[19]

sinful (or unjust) *ẓalūm^{an}* (Q.14:34; 9:109; 33:72)	self-sufficient *astaghna* (Q.96:7; 92:8)	ungrateful *kaffār^{un}* (Q.11:9; 14:34; 30:34; 32:10; 80:17)
despairing *la'ūs^{un}* (Q.11:9)	weak *da'īf^{an}* (Q.4:28; 30:54)	foolish *jahūl^{an}* (Q.33:72)
careless about your Lord *ma gharrak birabbik^{a}* (Q.82:6)	prays for evil the prayer meant for good *yad'u bishsharr^{i} du'aahu bilkhayr* (Q.17:11)	violent in his love for wealth *liḥubb alkhayr lashadīd* (Q.100:8)
unthankful *qalīl^{an} ma tashkurūn* (Q.7:10)	ungrateful to his Lord *lirabbih^{i} lakanūd^{un}* (Q.100:6)	exultant and boastful *fariḥ^{un} fakhūr^{un}* (Q.11.10)
rebellious *yaṭga* (Q.96:6)	arrogant (Q.90:5–7)	quarrelsome *khaṣim* (Q.16:4)
irritable *jazū^{an}* (Q.70:20; c.f. 30:36).	impatient *halūm^{an}* (Q.70:19).	ever hasty *'ajūl^{an}* (Q.17:11; 21:37)
liars about the judgment *kadhdhabūn biddīn* (Q.82:9)	inclined to evil *amāra bissū'* (Q.12:53)	remains proud *yusirr^{u} mustakbir^{an}* (Q.45:8)
turns away and becomes remote *a'ragh wa ni'a bijānibihi* (Q.17:83)	more quarrelsome than anything *akhthar shay jadal^{an}* (Q.18:54)	despairing when evil touches him *idha massahu ash-sharkān yu'sān* (Q.17:83)
in loss *fi khusr* (Q.103:2)	miserly *qatūr* (Q.17:100)	ingrate *kafūr* (Q.22:66)
niggardly *manū^{an}* (Q.70:20; c.f. 30:36)		

TABLE 18: Descriptions of humanity in the Qur'an

Based on such passages, one commentator finds support for the doctrine of universal sinfulness within the Qur'an.[20] The Prophet himself bemoaned human untrustworthiness: "People are just like camels, out of one hundred, one can hardly find a single camel suitable to ride."[21] There is certainly, in Muhammad's view, a cause for pessimism about humanity. He asked a contemporary, "What will be your condition when you will be left with the sediments of (worst) people?"[22] He felt that his was the finest generation: "The best of my followers are those living in my generation (i.e. my contemporaries), and then those who will follow the latter. . . . There will come after you, people who will bear witness without being asked to do so, and will be treacherous and untrustworthy, and they will vow and never fulfill their vows, and fatness will appear among them."[23] Ultimately "the righteous (pious) people will depart (die) in succession one after the other, and there will remain (on the earth) useless people like the useless husk of barley seeds or bad dates."[24] Already this trend was becoming apparent in a devaluation of the importance of sin. 'Anas told a later generation: "You people do (bad) deeds (commit sins) which seem in your eyes as tiny (minute) than [sic] hair while we used to consider those (very deeds) during the life-time of the Prophet as destructive sins."[25] He prophesied a time when honesty would become so rare among humanity as to be remarkable.[26]

Even in paradise, with all his needs fulfilled, a man will ask for land to grow crops which he will then pile up in heaps like mountains. Allah's disgust is shown by his comment, "Take, here you are, O son of Adam, for nothing satisfies you."[27] Human greed seems to persist beyond the grave. So does the desire for revenge. "The believers, after being saved from the (Hell) Fire, will be stopped at a bridge between Paradise and Hell and mutual retaliation will be established among them regarding wrongs they have committed in the world against one another."[28] Apparently not even salvation from hell and entry into paradise can curb these baser human instincts, according to the Hadith.

3. THE IMPACT OF ADAM

The problem appears to have begun with the disobedient action of the first humans. The punishment for this was to be cast down from paradise to earth for a period. "Therein you shall live and therein you shall die, and from there you shall be brought forth."[29] Eaton comments:

"They 'fell' together, equal in guilt as they had been in glory."[30] The movement from height to depth is conveyed in the following verse: "We created man in the best stature (mould), then we reduced him to the lowest of the low, except those who believe and do righteous deeds."[31]

Yet most Muslims are quick to deny the idea of a "fall" in Islam. "There is no Fall in the Qur'an, hence there is no Original Sin. Human beings are not born sinful into this world, hence do not need to be 'redeemed' or 'saved'. This is generally accepted in the Islamic tradition."[32] Barlas projects the Adam narrative back to an evolutionary pre-history. "There is no qur'anic narrative about original sin or Eve's culpability for the fall. . . . Indeed, there is no concept of the fall in Islam. Rather . . . the expulsion of the human pair from paradise marks the transition from consciousness to self-consciousness."[33]

However, Adam's action did not involve himself only (see Sidebar *Effects of Adam's Sin*).

> ## EFFECTS OF ADAM'S SIN
>
> Moses saw the effects of Adam's sin being passed on to his progeny forever, when he accused Adam: "You are the one who made people miserable and turned them out of Paradise."[a] Another hadith is even more specific: "You . . . led people astray and brought them out of the Garden."[b] Clearly, if Adam's sin had not affected subsequent generations in some way, then humans would have continued to have the same free access to Paradise that Adam and his wife initially enjoyed. Their action changed the human situation forever.

4. THE ROLE OF SATAN

Several hadith propose that the devil took advantage of Adam's weakness early on. "Allah's Apostle (peace be upon him) said: 'When Allah fashioned Adam in Paradise, He left him as He liked him to leave. Then Iblis [the devil] roamed round him to see what actually

---

a. B.6:260.

b. Muwatta 46:1. See http://sunnah.com/urn/416870

that was and when he found him hollow from within, he recognised that he had been created with a disposition that he would not have control over himself.'"[34] Another hadith suggests that Satan himself has filled this hollow void: "Satan circulates in the mind of a person as blood does (in his body) and . . . Satan might put some (evil) thoughts in your minds."[35]

This process appears to begin at birth: "When any human being is born, Satan touches him at both sides of the body with his two fingers."[36] The close contact continues throughout life. Every Muslim is told to wash out his nose three times each morning "because Satan has stayed in the upper part of his nose all the night."[37] Demonic interference is clearly personal and physical. One man slept through the call to prayer because "Satan urinated in his ears."[38]

5. SYNTHESIS

This combination of being created in the divine image and at the same time having Satan circulating in one's blood, sleeping in one's nose, and urinating in one's ear makes for a strange creature. C. S. Lewis' demonic antagonist referred to humans as "half spirit and half animal."[39] This analysis was shared by the Sheikh of al-Rabwah, Muhammad al-Demashqi (d.727/1327). He states about man: "He is just like an animal in his lust and hunger to develop the earth; and he is like angels in knowledge, worship and guidance."[40]

In a dream described in one hadith, Muhammad encountered people whose appearance displayed the best and worst of humanity. "There we met men who, half of their bodies, look like the most-handsome human beings you have ever seen, and the other half, the ugliest human beings you have ever seen." The reason for this form was explained to Muhammad: "They were those who mixed good deeds and bad deeds." Even more remarkable is the way in which their appearance became transformed. In the dream two (possibly angelic) visitors spoke to these half-handsome, half-ugly people: "'Go and dip yourselves in that river.' So they dipped themselves therein and then came to us, their ugliness having disappeared and they were in the most-handsome shape. The visitors said, 'The first is the Garden of Eden and that is your dwelling place.'" Then they added: "Allah forgave them."[41] This hadith will be discussed below.

6. HUMANS: INDIVIDUAL OR CORPORATE?

At times in Islamic theology, there is a clear expression of Allah's dealing with each individual on a personal level. This is found in the hadith: "Allah has appointed an angel in the womb, and the angel says, 'O Lord! A drop of discharge (i.e. of semen), O Lord! A clot, O Lord! A piece of flesh.' And then, if Allah wishes to complete the child's creation, the angel will say, 'O Lord! A male or a female? O Lord! Wretched or blessed (in religion)? What will his livelihood be? What will his age be?' The angel writes all this while the child is in the womb of its mother."[42] Every person has his or her unique future mapped out, according to this hadith.

At other times, there is a strong connection between Adam and humanity, as though the shared identity is the key feature. A person in hell is addressed by Allah: "While you were in the backbone of Adam, I asked you . . . not to worship others besides Me, but you insisted on worshipping others besides me."[43] This is based on a Qur'anic concept,[44] where the people are brought forth from the loins of Adam's offspring.[45]

Although Abdalati claims that, in the Muslim view, "sin is not hereditary, transferable, or communal in nature,"[46] the Hadith hint at a different picture. One account intimates that the first man passed some of his less noble characteristics on to his descendents. Adam in his earlier days had conferred forty of his own years upon David. Muhammad related the story: "When Adam completed his age life-span with only forty years remaining, there came to him the angel of death. Thereupon Adam said: 'Are there not forty years left in my life-span?' The angel said: 'Did you not confer your son (forty years)?' Adam denied it and so did his offspring. Adam forgot and ate (the fruit) of the tree and so his offspring also forgot; and he (Adam) sinned and his offspring sinned."[47] Clearly the first instance of an action has repercussive effects. The Prophet said, "No human being is killed unjustly, but a part of responsibility for the crime is laid on the first son of Adam who invented the tradition of killing (murdering) on the earth."[48] Adam's wife is also implicated in subsequent human failings. Muhammad stated: "But for Eve, wives would never betray their husbands."[49] Some sense of sin being inherited or innate is implied here. This thought is not unfamiliar to Muslims. "Islamic cultures . . . characteristically tend to have at least some sense of corporate responsibility for the misdeeds of others in the kinship network. Indeed the emphasis that Islamic cultures typically have on honour and shame may often mean that serious misdemeanours bring disgrace on the family, and even on the whole community for generations to come."[50] Although each person is an individual, one's true identity is drawn from a corporate association with Islam, as a part of the *Umma*, or with Adam, as a part of the human race (see Illustration 11). Adam's legacy of disobedience has continued to have an effect on succeeding generations.

Individual Muslims "in the Umma"

Individual Muslims "in Adam"

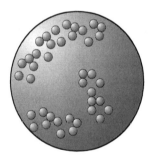

ILLUSTRATION 11: Comparing being "in the umma" with being "in Adam"

7. CONNECTIONS WITH BIBLICAL THEMES

The shared expression "in His image" in the Hadith provides a good starting point for a discussion on the nature of humanity from both Muslim and Christian perspectives. If people somehow express the image of God, then the prospect of a deeper bond with Him exists.

"The image of God in humankind means that there is a basic likeness between God and humankind which creates the possibility
of a personal relationship with God, and of God revealing himself
to humans."[51]

Although there are hints in that direction, Muslim theology in
general lacks the full-orbed depiction of the human condition which
is found in the Bible. People are neither very good nor very bad.
The biblical description of humanity being made "in the image of
God" receives a single mention in the Hadith, but its meaning is not
developed. At the same time the full depth of human depravity is
downplayed in the Qur'an by references to people who simply "forgot" (*nasiya*)[52] or were "neglectful" (*ghāfil*).[53] The way some Muslim
writers describe humanity suggests they are intentionally trying to
ignore the painful evidence of human history. Shabbir Akhtar writes
that "Muslims are religiously obliged to resist the tragic conclusion
that man has failed in some ultimate and irreversible way." He goes
on: "Muslims must, rightly or wrongly, refuse to concede the tragic
failure of man on pain of having no theology left to articulate."[54] To
stare distressingly obvious truth in the face can be an agonizing experience. Denial may appear to be the only option. Yet without proper
diagnosis, the appropriate treatment is unlikely to be prescribed.

Some value may still be extracted from the Hadith's description
above of humans performing a mixture of good and bad deeds. This
portrayal would seem to be applicable to everyone in some way. Few
people would admit to being perfect, and even fewer to being totally
depraved. This accords with the human condition of being created
in the image of God, and yet having fallen from grace.

The antidote which removed their repulsiveness in this account
was immersion in water. Their bad deeds were overlooked. This
hadith brings to mind the biblical statement, "he saved us, not
because of righteous things we had done, but because of his mercy.
He saved us through the washing of rebirth and renewal by the
Holy Spirit, whom he poured out on us generously through Jesus
Christ our Savior."[55] Baptism as the cleansing through washing is
also mentioned.[56] Baptism receives a single mention in the Qur'an:
"(Our religion is) the baptism of Allah; and who can baptize better than Allah?"[57] However, this concept is not at all developed

in Muslim theology. Analyses such as that given above provide a
starting point for discussions about the inner nature of people and
possible solutions to the human condition. We will look at the
Hadith's analysis of the human heart later.

NOTES

1. Gen 1:27; 5:1; 9:6; 1 Cor 11:7; Jas 3:9.
2. 2 Pet 1:4.
3. 1 Cor 3:9; 2 Cor 6:1.
4. Ps 8:4–8.
5. Sarwar, *Islam*, 141.
6. Q.95:4.
7. Q.17:70.
8. Q.2:30, 34; 6:165; 7:11; 15:28, 29, 27:62, 38:71–73.
9. Q.30:30. This may simply be the view that every child is natu-
    rally born a Muslim, but their parents convert them to Judaism,
    Christianity, or Magianism (B.2:440, 441, 467).
10. Q.33:72.
11. B.8:246. The Arabic phrase used in this hadith *'ala sūratihi* "accord-
    ing to His image" is identical with the term in the Van Dyke Arabic
    translation of the Bible : "And God created man in His image" *fa
    khalaq allāh al-insān 'ala sūratihi* (Gen 1:27). Zwemer was appar-
    ently unaware of this hadith when he commented that Allah "has no
    relations to any creature that partake of resemblance. The statement
    in Genesis that man was created in the divine image is to the Moslem
    blasphemy." Zwemer, *Doctrine of God*, 30.
12. Kamali, *Textbook*, 2.
13. Kateregga and Shenk, *Islam and Christianity*, 100–101.
14. Ibid., 15, 21.
15. B.2:18; 3:592, 730, 732; 4:14; 7:116, 128; 9:252.
16. Q.2:30; 6:165; 7:69, 74; 27:62; 35:39; 10:14, 73; 7:129.
17. Gen 1:26–30; 2:15–20.
18. Ps 51:5; Jer 17:9; Rom 7:15.
19. There are many additional verses which ascribe sinfulness to particu-
    lar individuals or to unbelievers who refused to accept Muhammad's
    message.

20. Haddad, *Principles,* chapters 11–12.

21. B.8:505.

22. B.1:467.

23. B.3:819, 820; 4:757; 5:2, 3; 8:436, 437, 652, 686.

24. B.8:442.

25. B.8:499.

26. B.8:504; 9:208.

27. B.9:610.

28. B.8:542.

29. Q.7.24.

30. Eaton, "Man," 361.

31. Q.95:4-6.

32. Hassan, "An Islamic Perspective," 107.

33. Barlas, "Women's readings of the Qur'ān," 259.

34. Sahih Muslim no. 1200 narrated by Anas ibn Malik from CD Alim/ Hadith/Sahih Muslim.

35. B.3:254, 251, 255; 4:333, 501; 8:238; 9:283.

36. B.4:506.

37. B.4:516.

38. B.2:245; 4:492.

39. Lewis, *Screwtape Letters*, 44.

40. Cited in *Arab Development Report 2003*, 19.

41. B.6:196; 9:171.

42. B.4:550.

43. B.4:551; 8:562.

44. Q.7:172.

45. Al-Hilali and Khan, *Translation of the meanings of the Noble Qur'an,* 226, give an alternative translation of this as "from Adam's loin his offspring."

46. Abdalati, *Islam in Focus*, 40–52.

47. Robson, *Mishkat al-Masabih* , vol. 1, p. 31.

48. B.9:6; 4:552; 9:423.

49. B.4:547.

50. Parsons, *Unveiling God*, 221.

51. Chapman, *The Bible*, 24.

52. E.g., Q.6:44.

53. E.g., Q.7:205.

54. Akhtar, *Faith*, 161.

55. Titus 3:5–6. God promised the Israelities: "I will sprinkle clean water on you, and you will be clean" (Ezek 36:25).

56. Eph 5:26.

57. Q.2:138.

10

THE FORGIVENESS OF SINS

LIKE THE QUR'AN AND THE BIBLE, the Hadith contain much information about sin and forgiveness. The Hadith contain lists of acceptable behavior[1] and forbidden actions.[2]

1. SINS INCUR PENALTIES

Sin is not ignored or glossed over, for a judgment is coming.[3] "Some people . . . will be scorched by Hell (Fire) as a punishment for sins they have committed, and then Allah will admit them into Paradise by the grant of His Mercy."[4]

The requirement for entry into paradise is that one's sins be forgiven. A single indiscretion can affect one's eternal destiny.[5] Thabit reported that "a man used to raise his voice over the voice of the Prophet and so all his good deeds have been annulled and he is from the people of Hell."[6]

The Bible is similarly clear about the dangers of disobeying God. "Everyone will die for his own sin," reported Jeremiah; "The wages of sin is death," stated Paul.[7]

2. SINS MUST BE PAID FOR

God's opposition to sin is a consistent theme of the whole Bible, from the judgment in the Garden of Eden to the grand assize with the ultimate destination of the evil ones in "the fiery lake of burning sulphur."[8] A general principle is that sin must be paid for—it is not simply overlooked. Abraham asks rhetorically: "Will not the Judge of all the earth do right?"[9] Jesus set a high standard: "I tell you that men will have to give account on the Day of Judgment for every careless word they have spoken."[10]

In the Hadith, sin may sometimes be paid for in this life. "And whoever indulges in any one of them (except the ascription of partners to Allah) and gets the punishment in this world, that punishment will be an expiation for that sin. And if one indulges in any of them, and Allah conceals his sin, it is up to Him to forgive or punish him (in the Hereafter)."[11] One man was told by Muhammad that his unnamed but legally punishable sin was forgiven because he had prayed along with the Prophet and his companions.[12]

In the Roman Catholic concept, sin is considered as "being in arrears" toward God. It can be paid for by performing good works or receiving indulgences through which, as a Jesuit priest expressed it, "we can make devastating inroads into our sinful debt." He concludes: "It is quite possible for any consecrated person to die with all temporal punishment for past forgiven sins removed."[13] This aspiration would be shared by many Muslims.

The means of achieving this in Islam are manifold. They would include saying prayers five times a day,[14] especially in Ramadhan[15] and particularly the night of *Qadr* (predestination or decree),[16] fasting during Ramadhan,[17] performing ablutions,[18] spending for Allah's sake,[19] or "even for the morsel of food which you put in your wife's mouth."[20] As the early Muslims dug the defensive trench around Medina, Muhammad prayed for their forgiveness.[21]

The Qur'an calls such good works "a beautiful loan to God,"[22] which God promises to multiply many times over.[23] The reward for one deed can be doubled[24] or even multiplied ten to seven hundred times.[25] A small good deed, such as giving a date as charity, will ascend to Allah who will bring it up for its owner as one does a baby horse until it becomes a mountain.[26]

3. SIN AND FORGIVENESS AS COMMERCIAL TRANSACTIONS

Deeds will be weighed on scales on the Day of Judgment.[27] For reciting a certain pious phrase one hundred times, "one hundred good deeds will be written in his accounts, and one hundred sins will be deducted from his accounts."[28] Muhammad told his followers to recite "two expressions which are very easy for the tongue to say, but they are very heavy in the balance."[29] Both the Qur'an and the Hadith use commercial language when describing sin and forgiveness.

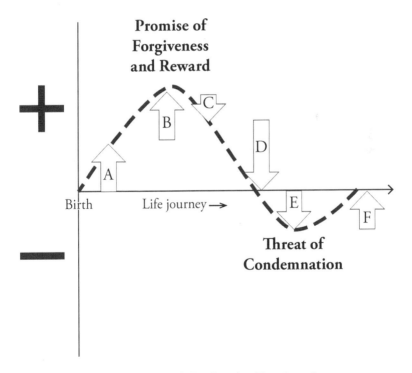

ILLUSTRATION 12: The Promise/Threat graph

The Promise/Threat Graph (Illustration 12) illustrates some of these principles in the Hadith. Good and bad deeds are spiritual credits or debits based on actions as one's life progresses (the dashed line in the diagram). The account starts at zero, for humans are seen as morally neutral at birth, for all people are born as Muslims, according to the Hadith.[30] The same applies to a convert to Islam. "His acceptance of Islam puts him squarely in the zero zone and lays out before him the arduous road of the Shari'ah . . . which he has yet to tread in order to lift himself out of the zero zone by his own efforts."[31] A good work (Action A) attracts reward when performed.[32] As Muhammad described it, "Any good deed which you will do for Allah's Sake, will upgrade and elevate you."[33] Reward and forgiveness are often bracketed together. A fighter's martyrdom immediately after he embraced Islam was described as "a little work, but a great reward."[34] Good works, such as worshiping only Allah, result in avoidance of punishment.

Further good works accumulate (i.e., Actions A + B), generating a surplus of merit. A man providing food for his wife would be rewarded. Simple actions, such as giving half a date in charity or saying a "good pleasant word," would help protect one from the fire.[35] Certain recited phrases are heavy on the weighing scales.[36] All purchases accrued merit, but for some unexplained reason, construction projects did not. "A Muslim is rewarded (in the Hereafter) for whatever he spends except for something that he spends on building."[37] Yet whoever builds a mosque on earth, "Allah would build for him a similar place in Paradise."[38]

Unacceptable actions (Action C) decrease any accrued merit. Some deeds involve a small loss. Keeping a dog for other than hunting or guarding accrued a daily loss of two *Qirats* (one third of a *dirham*).[39] Other actions cancel all previous merit (Action D),[40] e.g., whoever oppresses another will have his good deeds taken from him[41] as will a slave who befriends someone without his master's permission.[42] Sins of omission operate in this sphere: "Whoever leaves the 'Asr prayer, all his (good) deeds will be annulled."[43] Thus neglecting to do what is required has the same negative effect as performing a forbidden action.

Any sin (Action E) moves the actor towards condemnation, for "every soul is delivered to ruin by its own acts."[44] However, this too can be canceled out (Action F), e.g., "good deeds remove (annul) the evil deeds (small sins)."[45] Whoever recites a certain short prayer one hundred times a day "will be forgiven all his sins even if they were as much as the foam of the sea."[46] Life's trials, such as sickness, could result in cleansing from some sins.[47] Since the plague was seen as a punishment from Allah, those in a land afflicted by plague were advised not to leave it.[48] Presumably to remain and receive unmerited punishment in this life was better than fleeing and receiving punishment merited by one's sins in the hereafter.

The biblical perspective reveals sin as more insidious and persistent. It is not simply a ledger fluctuating between red and black, with a bottom line that can ultimately be balanced by hard work and good behavior. Sin indicates a universally experienced distortion within the human spirit. The Preacher of Proverbs asks: "Who can say, 'I have kept my heart pure; I am clean and without sin'?"[49] The answer is resoundingly negative—no one, neither Jew nor Gentile nor even the apostle Paul himself, could attain the high standards of a pure and righteous God: "There is no one righteous, not even one; there is no one who understands, no one who seeks God. All have turned away, they have together become worthless; there is no one who does good, not even one."[50]

4. THE UNFORGIVABLE SIN

The Bible's sole reference to unforgivable sin relates to those who were saying of Jesus: "He has an evil spirit."[51] It involves attributing the work of Christ to demonic origins.

Although most Muslims would claim that the only unforgivable sin in Islam is shirk (associating other deities with Allah),[52] the Hadith list other sins which are unforgivable. These include withholding water from travelers when you have a surplus, pledging obedience to a Muslim ruler only for worldly gain, and making a false oath while bargaining after the 'Asr prayer.[53] Claiming falsely to be someone's son would bar one from paradise.[54] On another occasion, Muhammad warned against presumption. "Whoever performs the ablution as I have done this time and then proceeds to the mosque and offers a two-Rak'at [bowing and prostrating] prayer and then sits there (waiting for the compulsory congregational prayers), then all his past sins will be forgiven." However, the value of one's prayers could be nullified by a simple action like breaking wind after ablutions.[55]

Even after assuring his followers that performing prayers perfectly would result in the forgiveness of all past sins, Muhammad immediately negates this assurance by adding, "Do not be conceited (thinking that your sins will be forgiven because of your prayer)."[56] The chances of success appear to be slim. At the judgment, Adam is asked to take out from all humanity those people condemned to the fire. When Adam asks how many this would be, the divine voice replies: "Out of every thousand (take out) nine-hundred and ninety-nine (persons)."[57]

5. UNSTABLE IDENTITY OF THOSE WHO SIN

Moreover the Hadith complicate matters by altering the definition of a believer. One day Muhammad announced a word from Allah: "In this morning some of my slaves remained as true believers and some became non-believers."[58] Those who attributed the recent rain to a star became unbelievers, while those who gave the credit to Allah remained believers. A man who wanted to kill a disbeliever who then converted to Islam in the heat of battle was told by Muhammad that "you would be in the position in which he was before he said the sentence."[59] Those who kill other Muslims "become disbelievers."[60] Another time the Prophet said:

> When an adulterer commits illegal sexual intercourse, then he is not a believer at the time he is doing it, and when a drinker of an alcoholic liquor drinks it, then he is not a believer at the time of drinking it, and when a thief steals, then he is not a believer at the time of stealing, and when a robber robs, and the people look at him, then he is not a believer at the time of doing robbery.[61]

It appears that one moves in and out of faith by belief and actions—good or otherwise (see Illustration 13). Commenting on this saying, Ibn Abbas claims that repentance returns the person to faith.[62] There seems to be no stability of identity. One's spiritual status is transformed quickly, contingent on one's actions. Nasr comments: "The life of the Muslim moves like a winding road toward a mountain top, vacillating from one side to another between rigor and mercy, fear of God's retribution and trust in His forgiveness."[63] The overall impression is of religious undulation and uncertainty.

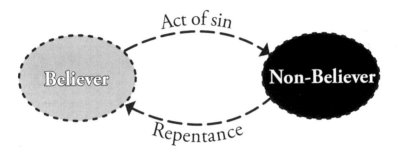

ILLUSTRATION 13: Switching between "believer" and "non-believer" status

6. UNCERTAIN OUTCOME FOR THOSE WHO SIN

Even if a person avoided the major sins, how could he know if his good deeds would outweigh his bad deeds? On his deathbed, the Caliph 'Umar was reminded of his great accomplishments, but even these did not seem enough.

> A young man came saying, "O chief of the believers! Receive the glad tidings from Allah to you due to your company with Allah's Apostle and your superiority in Islam which you know. Then you became the ruler (i.e. Caliph) and you ruled with justice and finally you have been martyred." 'Umar said, "I wish that all these privileges will counterbalance (my shortcomings) so that I will neither lose nor gain anything."[64]

In another account, he stated: "If (at all) I had gold equal to the earth, I would have ransomed myself with it from the punishment of Allah before I meet Him."[65] This was despite Muhammad's assurance that 'Umar would enter paradise.[66] When one of the *muhājirūn* (immigrants from Mecca) died in Medina, a fellow Muslim claimed that Allah had blessed the deceased. Muhammad corrected him: "As regards Uthman, by Allah, he has died and I really wish him every good, yet, by Allah, although I am Allah's Apostle, I do not know what will be done to him."[67]

7. CONNECTIONS WITH BIBLICAL THEMES

Muslim and Christian understandings differ on sin, how God responds to it, and how to repent. For Muslims, according to Rodinson,

> sin was a fault, a disobedience, a mark of ingratitude, an omission brought about by an unjustified preference for the goods of this world. It never elicited from God the laments of the betrayed lover, weeping to see faithless man reject his love, which run through all the pages of the Old and New Testaments. Such a piteous appeal for the love of a weak creature would be inconceivable coming from the Master of the worlds of the Koran, who reaches the uttermost limits of his goodness in himself deigning to love and to forgive.[68]

Although it never quite reaches to the levels of biblical revelation, one particular story in the Hadith illustrates a kind of "softening" in Allah.

> The Prophet said, "Amongst the men of Bani Israel there was a man who had murdered ninety-nine persons. Then he set out asking (whether his repentance could be accepted or not). He came upon a monk and asked him if his repentance could be accepted. The monk replied in the negative and so the man killed him. He kept on asking till a man

advised to go to such and such village. (So he left for it) but death overtook him on the way. While dying, he turned his chest towards that village (where he had hoped his repentance would be accepted), and so the angels of mercy and the angels of punishment quarrelled amongst themselves regarding him. Allah ordered the village (towards which he was going) to come closer to him, and ordered the village (whence he had come), to go far away, and then He ordered the angels to measure the distances between his body and the two villages. So he was found to be one span closer to the village (he was going to). So he was forgiven.[69]

The connections with the story of the prodigal son[70] and the repentant thief on the cross[71] are patent. God does not require good works in order for sin to be forgiven. "By observing the law, no-one will be justified."[72] In this Hadith narrative, God intervenes in the physical world to save the undeserving man. As the Bible says: "It is God who justifies."[73] Yet He does so according to standards of justice—the fortunate man was heading toward, and was one span closer to, the village where he hoped his repentance would be accepted. The only requirement was the most basic turning toward God.[74] Are there any implications in this to help Christians involved in ministry to Muslims?

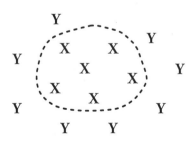

ILLUSTRATION 14: A "bounded set"

Some involved in cross-cultural ministry have struggled with these issues and have developed various responses, including how they view conversion. There are two basic approaches to conversion and affiliation.[75] The first is expressed in the term "bounded sets" (see Illustration 14) where objects (in this case, people) are defined by their position in relation to the boundary. Any person is either "inside" (X) or "outside" (Y) the set. The key element is their location. From a spiritual perspective, this might include membership of the church, etc. Those inside the set have been accepted as members of the set because they fulfill certain criteria. It is based on a one-time static analysis.

A second way of viewing conversion is through the paradigm of "centered sets" (see Illustration 15). The focus of this model is not a boundary line but the center. The defining issue is not current proximity to the center, but rather movement toward the hub (i.e., A, B, and E), rather than away from it (C and D). It is a more dynamic situation, since the positions will change over time.

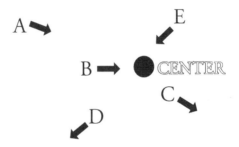

ILLUSTRATION 15: A "centered set"

According to some hadith, the performance of a sufficient number of good works is no guarantee of entry to paradise: the better indicator of ultimate success was orientation toward the goal. The stories of the Hadith of the repentant killer who "turned his chest," the returning prodigal son who "came to his senses . . . got up and returned to his father," and the thief on the cross beside Jesus all depict people who are realigning their lives toward the center, even though they may be "a long way off" and can boast no good works to merit any acceptance. They had all come to a point of "conversion" without earning it by their righteous deeds. This is crucial to the topic at hand. As Richard Peace observed, "How we conceive of conversion determines how we do evangelism."[76]

There are different understandings of how to turn back to God. Rodinson contrasts Muslim and Christian understandings. For a Muslim, "the sinner's repentance was much more the regretful acknowledgement of a mistake, an unfortunate oversight, than the anguished desolation of a creature who, craving love, has momentarily strayed or failed to see the offer of a boundless affection until too late."[77] Another writer reminds us that "repentance is not the first step towards grace, but a response to grace."[78]

The task of evangelism and assessing the spiritual status of those being addressed is a risky venture, for what is at stake is one's eternal destiny. "It will be said to the people of Paradise, 'O people of Paradise! Eternity (for you) and no death,' and to the people of the Fire, 'O people of the Fire, eternity (for you) and no death!'"[79] The Bible likewise refers to heaven[80] and hell[81] as places of eternal abode.

So what is the role of good works? Can they be used to win one's acceptance before God? Some hadith suggest that this is not always the case, as the next chapter shows.

NOTES

1. E.g., B.1:505.

2. E.g., B.4:28.

3. B.1:17; 5:232, 233; 6:419; 9:12, 37, 320, 560.

4. B.9:542.

5. E.g., B.4:175; 7:717.

6. B.4:810.

7. Jer 31:30; Rom 6:23.

8. Rev 21:8.

9. Gen 18:25.

10. Matt 12:36.

11. B.1:17; 5:232; 6:417; 8:775, 793; 9:320, 560.

12. B.8:812.

13. McAuliffe, "Forestalling the pains of purgatory," 291. This concept is still widely believed and practiced. See http://www.newadvent.org/cathen/07783a.htm (accessed October 14, 2015).

14. B.1:504, 506.

15.   B.1:36.

16.   B.1:34.

17.   B.1:37.

18.   B.1:161.

19.   B.1:53.

20.   B.1:53, 576; 5:693; 8:384, 725.

21.   B.5:424, 425.

22.   Q.5:12.

23.   Q.2:245.

24.   B.1: 97.1; 4:255, 655.

25.   B.1:40; 8:498; 9:592.

26.   B.2:491; 9:525.2 .

27.   B.6:206; 9:508.

28.   B.8:412.

29.   B.8:415, 673: 9:652.

30.   B.2:440, 441, 467.

31.   Al-Faruqi, *Ethics*, 226.

32.   B.7:572.

33.   B.6:693, 273.

34.   B.4:63.

35.   B.8:547, 548, 568.

36.   B.8:673.

37.   B.7:576.

38.   B.1:441.

39.   B.7:390.

40.   B.2:532; 6:62.

41.   B.3:629.

42.   B.8:747; 3:94; 4:397, 404; 9:403.

43.   B.1:528.

44.   Q.6:70; 34:50.

45.   B.1:504; 6:209 cf. Q.11:114; 4:31.

46.   B.8:414.

47.   B.9:562.

48.   B.9:104.

49.   Prov 20:9.

50. Rom 3:10–12 quoting Ps 14:1–4; 53:1–3; Eccl 7:20.

51. Mark 3:28–30.

52. Based on Q.4:48, 116, B.7:850; 8:507. Abdalati, *Islam in Focus*, 23–40.

53. B.3:838.

54. B.8:758, 759.

55. B.9:86.

56. B.8:441.

57. B.4:567; 6:265; 8:537.

58. B.1:807; 2:148; 5:468.

59. B.9:5.

60. B.8:187; 9:7, 8.

61. B.3:655; 7:484; 8:763, 801.

62. B.8:800.2.

63. Nasr, "God," 318.

64. B.2:475; 5:50, 254.

65. B.5:41.

66. B.5:42; 8:235; 9:367.

67. B.3:852.

68. Rodinson, *Muhammad*, 235.

69. B.4:676.

70. Luke 15:11–32.

71. Luke 23:39–43.

72. Gal 2:16.

73. Rom 8:33.

74. The Qur'an, however, suggests a certain arbitrariness about Allah in response: "He forgives whom he pleases and He punishes whom He pleases" (Q.5:18).

75. Hiebert, *Anthropological Reflections*.

76. Peace, *Conversion*, 286.

77. Rodinson, *Mohammed*, 236.

78. Adam, *Hearing God's Words*, 28.

79. B.8:553, 552, 556.

80. 1 Thess 4:17; 1 Cor 9:25.

81. Luke 16:26; Jude 1:13; Rev 20:10.

11

THE INADEQUACY OF WORKS

1. ACTIONS ARE NOT A CLEAR SIGN
OF ONE'S FINAL DESTINY

Actions are an unclear indication of a person's ultimate fate, for, as the Prophet said: "Your deeds will not make you enter Paradise."[1] Israr Khan concedes that "the tradition does not give any credit to good deeds at all."[2] Muhammad stated: "A man may do what seem to the people as the deeds of the dwellers of Paradise but he is from the dwellers of the Hell-Fire and another may do what seem to the people as the deeds of the dwellers of the Hell-Fire, but he is from the dwellers of Paradise."[3]

This concurs with two of Jesus' sayings. He announced to his disciples: "Many will say to me on that day, 'Lord, Lord, did we not prophesy in your name, and in your name drive out demons and perform many miracles?' Then I will tell them plainly, 'I never knew you. Away from me, you evildoers!'"[4] Yet the criminal crucified beside him was told, "I tell you the truth, today you will be with me in paradise."[5]

2. MUHAMMAD'S WORKS DID NOT GUARANTEE HIS ENTRY TO PARADISE

Significantly, the Prophet himself expressed uncertainty about his personal destiny. He was so fearful of the possibility of hell-fire that he repeatedly implored Allah about it.[6] Aisha reported him "seeking refuge with Allah from the punishment in the grave in every prayer he prayed."[7] He regularly entreated, "O Allah! I seek refuge with You from the punishment of the Fire, the afflictions of the grave, (and) the punishment in the grave."[8] His deathbed prayer was, "O Allah! Excuse me and bestow Your Mercy on me and let me join with the highest companions (in Paradise)."[9] Due to performing *ruqya* (reciting Qur'anic verses over the sick),[10] Muhammad had apparently disqualified himself from being among the 70,000 Muslims guaranteed paradise "who will neither have any reckoning of their accounts nor will receive any punishment."[11]

After a vision, he noted: "Hell became so near to me that I said, 'O my Lord, will I be among those people?'"[12] At a funeral discussion about the ultimate state of the deceased, Muhammad admitted to his followers: "By Allah, though I am the Apostle of Allah, yet I do not know what Allah will do to me, nor to you."[13] This accords with his statement in the Qur'an to his followers: "nor do I know what will be done with me or with you."[14] Once he confidently stated: "Whosoever will meet Allah without associating anything in worship with Him will go to Paradise." When asked if this should be announced publicly, he averred: "No, I am afraid, lest they should depend upon it (absolutely)."[15]

Despite this, he informed certain individuals that they would enter Paradise,[16] including Thābit bin Qais,[17] Fātima,[18] 'Umar,[19] 'Ukasha bin Muhsin,[20] and a man who was killed as a martyr.[21] After Haritha was killed in the battle of Badr, Muhammad assured the young soldier's mother that "he is in Paradise."[22] He also reported Allah's statement that a blind person would enter paradise in compensation for the loss of his eyes.[23] Paradise was also guaranteed for those who could "guarantee (the chastity of) what is between his two jaw-bones and what is between his two legs (i.e. his tongue and his private parts)."[24] On another occasion, Muhammad noted the futility of good works to obtain salvation, even for himself (see Sidebar *Muhammad Uncertain of Paradise*).

The echo from Ephesians 2:8–9 is deafening: "For it is by grace you have been saved through faith—and this is not from yourselves, it is the gift of God—not by works, so that no one can boast." One is reminded of the divine prophecy found in Isaiah: "I will expose your righteousness and your works, and they will not benefit you."[25] Paul builds on this concept: "A man is not justified by observing the law but by faith in Jesus Christ." He informs Timothy that God saved us "not because of anything we have done but because of his own purpose and grace."[26] For Christians, good works are a consequence of salvation, not the cause of it.[27]

> **MUHAMMAD UNCERTAIN OF PARADISE**
>
> Abū Huraira reported: "I heard Allah's Apostle saying, 'The good deeds of any person will not make him enter Paradise.' (i.e. None can enter Paradise through his good deeds.) They (the Prophet's companions) said, 'Not even you, O Allah's Apostle?' He said, 'Not even myself, unless Allah bestows His favor and mercy on me.'"[a] Aisha concurred: "The Prophet said, 'Do good deeds properly, sincerely and moderately, and receive good news because one's good deeds will not make him enter Paradise.' They asked, 'Even you, O Allah's Apostle?' He said, 'Even I, unless and until Allah bestows His pardon and Mercy on me.'"[b]

3. THE RELATIONSHIP BETWEEN FAITH AND WORKS

An indicator of the relationship between faith and works would be a deathbed conversion. A religious system such as Christianity based on faith alone would recognize the salvific efficacy of such a last-minute commitment. The thief on the cross beside Jesus is the classic example.[28] However, a works-based religious system such

---

a. B.7:577.

b. B.8:474.

as Islam, if strictly applied, should question it, since the person would be unable to perform any good works to save himself. Muhammad worked hard to convince his dying uncle Abū Talib to pronounce the *shahāda*, promising to intercede for his uncle if he accepted Islam.[29] He also stated that all one's previous good works would be counted.[30] However, these still might not have been enough to save his uncle from the hell-fire.

4. CONNECTIONS WITH BIBLICAL THEMES

The Bible is unequivocal about the basis of salvation: "If you confess with your mouth, 'Jesus is Lord' and believe in your heart that God raised him from the dead, *you will be saved*."[31] Jesus was emphatic: "I tell you the truth, whoever hears my word and believes him who sent me has eternal life and will not be condemned; he has crossed over from death to life."[32] Paul writes very clearly: "And if by grace, then it is no longer by works; if it were, grace would no longer be grace."[33]

The Muslim uncertainty about salvation casts the Christian understanding of hope in a positive light. Writing about Indonesian Muslims who have come to faith in Christ, Greenlee notes that "assurance of salvation remains the most significant reason for the conversions, even among those informants who fervently exalt the power aspects of the Gospel."[34]

On one occasion, Muhammad seemed to grasp the important distinction between works performed to earn merit in order to gain one's salvation, and those performed out of gratitude for a salvation that had already been won. "The Prophet used to offer night prayers till his feet became swollen. Somebody said to him, 'Allah has forgiven you, your faults of the past and those to follow.' On that, he said, 'Shouldn't I be a thankful slave (of Allah)?'"[35] Prayer becomes an expression of gratefulness to God, rather than an exercise to gain religious merit.

Muhammad spoke of God's "screening" work with believers. "Allah will bring a believer near Him and shelter him with His screen and ask him: 'Did you commit such-and-such sins?' He will say: 'Yes, my Lord.' Allah will keep on asking him till he will confess all his sins and will think that he is ruined. Allah will say: 'I did screen your sins in the world and I forgive them for you today', and then he will be given the book of his good deeds."[36] One is reminded of the biblical statement: "God was reconciling the world to himself in Christ, not counting men's sins against them."[37]

However, this teaching about assurance raises the question of justice and equity. Is sin simply overlooked by God, or does some price need to be paid? Are atonement and/or expiation necessary, or even possible? The next section addresses these important questions.

NOTES

1. B.8:471, 474.

2. Khan, *Authentication,* 57. Because this conflicts with the Qur'an's teaching about good works (Q.2:25, 82, 277; 3:57; 4:57, 122, 173; 11:23; 14:23; 18:107; 22:14, 23, 50, 56; 29:58; 31:8; 32:19; 42:22; 47:12; 85:11, etc.), Khan rejects the authenticity of this hadith.

3. B.5:514. The similarity to Ezekiel 33:12–16 may be more apparent than real, for the element of repentance is missing in the Hadith's account.

4. Matt 7:22–23.

5. Luke 23:43.

6. B.1:795; 2: 159, 164, 458, 459; 4:76, 77; 6:320; 8:375, 376, 377. The Qur'an presents this uncertainty as a common issue (Q.26:51; 26:82; 66:8), despite affirming that those who believe "have assurance in the hereafter" (Q.2:4; 31:4).

7. B.2:454.

8. B.1:795; 2:459; 4:76, 77; 6:230; 8:375, 376, 377, 378, 381, 385, 386, 387, 388.

9. B.7:578.

10. B.7:640, 642.

11. B.8:549, 479; 7:648; 8:549, 550.

12. B.1:712; 3:552.

13. B.5:266; 2:334, 335; 9:131, 145.

14. Q.46:9.

15. B.1:131; also 4:108.

16. Many Muslims know of *al-`Ashara al-Mubasharîn bi-l-Janna* ("the ten promised Paradise"), but these are not recorded in al-Bukhari. These are listed in the Hadith of Abu Dawūd 41:4632 http://sunnah.com/abudawud/42 and Tirmidhi 46:3747 http://sunnah.com/tirmidhi/49

17. B.4:810.

18. B.4:819.

19. B.5:42.

20. B.7:606; 8:549, 550.

21. B.5:377.

22. B.8:558, 572.

23. B.7:557.

24. B.8:481.

25. Isa 57:12.

26. 2 Tim 1:9.

27. Gal 2:16 ; Tit 3:7–8.

28. Luke 23:43.

29. B.2:442; 5:223; 6:295; 8:762.

30. B.1:78; 2:517; 3:423; 8:21.

31. Romans 10:9, emphasis mine. The Bible is not universalistic regarding salvation, i.e., that all people will be saved. There are conditions to be fulfilled. The primary action of faith (see John 6:28–29) must be accompanied by deeds which illustrate the faith (Jas 2:14). These deeds will play some role in the judgment process (see Matt 25:37 ff.; Rev 20:12). There seems also to be the potential of falling away (Luke 9:62; Heb 6:4–6).

32. John 5:24.

33. Rom 11:6.

34. He is citing Bard Lokken Knapstad, "Show us the Power: A Study of the Influence of Miracles on the Conversion Process from Islam to Christianity in an Indonesian Context," MA thesis (Oslo: Norwegian Lutheran School of Theology, 2000) in Greenlee, "How Is the Gospel Good News for Muslims?"

35. B.6:360; 8:478. The Qur'an states to the Jews: "We forgave you so that you might be grateful" (Q.2:52).

36. B.3:621; 6:207; 8:95, 96; 9:605.

37. 2 Cor 5:19.

12

AVOIDING PUNISHMENT
FOR ONE'S SINS

1. THE QUR'AN DISAVOWS HUMAN
ATONEMENT BUT THE HADITH AFFIRMS IT

The Qur'an appears to deny some core Christian beliefs. Yusuf Ali claims that "the theological doctrine of blood sacrifice and vicarious atonement [is] rejected by Islam."[1] According to the Qur'an, each person is responsible for his or her own sin: "Whoever earns a sin, he earns it only against himself."[2] "And whatever of misfortune befalls you, it is because of what your hands have earned."[3] The equation appears to be simple: Good is rewarded[4] and evil is punished.[5] Good and bad deeds only benefit or disadvantage the person who did them: "Whoever works righteousness benefits his own soul; whoever works evil, it is against his own soul."[6] The impression given is of a simple and clear correspondence between an action and its consequence, between a person's good or bad behavior and his or her reward or punishment (see Figure 1).

A person completes a GOOD deed ⟶ That person receives the appropriate REWARD
A person performs a BAD deed ⟶ That person receives the appropriate PUNISHMENT

FIGURE 1: The apparent teaching of Islam

Deeds will be weighed on scales on the Day of Judgment, and every soul is *yubsal* (delivered) by what it has earned. Any form of substitution is disallowed.[7] Those who offer to bear the sins of others are liars and will bear their own sins and other loads besides.[8] Moreover, the transferral of guilt is prohibited. "And whoever earns a fault or a sin and then throws it on to someone innocent, he has indeed burdened himself with falsehood and a manifest sin."[9] Yusuf Ali reiterates his point: "There can be no vicarious atonement."[10] In this chapter we will deal with bad deeds and punishment and see that this apparently clear teaching did not always apply.

2. SOME SINFUL ACTIONS WOULD BE OVERLOOKED

The principle of punishment being visited upon those who sinned was not always carried out. Some pagans who converted to Islam were burdened by their shameful history of murder and sex, particularly when they heard a verse recited describing these as unacceptable acts.[11] They said, "O Muhammad! Whatever you say and invite people to, is good: but we wish if you could inform us whether we can make an expiation for our (past evil) deeds." As a result, the following verse was revealed: "Say: O My slaves who have transgressed against their souls! Despair not of the Mercy of Allah."[12]

When a man was accused of being a hypocrite, Muhammad ascertained that he had recited the first sentence of the *shahāda*, and then pronounced: "Nobody will meet Allah with that saying on the Day of Resurrection, but Allah will save him from the Fire."[13]

The avoidance of punishment was, however, conditional on not doing evil after accepting Islam. A man said: "'O Allah's Apostle! Shall we be punished for what we did in the Pre-Islamic Period of ignorance?' The Prophet said, 'Whoever does good in Islam will not be punished for what he did in the Pre-Islamic Period of ignorance and whoever does evil in Islam will be punished for his former and later (bad deeds).'"[14]

At another time, this general ruling received a more specific response.

Allah's Apostle said, "Someone came to me from my Lord and gave me the news (or good tidings) that if any of my followers dies worshipping none (in any way) along with Allah, he will enter Paradise." I asked, "Even if he committed illegal sexual intercourse (adultery) and theft?" He replied, "Even if he committed illegal sexual intercourse (adultery) and theft."[15]

In this case, no penalty for these illicit actions is described. Others who had avoided certain sins (such as cauterization, treatment by recitation of Qur'anic verses, and seeing evil omens) and had put their trust in the Lord alone "will neither have any reckoning of their accounts nor will receive any punishment."[16] A man committed a sin twice, and asked for forgiveness each time and received it.

Then he remains without committing any another sin for a while and then commits another sin (for the third time) and says, "O my Lord, I have committed another sin, please forgive me," and Allah says, "My slave has known that he has a Lord Who forgives sins and punishes for it. I therefore have forgiven My slave (his sin), he can do whatever he likes."[17]

A person performs an EVIL deed ⟶ That person is NOT PUNISHED

FIGURE 2: Sins may escape punishment without expiation

Sins which did not become evident in public may be forgiven or punished at the divine discretion, for "whoever commits any of those sins and Allah does not expose him, then it is up to Allah if He wishes He will punish him or if He wishes, He will forgive him."[18] Some sins are not punished. See Figure 2.

3. PUNISHMENT FOR A BAD DEED CAN BE PAID FOR BY EXPIATION

However, it is possible that a person might perform a bad deed and the deed is not overlooked, yet the sinner does not receive any punishment for that deed. This happens through the process of expiation. The verb *kaffar* (expiate) occurs fifteen times in the Qur'an.[19] It is significant that, as a verb, only Allah expiates the evil which believers have done. "Whoever believes in Allah and performs good deeds, He will expiate him from his sins and will admit him to Gardens."[20] It is always a divine and never a human initiative. The noun *kaffārah* (expiation) occurs three times.[21] As a noun, however, it is the action that can be taken by individuals to remove some of their sins.

The Hadith strengthens this second meaning. Fifty-four accounts in al-Bukhāri mention *kaffar* or *kaffārah*, but in the Hadith it becomes human activity which can expiate sin. In fact, "every (sinful) deed can be expiated."[22] "A man's afflictions (i.e. wrong deeds) concerning his relation to his family, his property and his neighbors are expiated by his prayers, giving in charity and enjoining what is good and forbidding what is evil."[23] Saying the five daily prayers regularly annulled evil deeds,[24] as did performance of the 'Umra (shorter pilgrimage).[25] Sometimes the payment of money was required. The sin of encouraging others to gamble could be canceled by giving some money in charity.[26] "The *Kaffarah* for having intercourse with menstruating women is one dinar if the blood is completely red and half a dinar when the blood is (somewhat) yellow."[27] The penalty for murder was death: "*al-qisās* (the Law of Equality in punishment) is prescribed for you in case of murder."[28] However, an alternative is permitted. If the killer was forgiven by the relatives of the deceased, he could purchase his own life through compensatory *diya* (blood money).[29] The murderer's life could be saved by the payment of a price. Over fifteen hadith deal with this practice.[30]

Although certain rituals were mandatory, they could be circumvented if some reparation was made. Fasting, despite being compulsory,[31] might be replaced by feeding a needy person instead.[32] The term used is *fidya* (ransom), and it applied for those unable to complete the *Hajj* or *Umra*.[33] It is defined as "compensation for a missed or wrongly practiced religious obligation (like in *Hajj*), usually in the form of money or foodstuff or offering (animal by slaughtering it)."[34] Shaving one's head before *Hajj* to deal with head-lice was seen as a transgression—the required payment included feeding the poor or offering a sacrifice.[35]

Some sins were expiated by reversing the action or rectifying the damage caused. The Prophet said, "Spitting in the mosque is a sin and its expiation is to bury it."[36] Allah's Apostle said: "Whoever amongst you swears, (saying by error) in his oath 'By Al-Lat and Al-'Uzza' [the names of two pagan idols], then he should say, 'None has the right to be worshipped but Allah.'"[37]

At other times, there was no apparent connection between the sin and the expiatory action. One man, for example, was admitted to Paradise for giving water to a thirsty dog.[38] In another version of the story it is a Jewish prostitute who is forgiven by way of the same act.[39] A man who had performed no good deeds asked his family to burn his body when he died and crush and scatter the ashes, out of fear of Allah. So Allah forgave him.[40] Aisha "manumitted forty slaves as expiation for her [broken] vow."[41] This was an illustration of Muhammad's pledge: "If I take an oath to do something and later on I find something else better than the first one, then I do what is better and make expiation for my oath."[42] See Figure 3.

Sin could even be expiated passively, by an unintended and undesired event. "No fatigue, nor disease, nor sorrow, nor sadness, nor hurt, nor distress befalls a Muslim, even if it were the prick he receives from a thorn, but that Allah expiates some of his sins for that."[43] Any sickness would annul sins.[44] Losing two or three children would protect a Muslim man or woman from the fire of hell.[45] In fact, too easy a life could mean that one's rewards were being given early, in this life rather than the next.[46] A shorter and more difficult life might indicate that "they did not take anything from their rewards in this world."[47]

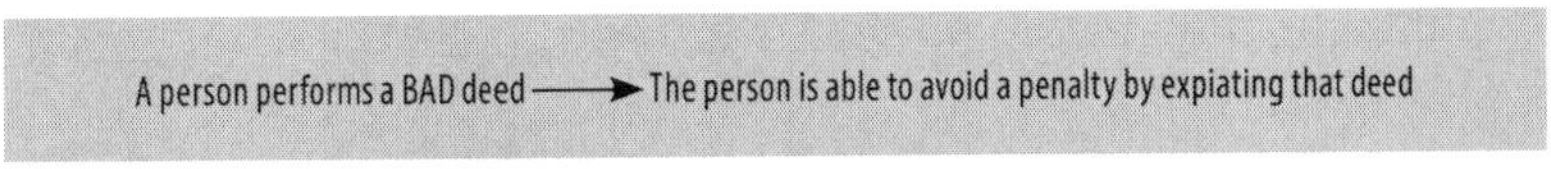

A person performs a BAD deed ⟶ The person is able to avoid a penalty by expiating that deed

FIGURE 3: The Principle of Expiation

Moreover, the Hadith do not affirm the general Qur'anic adage that sin is always punished and good is always rewarded. The Hadith points out other ways punishment was avoided for sins committed. These are outlined here.

4. SINS COULD BE PASSED ON TO OTHERS

In the Qur'an, those who led others astray would carry not only their own 'awzār (burdens) but also the 'awzār of those they had misled.[48] There is also a saying attributed to Abel about his brother Cain coming to attack him: "If you do stretch your hand against me to kill me, I shall never stretch my hand against you to kill you, for I fear Allah; the Lord of the worlds. Verily, I *intend to let you draw my sin on yourself* as well as yours."[49] Yusuf Ali suggests an interpretation of these verses: "The unjust murderer not only carried on himself the burden of his own sin, but also the burden of his victim's sins. The victim, in suffering a wrong or injustice, is forgiven his own sins."[50] In fact, the burden of sin continues to be piled on Cain throughout history, according to the Hadith. "None is killed unjustly, but the first son of Adam will have a part of its burden."[51]

Bad deeds and good ones were conveyable to other people. "Whoever has wronged his brother, should ask for his pardon (before his death), as (in the Hereafter) there will be neither a Dinar nor a Dirham [two types of Arab currency]. (He should secure pardon in this life) before some of his good deeds are taken and paid to his brother, or, if he has done no good deeds, some of the bad deeds of his brother are taken to be loaded on him (in the Hereafter)."[52]

In some cases of *diya* (blood-money for killing a person), the payment was a male or female slave to be given to the family of the murdered person.[53] In these instances an innocent slave paid for the crime of the murderer by continuing to suffer bondage, but now in the household of the murdered person. This principle is outlined in Figure 4.

A person performs an EVIL deed ———▶ A DIFFERENT person receives the punishment

FIGURE 4: Sins may result in transference of punishment

5. SINS COULD BE EXPIATED BY THE ACTION OF AN INNOCENT PERSON

Sometimes it happened that the innocent could willingly pay the price for the guilty. A man who indulged in sexual intercourse with his wife when he should have been fasting was told by Muhammad to do several things, including freeing a slave, to expiate his sin. He was unable to fulfill any of the requirements. Consequently Muhammad gave him a basket of dates to distribute to the poor as expiation. Since the man knew no family poorer than his own, Muhammad told him to keep the dates for himself. Apparently the man's sin was expiated by his action of giving the basket of dates to his own poor family, even though he did not pay for the dates himself. Muhammad, although innocent of the man's sexual act, paid for the sin of the guilty man by forgoing his dates.[54] When Abdullah bin Sahl was murdered by an unknown assailant, Muhammad himself paid the one hundred camels worth of *diya* (blood money) to the victim's family.[55] If a person guilty of killing someone had no financial resources or was unable to pay the *diya* or blood debt, others, including relatives and friends, could pay this money on behalf of the killer.[56] Clearly an innocent person could pay the price for the sins of others. See Figure 5.

A person PERFORMS a BAD deed ———▶ An INNOCENT person PAYS THE PENALTY

FIGURE 5: A volunteer may take on the punishment for another's sin

6. CONNECTIONS WITH BIBLICAL THEMES

"Expiation" or "atonement" is found in the Old Testament nearly 120 times both as a noun (Hebrew *kippur*) and a verb (Hebrew *kaphar*). It refers to a "covering" or "appeasement" (either physical or spiritual), and invariably refers to the sacrifice system established by God, where an animal died in the place of a sinner. The sacrifices were a divine provision whereby the judgment against sin could be averted by the shedding of blood. The New Testament mentions "expiation" four times, and always in the context of the death of Christ.[57] When the Islamic documents are compared with the biblical records, a progression in meaning is found (see Figure 6).

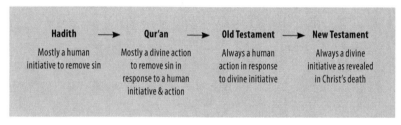

FIGURE 6: There is a progression in the meanings of expiation

This is an anomaly: the Hadith generally moves closer to the biblical view in some ways.

The Hadith principle that a person can commit a sin without the person paying the punishment for it (see Figure 2) finds an echo in the Bible. It points to the "blessed" man, described in the Psalms, "whose transgressions are forgiven, whose sins are covered . . . whose sin the Lord does not count against him."[58] Sometimes reparation for a sin might be paid, as in the case of theft or extortion[59] (see Figure 3).

Rather than exacting a justly deserved punishment against the offended, God is praised as One who "does not treat us as our sins deserve or repay us according to our iniquities."[60] This does not mean that the sins are simply ignored, for the punishment must be borne by another (see Figure 4). The prophecy of Isaiah described an innocent one who paid the price for the evil deeds of others. He "was pierced for our transgressions . . . crushed for our iniquities,

the punishment that brought us peace was upon him."[61] Citing this
passage, Peter wrote of Jesus: "He himself bore *our* sins in *his* body on
the tree, so that we might die to sins and live for righteousness; by *his*
wounds *you* have been healed"[62] (see Figure 5). Peter points out the
exchange principle that was operating: "For Christ died for sins once
for all, the righteous for the unrighteous, to bring you to God."[63]

NOTES

1.	Ali, *The Holy Qur'an: English translation*, 268, n. 66.3.
2.	Q.4:111; 6:164.
3.	Q.42:30.
4.	Q.2:286; 4:124.
5.	Q.2:281; 4:123; 53:31.
6.	Q.41:46; 17:7, 15; 45:15.
7.	Q.29:12.
8.	Q.29:13.
9.	Q.4:112.
10.	Ali, *The Holy Qur'an: English translation*, 1643, n. 5113.
11.	Q. 25.68.
12.	Q.39.53; B.6:334.
13.	B.9:71.
14.	B.9:56.
15.	B.2:329, 330; 3:573; 4:445; 7:717; 8:285, 450, 451; 9:579.
16.	B.8:549, 479; 7:648.
17.	B.9:598.
18.	B.9:320.
19.	Q.39:35; 5:65; 47:2; 2:271; 3:193, 195; 4:31; 5:12; 8:29; 29:7; 39:35; 48:5; 64:9; 65:5, 8.
20.	Q.64:9.
21.	Q.5:45, 89, 95.
22.	B.9:629.
23.	B.4:786; 1:503; 2:516; 3:119; 9:216.
24.	B.1:506.
25.	B.3:1.

26. B.6:383; 8:128, 645.

27. From CD Islamic Scholar/Hadith/Mishkat.

28. Q.2:178. This is the application of *lex talionis* "life for life, eye for eye, tooth for tooth, etc." as in Ex 21:23–25.

29. Q.2:178, 4:92; 17:33.

30. E.g., B.1:111,112; 4:283.

31. E.g., Q.2:183.

32. Q.2:184.

33. Q.2:196.

34. Al-Hilali and Khan, *Translation of the meanings of the Noble Qur'an*, 866.

35. Q.2:196 and B.5:504; 6:42; 7:604.

36. B.1:407.

37. B.8:645.

38. B.1:174; 3:551, 646; 8:38.

39. B.4:538, 673.

40. B.4:659, 684, 685, 688; 8:488; 9:597, 599.

41. B.8:98; 4:708.

42. B.8:618–622; 8:708, 709.

43. B.7:545, 544, 550, 551.

44. B.7:560, 564, 565, 566, 571.

45. B.2:341; 8:650; 9:413.

46. B.2:364, 365; 5:237, 253, 376, 378, 408.

47. B.2:366; 5:237, 253, 378; 8:455.

48. Q.16:25; 29:13.

49. Q.5:28–29 (emphasis mine).

50. Ali, *The Holy Qur'an: Text, Translation and Commentary*, 251 n.732.

51. B.9:423, 6; 4:552.

52. B.8:541.

53. B.9:41, 42.1, 42.2, 45, 420.

54. B.3:156–158, 772; 7:281; 8:110, 185, 700, 701, 702, 8111.1, 111.2.

55. B.4:398; 8:164; 9:36–37.

56. B.9:44-45.

57. Rom 3:25 (Greek *hilasterion*) and Heb 9:5, referring to Old Testament atonement as a picture of Christ's sacrifice; 1 John 2:2; 4:10 (Greek *hilasmos*).

58. Ps 32:1–2.

59. Ex 22:1; Luke 19:8.

60. Ps 103:10.

61. Isa 53:5.

62. 1 Pet 2:24 (emphasis mine).

63. 1 Pet 3:18.

13

GAINING REWARD

EVERY DEED AND ITS IMPLICATIONS are not as inevitably linked as is sometimes supposed. Just as a bad deed does not always lead to punishment, a clear one-to-one correspondence of a good action leading to its inevitable positive consequence is not always evident. The Hadith provide other perspectives which open up new possibilities.

1. NON-COMPLETION OR INADEQUATE COMPLETION OF A GOOD DEED WAS SOMETIMES ACCEPTABLE

Simply preparing for and intending to carry out an obligation would be counted as equivalent to fulfilling that duty if one was prevented from doing so.[1] A man was told by Muhammad that he would be rewarded for his intention to give gold coins in charity, even though he never gave them.[2] A person's circumstances, both personal and physical, may mean that the reward of a full *Hajj* could be received, despite not completing it.[3] When pilgrims performed their *Hajj* rituals out of sequence, potentially canceling their reward, Muhammad comforted them with: "Do it (now) and there is no harm."[4] One commentator concludes from these events that "the 'intent' of the believer . . . is of more account than his doing."[5] Intention may overrule completion (see Figure 7).

> A person inadequately completes a GOOD deed ⟶ That person STILL receives the appropriate REWARD

FIGURE 7: Incomplete good deed may bring reward

2. A PERSON COULD GAIN A REWARD FROM THE ACTION FOR OTHERS

A non-beneficiary could perform an action to benefit others. Muhammad sacrificed a sheep[6] and cows[7] on behalf of his wives. Some of his companions were given a sheep to sacrifice for themselves.[8] A woman who selflessly gave food in charity would be rewarded, but the same reward would be received by her husband who earned the money to buy the food, as well as by the shopkeeper who sold her the food.[9] A man would receive half the reward of his wife's charitable giving from his wealth, although she did so without his orders.[10] Clearly, rewards could be accounted to those vaguely associated with and perhaps unconscious of the good deed. Likewise animals could win merit for their owners. The horse of a *mujāhid* (Muslim fighter) could earn reward for its rider by consuming food and drink; even its footsteps when grazing and the dung and urine it produced would be counted.[11] Rewards could be transmitted to others (see Figure 8).

> A person carries out a GOOD deed ⟶ A DIFFFERENT person receives the appropriate REWARD

FIGURE 8: Rewards for good deeds are transferable

Moreover, rewards were transferable over time. All good deeds performed before becoming a Muslim would be counted.[12]

3. A LIVING PERSON COULD PAY IN SUBSTITUTION FOR A DEAD PERSON

Islamic law allows for transferral of economic debt: *Hawālah* is "the transference of debt from one person to another. It is an agreement whereby a debtor is released from a debt by another becoming responsible for it."[13] In many cases, a debtor had died leaving behind no finances, so others undertook to do what the deceased could no longer do for himself.[14] Business could be carried by proxy, with another person acting as the representative of the buyer or seller when authorized to do so.[15]

This was also permitted for spiritual debts, by analogical connection. When a woman asked about the acceptability of fulfilling her dead mother's vow to perform the *Hajj,* Muhammad inquired: "If your mother had been in debt, would you have paid her debt?" She said, "Yes." He said, "So you should pay what is for Him as Allah has more right that one should fulfill one's obligations to Him."[16] Another woman was allowed to perform *Hajj* on her sick father's behalf,[17] and several did so in the place of those who had died.[18] A relative was permitted to fast on behalf of a dead person,[19] and guardians were required to make up missed days of fasting for the deceased.[20] Unfulfilled vows could be carried out on behalf of the deceased.[21] In each of these cases, the reward was accrued by the person who had died, to be accessed on the Day of Judgment.

Although the Qur'an forbids the posthumous payment of *sadaqa,*[22] Muhammad allowed this when people wanted to give alms on behalf of the dead.[23] The deceased who benefited from it would shield the givers from the hell-fire.[24] Moreover, the living could and did pray for the dead. Muhammad was commanded to do so[25] and was often found praying at funerals.[26] This implies that one can intercede for others who cannot pray for themselves. In fact, some would come out of the fire through the intercession of others,[27] particularly of Muhammad.[28] Islam's prophet had claimed this right for himself,[29] and his followers were told to pray for it to be given to Muhammad.[30] This would be Muhammad's one invocation that would be "definitely fulfilled by Allah."[31]

It appears, then, that most of the main pillars of Islam can be performed by someone for the benefit of others (see Table 19).

Shahada for others	Not possible
Prayer for the dead	This is *du'a*, not *salāt* B.2:403-408, 411, 412
Fasting for the dead	B.3:174, 173
Giving alms for the dead	B.2:470; 4:19, 22,24; 2:499
Performing *Hajj* for the dead	B.9:418; 2:589; 5:682; 8:247; 3:77-79

TABLE 19: The Pillars of Islam fulfilled by others

This principle is outlined in Figure 9.

A LIVING PERSON does a GOOD DEED ⟶ A DEAD PERSON receives the REWARD

FIGURE 9: Rewards for good deeds are transferable to the dead

4. A SINGLE ACTION COULD HAVE POSITIVE ETERNAL CONSEQUENCES

Some actions apparently expiated all of a person's sins. For example, Muhammad refused to execute Hatib, who had betrayed him by relaying information to the Prophet's enemies. Hatib had fought alongside the Prophet in the battle of Badr. Muhammad said: "Maybe Allah looked at the Badr warriors and said, 'Do whatever you like, as I have granted Paradise to you,' or said, 'I have forgiven you.'"[32] All of a worshiper's past sins could be forgiven if his "Amen" at the completion of prayers coincided with that of the angels.[33] Such a process may have applied to Muhammad himself, for it was said that his past and future sins had been forgiven.[34] Despite this, Muhammad continued to pray for such forgiveness.[35] Blindness carried the special divine promise that if the afflicted person "remains patient, I will let him enter Paradise in compensation."[36] The reward of *Hajj Mabrūr* (the one accepted by Allah) "is nothing except

Paradise"[37]—the same promise extended to the first Muslims to undertake a naval expedition or if he was among the first Muslims to invade Caesar's city.[38] A single act of memorizing the ninety-nine names of Allah would allow entry to paradise.[39] Muhammad spoke of forty such deeds which could result in paradise for those who performed them.[40] Figure 10 describes this principle.

A person carries out a SINGLE GOOD deed ——▶ RESULTS of that deed are ETERNAL

FIGURE 10: Effects of a single good deed may be everlasting

5. THE POSITIVE ACTION OF ONE PERSON COULD HAVE BENEFICIAL IMPLICATIONS FOR MANY OTHERS

The concept of the *fard kifāyah* (sufficiency duty) occurs in Islamic theology. "It is a collective duty—an obligation which, if performed by one person, suffices for the rest; as it does not have to be performed essentially by all."[41] The action of one person or a small portion of the nation, such as soldiers fighting to defend their homeland, could bring assistance to the whole community. The opposite is *fard 'ayn* or *fard wājib* (obligatory duty)—a requirement which every individual must perform, e.g., daily prayers and fasting.[42] 'Umar, for example, is described as "the door" holding back the affliction which threatened the Islamic community.[43] This principle is summarized in Figure 11.

The POSITIVE action of ONE person ——▶ BENEFITS for MANY OTHERS

FIGURE 11: Effects of a good deed may be extended to others

This links with some modern-day versions of Islam. According to Johnson, South Asian Muslims "see themselves as linked to others in a deep way, particularly with leaders. As Muslims they had considered linkage with the prophet Muhammad as the means of salvation."[44]

6. REWARDS AND PUNISHMENTS COULD CROSS THE LIFE/DEATH BOUNDARY

Punishment now means no punishment later, for sins expiated for in this life would not be punished in the next. "And if one of you commits any of these sins and is punished in this world then that will be his expiation for it."[45] Sins could also be expiated in this life by suffering the legal punishment for that action.[46] This explains why a man confessed his illegal sexual intercourse to Muhammad and accepted the judgment of stoning,[47] so he would not have to face the punishment for his sin in hell (see Figure 12).

A SIN is paid for IN THIS LIFE ⟶ It receives NO PENALTY in THE NEXT LIFE

FIGURE 12: Temporal actions can have eternal effects

7. CONNECTIONS WITH BIBLICAL THEMES

The six principles outlined above can be pointers to biblical teaching. The Hadith propose that non-completion of a spiritual goal does not necessarily disqualify the actor from reward (see Figure 7). The apostle Paul explains his own incomplete path of discipleship: "Not that I have already obtained all this, or have already been made perfect, but I press on to take hold of that for which Christ Jesus took hold of me . . . I press on towards the goal."[48] Intention and purpose are an important step toward, and at times as crucial as, actual completion of one's aspiration. The psalmist speaks of God's paternal lenience: "As a father has compassion on his children, so the Lord has compassion on those who fear him; for he knows how we are formed, he remembers that we are dust."[49]

For those incapable of becoming good enough to save themselves, God provides an alternative way (see Figure 8). In Roman Catholic theology, one's accrued benefit can be passed on to others when individuals "contribute generously to the spiritual treasury of the Church by acquiring much more expiatory wealth than they themselves need."[50]

However, most Protestant Christians would not accept this concept, holding that Christ alone can perform this service. From a Christian perspective, the holiness attained by Christ can be transferred to others. He prays to his heavenly Father for his followers: "Sanctify them (Greek *Hagiazo* lit. "make them holy") by the truth. . . . For them I sanctify myself, that they too may be truly sanctified."[51] Paul announces that "God made him who had no sin to be sin for us, so that in him we might become the righteousness of God."[52]

The Hadith imply that the good works of one person can be transferred to the benefit of another (see Figure 9). However, from a Christian perspective, there are many assumptions that are implicit or explicit in this scheme. It presupposes that the relationship between God and humanity is positive or at least neutral, and that these actions are possible to perform, and that they will be accepted by God.

By contrast, Paul reminds humanity of its parlous state before God. Rather than being in a position to offer services for others that would be acceptable to God, people are, apart from His mercy, spiritually lifeless. "As for you, *you were dead* in your transgressions and sins. . . . But because of his great love for us, God, who is rich in mercy, made us alive with Christ even when *we were dead* in transgressions—it is by grace you have been saved."[53] God's love is shown by his gracious response to those who are spiritually unresponsive to him. In a very real sense, as the Hadith hint, good works can cross the life/death barrier, but here it is to the benefit of the spiritually dead (see Figures 9 and 12).

A solitary feat by one person could have eternal consequences for many (see Figures 10 and 11). It is clear that a single act, as opposed to a "long obedience in the same direction,"[54] could have a salvific outcome in the biblical context. Isaiah contrasts a multitude of people who make many wrong choices with one individual's act of obedience and dedication which absorbs all these sins. "We all, like sheep, have gone astray, each of us has turned to his own way, and the Lord has laid on him the iniquity of us all."[55] The writer to the Hebrews declares that "by one sacrifice he has made perfect forever those who are being made holy."[56] This has implications for the Christian understanding of the comprehensive significance of the death of Christ.[57]

In a prophetic word, the high priest Caiaphas declared to the Jews about Jesus: "It is better for you that one man die for the people than that the whole nation perish."[58] This is a helpful pointer to Christ's "federal headship," in which his salvific action results in benefit for all those who are "in Christ."[59] Under "federal headship," the leader is responsible for the welfare (or otherwise) of the whole nation. The Qur'an speaks of the close identification of the life and death of an individual with that of the whole world. It states that "if anyone killed one person, …it would be as if he killed all mankind, and if anyone saved a life, it would be as if he saved the life of all mankind."[60] The Bible presents this as a way of looking at humanity. "For as in Adam all die, so in Christ all will be made alive."[61] One person is taken as the representative of all humanity—either Adam in the old humanity, or Christ in the new humanity. People will be affected, negatively or positively, by the actions of the one with whom they are identified. Romans 5:12–21 elaborates on this.[62]

This strikes a chord with the collectivist attitude of the early Arabs:

> The clan defined the mental universe of the Bedouin. . . .
> Without the clan, the individual had no place in the world,
> no life of his own. The language of the Bedouins offered no
> way to express the concept of individuality or personality.
> The term *wajh* (face), although applied to the chief, was
> really a concept designating the persona of the group rather
> than the individuality of the shaykh [leader] as a person.[63]

An insult about the leader was an insult on the whole clan, and an honor bestowed on the leader dignified all who followed him. However, it placed great store on the actions of the leader. When the Byzantine emperor Heraclius was challenged in Muhammad's letter to him to accept Islam, the threat was made, "but if you reject this, you will be responsible for the sins of all the people of your kingdom."[64] The prophet Isaiah spoke of the Suffering Servant in such terms: "He took up our infirmities and carried our sorrows. . . .

He was pierced for our transgressions, he was crushed for our iniquities; the punishment that brought us peace was upon him, and by his wounds we are healed. . . . The Lord has laid on him the iniquity of us all. . . . For he bore the sin of many."[65]

Jesus applied a similar approach on his teaching about sin. "If your right eye causes you to sin, gouge it out and throw it away. It is better for you to lose one part of your body than for your whole body to be thrown into hell. And if your right hand causes you to sin, cut it off and throw it away. It is better for you to lose one part of your body than for your whole body to go into hell."[66] Dealing with sin requires radical action. The most radical response to sin was the sacrifice of Christ.

Christ's death took place at a point in history. Could it apply across all historical ages? The Bible suggests that this event was not bounded by time. "Revelation's description of [Jesus] as the lamb slain before the foundation of the world (Rev 13:8) [indicated] that his death had significance beyond the earthly chronology in which it had occurred."[67] Paul writes that God's grace "was given us in Christ Jesus before the beginning of time, but it has now been revealed."[68] Jesus is designated as a priest like Melchizidek "without father or mother, without genealogy, without beginning of days or end of life,"[69] "but because Jesus lives forever, he has a permanent priesthood. Therefore he is able to save completely those who come to God through him, because he always lives to intercede for them."[70] He died "not for our sins only, but for the sins of the whole world."[71] On the basis of the coming death of the promised Redeemer, previous sins were not penalized. "God presented him as a sacrifice of atonement, through faith in his blood. He did this to demonstrate his justice, because *in his forbearance he had left the sins committed beforehand unpunished*—he did it to demonstrate his justice at the present time, so as to be just and the one who justifies those who have faith in Jesus."[72] As the pre-existent and eternal Son of God, Jesus exercised a ministry which has implications beyond historical time.

NOTES

1. B.2:703, 704. Muhammad said over the corpse of the martyred shepherd Al-Aswad that "he has with him now his two wives from the dark-eyed houris," despite "never having prayed a single prayer" because he had only recently accepted Islam. Ibn Ishaq, *Sira,* 519.

2. B.2:503.

3. B.2:631; 3:86.

4. B.1:83.

5. Levy, *The Social Structure of Islam,* 218.

6. B.2:767, 778.

7. B.1:293; 4:201; 7:455.

8. B.3:679.

9. B.2:506, 518, 520, 521.

10. B.7:123, 273.

11. B.4:44,105, 112; 6:486; 9:454.

12. B.1:78; 2:517; 3:423; 8:21. Conversely, oaths made in the pre-Islamic period had to be fulfilled (B.4:372).

13. Al-Hilali and Khan, *Translation of the meanings of the Noble Qur'an,* 868. *Hawalah* is also a financial transfer system often used in money laundering for criminal or terrorist purposes. See http://www.interpol.int/public/financialcrime/moneylaundering/hawala/default.asp (accessed October 15, 2015).

14. B.3:486–495.

15. B.3:496–512.

16. B.9:418.

17. B.2:589; 5:682; 8:247.

18. B.3:77–79.

19. B.3:174.

20. B.3:173, 174. This was despite another hadith: Yahya related to me from Malik that he had heard that Abdullah ibn Umar used to be asked, "Can someone fast for someone else, or do the prayer for someone else?" and he would reply, "No one can fast or do the prayer for anyone else." Cited in Muwatta 18:43 from http://sunnah.com/malik/18 accessed October 14, 2015

21. B.4:23; 8:689, 690; 9:90.1.

22. Q.63:10–11.

23. B.2:470; 4:19, 22, 24.

24. B.2:499.
25. Sahih Muslim 4:2127 from http://sunnah.com/muslim/11 (accessed October 14, 2015)
26. E.g., B.2:403–408, 411–412.
27. B.8:563.
28. B.8:571.
29. B.1:331, 429; 2:553.
30. B.1:588; 6:243.
31. B.9:556.
32. B.5:319, 572; 4:251, 314; 6:412, 413; 8:276; 9:72.
33. B.1:747, 748, 749, 762; 4:446, 451; 6:2; 8:411.
34. B.1:19; 6:3; 7:1; 8:570; 9:507, 532.3.
35. B.2:221; 9:482, 590.
36. B.7:557.
37. B.3:1.
38. B.4:175.
39. B.3:894; 9:489.
40. B.3:800.
41. Al-Hilali and Khan, *Translation of the meanings of the Noble Qur'an*, 866.
42. This has been applied to *jihād*, but scholars have differed as to whether fighting was *fard kifāyah*, or *fard wājib*. An example was Q.9:122, where some Muslims would fight and others stay behind. Firestone, *Jihad*, 60–61. Al-Ghazālī applied *fard kifāyah* to scientific research. It was a community obligation but did not need to be carried out by every individual. Anwar, Sabieh, "Is Ghazālī really the Halagu of Science in Islam?," *Monthly Renaissance* (October 2008), 18 (10), http://www.monthly-renaissance.com/issue/content.aspx?id=1016 (accessed October 15, 2015)
43. B.2:516; 9:216; 1:503.
44. Callum Johnson, "Of Status and Salvation: Views on Isa as Masih from South Asia," quoted in Greenlee, "How is the Gospel *Good* News for Muslims?"
45. B.5:232; 1:17; 8:793.
46. B.1:17; 6:417; 8:775, 793, 817; 9:320, 560.
47. B.7:195,196; 8:806, 810, 814; 9:280.
48. Phil 3:12, 14.

49. Ps 103:13–14.

50. McAuliffe, "Forestalling the pains of purgatory," 291.

51. John 17:19.

52. 2 Cor 5:21.

53. Eph 2:1, 4–5; Col 2:13 (emphasis mine).

54. Friedrich Nietzsche's term, used as the title of the book by Peterson, *A Long Obedience in the Same Direction.*

55. Isa 53:6.

56. Heb 10:14.

57. 2 Cor 5:14.

58. John 11:50.

59. E.g., 2 Cor 5:17.

60. Q.5.32

61. 1 Cor 15:22.

62. The idea is developed by Irenaeus in *Contra Haeresium,* http://www.ccel.org/ccel/schaff/anf01.ix.i.html (accessed October 15, 2015) and Augustine's *City of God,* http://www.ccel.org/ccel/schaff/npnf102.iii.html (accessed October 15, 2015).

63. Lapidus, *History,* 14.

64. B.4:187; 6:75.

65. Isa 53:4–6, 12.

66. Matt 5:29–30; 18:9–10/Mark 9:43–47.

67. Parsons, *Unveiling God,* 220. One hadith indicates that suffering continues in the body after death (Muslim 30:96).

68. 2 Tim 1:9–10.

69. Heb 7:3.

70. Heb 7:24–25.

71. 1 John 2:2.

72. Rom 3:25–26 (emphasis mine).

14

PICTURES OF THE CROSS

1. THE SINLESSNESS OF CHRIST

(a) Descriptions of Christ's sinlessness

Christ is understood in the Islamic texts as being without fault from the moment of his birth. The angel Gabriel declared to Mary: "I am but a messenger from your Lord to give you a boy most pure." The expression "most pure"[1] means blameless, guiltless, and sinless, according to the Muslim scholars al-Baidawi,[2] al-Tabari, and al-Zamakhshari.[3] The classical commentator Fakhr al-Din al-Razi (d.606/1209) stated: "Faultless *(zakiyyan)* means three things: First, that he is without sin; secondly that he grew in integrity, as it is said that he who has no sin is chaste and in the growing plant there is purity; thirdly, he was above reproach and pure."[4] The Hadith strongly hint at Christ's sinlessness since he was spared the satanic touch at birth. "The Prophet said, 'When any human being is born, Satan touches him at both sides of the body with his two fingers, except Jesus, the son of Mary, whom Satan tried to touch but failed, for he touched the placenta-cover instead.'"[5] Another account has an etiological focus: "No child is born but that, Satan touches it when it is born where upon it starts crying loudly because of being touched by Satan, except Mary and her Son."[6]

This contrasts with the boy Muhammad, whose chest was split open by the angels and his heart cleansed.[7] When Muhammad describes the people's search for mediators on the Day of Resurrection, each prophet outlines their incapability for the task due to their sins, which are listed. Even of Islam's prophet, it is said: "Allah forgave your early and late sins." However, only one is described as sinless: "Jesus will not mention any sin."[8] Abū Huraira reported: "I heard Allah's Apostle saying, 'By Allah! I ask for forgiveness from Allah and turn to Him in repentance more than seventy times a day.'"[9]

(b) Connections with biblical themes

Jesus challenged his contemporaries, "Can any of you prove me guilty of sin?"[10] The Bible affirms his sinlessness.[11] This is important in Christian thinking.

First, it reflects the divine holiness which God-in-the-flesh fully exhibits.

Secondly, the sinlessness of Christ placed him beyond Satan's power. Adam's sin brought all of his offspring under the dominion of Satan, who is variously described as "the prince of this world"[12] or "the god of this age"[13] and "the ruler of the kingdom of the air,"[14] whose kingdom is "the dominion of darkness."[15] John notes that "the whole world is under the control of the evil one."[16] As the promised "seed" of the woman,[17] born of a virgin,[18] Jesus came into the world in a manner which eschewed the stain of sin. He entered human life and lived beyond the influence of the devil. He demonstrated this by overcoming Satan's temptations[19] and casting out demons with authority.[20] Jesus came to regain what Adam had lost. Some scholars[21] have suggested that the Qur'an has a distant echo of the doctrine of the second Adam:[22] "Truly the likeness of Jesus, in God's sight, is as Adam's likeness,"[23] just as Adam is described in the Bible as "a pattern of the One to come."[24]

Thirdly, Christ alone was qualified to be the sinless sacrifice,[25] "the lamb without blemish or defect."[26] The Qur'an rightly claims: "No bearer of burdens can bear the burden of another."[27] Jesus alone had no burden of personal sin to bear, so he was able to bear the sin burden of others.[28]

It should be noted that the Hadith present some antagonism toward the cross. Aisha commented: "I never used to leave in the Prophet's house anything carrying images or crosses but he obliterated it."[29] When Jesus returns, He is said to "break the cross."[30] This may be related to the Qur'an's apparent denial of the crucifixion.[31] This verse is, however, capable of several interpretations.[32]

2. SACRIFICE AND RANSOM

(a) Sacrifice

Sacrifice is mentioned 155 times in al-Bukhārī's collection. Topics addressed include the necessity and sanctity of sacrifice,[33] timing of the ritual and consecration[34] of those performing the sacrifice,[35] grades of sacrifices,[36] acceptable sacrifices,[37] and the preparation of the animals.[38] *Aqiqa*, the sacrifice of an animal at the birth of a child, parallels the Jewish practice.[39] A common saying was, "May my parents be sacrificed for you."[40] No *Hajj* would be valid without a sacrifice,[41] and non-fulfillment of a ritual requirement (e.g. shaving one's head after *Hajj*) could be atoned for by the slaughter of a sacrificial animal.[42] Clearly sacrifice played a significant role in the early Muslim community. It conveyed the concept of exchange, where the death of a living creature accrued benefit to the person on whose behalf the offering was made.

(b) The ransom theme

Another motif in the Hadith is that of ransom. During raids and battles in the early years of Islam, captives and prisoners of war were often taken. They were either kept as slaves or sold back to their original tribes for ransom. Both holding enemy captives for ransom and paying for the release of Muslim captives was legislated for Muslims[43] and encouraged by Muhammad.[44] He provided money from foreign tribute to redeem Muslim captives.[45] Rather than simply accepting their captivity or depending only on their ability to escape, these captives relied on others to pay a price in order for them to be set free.

(c) Connections with biblical themes

The sacrificial system receives substantial coverage in the Old Testament. Key elements included the violent and premature death of a living being to atone for the sins of those presenting it. Sacrifice was a means of dealing with the pollution and uncleanness brought by sin. It returned the beneficiary to a position of sanctity and holiness (see Illustration 16).[46] In the New Testament, Jesus' death is presented as the sacrifice which atones for human sin.[47]

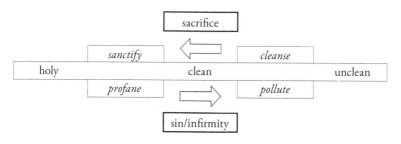

ILLUSTRATION 16: The sin-sacrifice cycle

He is described as "the lamb of God who takes away the sins of the world."[48] Jesus Himself spoke of His flesh which He would "give for the life of the world,"[49] and claimed that He would lay down His life for others.[50]

Ransom is another of the images used of the death of Christ.[51] By doing for humanity what they could not do for themselves, Jesus' death is seen as efficacious in liberating people from bondage to Satan.[52] The release of captives was promised in the Nazareth Manifesto[53] and experienced personally by the convicted criminal Barabbas at the Passover.[54] The only mention of the foundational verb *fada* (ransom) in the Qur'an[55] describes the work of God who ransomed Abraham's son with a "mighty sacrifice."[56] The connection between Abraham's offering of his son and the death of Christ as the Son of God has been made by several scholars.[57] Ransom and redemption are key elements in understanding the death of Christ.[58]

3. OTHER PICTURES OF THE CROSS

Substitutionary atonement, sacrifice, and ransom/redemption are not
the only depictions of the meaning of the cross found in the Bible.
There are several representations which have parallels in the Hadith.

(a) Betrayed hospitality

In Arab culture, both host and guest must be honored and respected
by the other. To abuse the hospitality of others is a heinous act, as
exemplified by the oft-repeated story of the treacherous men of 'Ukl
tribe.[59] For his part, the host must munificently provide for and vigorously protect his guests, whatever the cost.[60] Several hadith speak of
the importance of offering generous hospitality,[61] a trait exhibited by
Muhammad[62] and Abū Bakr.[63] Allah is the perfect host, munificently
preparing a place of welcome for the faithful in paradise.[64] Neglecting
to invite visitors to stay is seen as culpable,[65] for "your guest has a right
on you."[66] Protection of one's guests from their enemies became an
issue when Muhammad signed a treaty with the Quraish.

> When Suhail bin Amr agreed to the treaty (of Hudaibiya),
> one of the things he stipulated then, was that the Prophet
> should return to them (i.e. the pagans) anyone coming to
> him from their side, even if he was a Muslim; and would not
> interfere between them and that person. *The Muslims did
> not like this condition and got disgusted with it.* Suhail did not
> agree except with that condition. So, the Prophet agreed to
> that condition and returned Abu Jandal to his father Suhail
> bin 'Amr.[67]

This was in clear contravention to the mores of Arab hospitality.
Muhammad himself had taught that a "Muslim is a brother of
another Muslim. So he should . . . [not] hand him over to an
oppressor."[68] After a new convert to Islam, Abū Basir, fled from
Mecca to Medina, Muhammad surrendered him to the Quraish.
He escaped again, but refused to return to live among the Muslims
in Medina since Muhammad would have delivered him again to

the Meccans.[69] The asylum that was required and expected by social custom was not provided.

(b) The warrior's victory over oppressive powers

The Hadith identify a conflict between humanity and the spiritual powers. Although Muhammad one time claimed to have choked Satan,[70] he lived in constant fear of the devil[71] and was bewitched with a spell[72] that lasted for a year.[73] "The Evil Eye is a fact," he declared.[74] Apparently the demonic was a sphere in which Muhammad could not gain victory.

(c) An act of martyrdom

Martyrdom is highly esteemed in Islam. Dying "in the way (or cause) of Allah" assures entrance to paradise,[75] a promise reiterated in the Hadith.[76] Martyrs are not considered as dead, but still alive.[77] Throughout the Hadith, martyrdom is glorified. Umar prayed for it,[78] and Muhammad prophesied that Umar and Uthman would be martyrs.[79] Muhammad expressed his own wish for multiple martyrdoms,[80] a desire he claimed would be shared by all those who had sacrificed their lives.[81] He prayed that he would be in the company of the martyrs after his death.[82] He invoked evil on those who killed them,[83] and pledged to be a witness for some martyrs on the Day of Resurrection.[84] When Muhammad unsuccessfully asked creditors to excuse a martyr's debts, he prayed a blessing on the deceased man's property so the debts could be paid.[85] Since the al-Ansar tribe contributed the most martyrs, they will have superiority on the day of Resurrection.[86]

Interestingly, death in battle for Islam was not the only form of martyrdom; other options included death by plague,[87] drowning, abdominal disease, being buried alive by a falling building,[88] and when protecting one's own property.[89] The reward for one man's martyrdom was forfeited because he had taken some booty illegally.[90] Another Muslim, mortally wounded fighting for Islam, was pronounced by Muhammad as destined for the hell-fire for committing suicide to end his pain.[91] Angels shielded the corpse of the martyr with their wings,[92] and the martyrs were buried unwashed, with their blood and wounds evident.[93] Muhammad did not pray funeral prayers for them,[94] presumably because they had gone straight to paradise and needed no intercession. However, on one occasion he prayed the funeral prayer for some martyrs eight years after they died.[95] On the Day of Resurrection, the wounds of Muslim warriors will flow again, and their blood will smell like musk.[96] In paradise martyrs receive superior accommodation, above that of "the common believers."[97]

(d) Connections with biblical themes

The New Testament also portrays the hospitality/rejection/betrayal theme. As a host, Jesus served his guests[98] and later shielded them from their enemies.[99] He is presented as the perfect guest, for he went around doing good,[100] even providing for the needs of the other guests, and thereby protecting the reputation of his hosts.[101] Despite this, he was not always welcomed or treated honorably. The motif of violated hospitality codes in refusing to receive an honored guest is found in all four gospels.[102] There is also the ignominy of "handing over" a guest to his enemies, particularly of a fellow Jew to the hated gentile Roman occupiers.[103] This is used "to underline the seriousness and corporate shame that resulted from the rejection of Jesus."[104] Witherington notes that the "strong and polemical language" in Acts 3:13–14 aims to bring people "to the point of repentance by a 'shock and recognition' technique and then to open them up to reception of the restoration and blessings promised in Christ."[105] A recurring theme in Acts is, "You handed him over/killed/crucified/put him to death . . . but God raised him up."[106] The cross is presented as human sin in betraying the guest who came down from heaven, but the resurrection is God's vindication of his anointed one. The Hadith makes no mention of Christ's resurrection, but it does refer to some men who were brought back to life three days after they died in order to hear Muhammad's words of judgment.[107] Jesus explained that he was leaving the earth in order to prepare the rooms in his Father's house, and would return to collect his guests.[108]

The Bible also presents the cross as a conquest over the hostile evil powers that had enslaved humanity.[109] "The reason the Son of God appeared was to destroy the devil's work."[110] Just before his death, Jesus proclaimed: "Now will the prince of this world be driven out."[111]

Jesus is presented as the warrior who goes to fight on behalf of His oppressed people, building on the God-as-Warrior theme of the Old Testament.[112] The human debt of disobedience, which was being used by the powers as a means of controlling men, was canceled by Jesus' death on the cross. Like a hero who exposes the cowardice of a bully by standing up to him in front of everyone, Jesus had disarmed the powers and principalities, making a public spectacle of them, by His triumph on the cross.[113] Unlike the hireling who fled from the attacking wolf, the Good Shepherd stood his ground and lay down His life for his sheep.[114] However, in this apparent defeat was victory. The angel in John's vision of heaven announced that the lamb, which looked as if it had been slain, had triumphed.[115] The resurrection of Christ is crucial to this scenario. In having absorbed the worst that Satan could hurl against Him, Jesus stood up again, for He had "destroyed death."[116] Through His death, Christ was able to "destroy him who holds the power of death—that is, the devil."[117] Then the triumphant question is asked: "Where, O Death, is your victory? Where, O Death, is your sting?"[118]

Some see Jesus' crucifixion as a martyrdom—a voluntary and violent death for a cause.[119] He had outlined his motive: "Greater love has no one than this, that he lay down his life for his friends."[120] He was clear that his life was freely given. "No one takes it from me, but I lay it down of my own accord."[121] Unlike the early Muslim martyr Khubaid, who deprecated his oppressors with "O Allah, kill them all without exception,"[122] Jesus prayed for the forgiveness of his executors.[123] According to the Qur'an[124] and the Bible,[125] Jesus ascended to heaven and is alive now, as the Muslim martyrs are said to be. Referring to Revelation 5:6, Parsons notes: "The popular Muslim belief that the resurrected body in heaven will have the wounds and disfigurements of the earthly body, makes Revelation's portrait of the lamb looking as if it had been slain, a particularly striking image for a contextualised christology."[126] Significantly, it is the wounds of the resurrected Christ, proof of the passion, which elicit from the doubting Thomas his exclamation of faith: "My Lord and My God!"[127]

These pictures of the atonement present different views of the death of Christ, some depicted as more active or passive (see Illustration 17).

ILLUSTRATION 17: Representation of different views of the death of Christ

If Christ's death has such redemptive and transforming power, then how is it appropriated to others? How can people tap into its benefits?

NOTES

1. Q.19.19.

2. He uses the term *Tāhir min ul-dhunūb* "pure from sins." al-Baidawi, *Anwār al-tanzīl*, 9. This could also be understood in the context of *ismah* "faultlessness," which is seen to apply to all prophets. See the extended discussion in http://www.almujtaba.com/articles/aqaed/000018.html (accessed October 14, 2015).

3. al-Masih, *A Question*, 13.

4. Al-Fadi, *Person of Christ*, 10.

5. B.4:506.

6. B.6:71.

7. B.1:345; 5:227; 9:608.

8. B.6:236.

9. B.8:319.

10. John 8:46.

11. Heb 4:15; 1 John 3.7; 2 Cor 5:21.

12. John 14:30.

13. 2 Cor 4:4.

14. Eph 2:2.

15. Col 1:13.

16. 1 John 5:19.

17. Gen 3:15.

18. Isa 7:14.

19. Luke 4:1–13.

20. Luke 4:36.

21. Cragg, *Jesus and the Muslim,* 32; Guillaume, *Islam,* 196; Robinson, *Christ in Islam and Christianity,* 12, 69.

22. 1 Cor 15:20–28, 45–49; Rom 5:12–19.

23. Q.3.59.

24. Rom 5:14.

25. Heb 9:14.

26. 1 Pet 1:19 cf. Ex 12:5.

27. Q.17:15; 6:164; 35:18; 39:7; 53:38.

28. 1 Pet 2:24.

29. B.7:836.

30. B.3:425, 656; 4:657.

31. Q.4:157.

32. See, for example, Elder, "Crucifixion," 242–258.

33. E.g., B.1:67.

34. Head-shaving of those performing sacrifice as a part of the *Hajj* ceremony may be related to the Nazirite vows of the Old Testament (Num 6:8–11) or purification rites mentioned in the New Testament (Acts 21:24).

35. E.g., B.1:84.

36. B.2:6.

37. B.2:75.

38. E.g., B.2:617.

39. B.7:380; Luke 2:23–24.

40. E.g., B.1:711.

41. B.2:191.

42. B.7:604.

43. E.g., B.1:111; 9:40, 50.

44. E.g., B.3:714; 4:284; 5:535; 7:286.

45. B.1:413; 4:284.

46. Diagram taken from "Sacrifice in the Old Testament," http://christianthinktank.com/cross2.html (accessed October 14, 2015).

47. Rom 3:25; Eph 5:2; Heb 9:26 et al.; 1 John 2:2; 4:10.

48. John 1:29.

49. John 6:51.

50. John 10:11, 15.

51. Matt 20:28/Mark 10:45; 1 Tim 2:5; Heb 9:15.

52. Col 2:13–15; Heb 2:15.

53. Luke 4:18.

54. Matt 27:15–26/Mark15:6–15/Luke 23:18–25.

55. The noun *fidya(t)* is mentioned three times (Q.2:184, 196; 57:15) and derivative verbs Form III *fāda* (Q.2:85) and Form VIII *iftada* (Q.2:229; 3:91; 5:36; 10:54; 13:18; 39:47; 70:11) occur occasionally.

56. Q.37:107.

57. See, for example, Reuven Firestone, "Merit, Mimesis, and Martyrdom: Aspects of Shi'ite Meta-historical Exegesis on Abraham's Sacrifice in Light of Jewish, Christian, and Sunni Muslim Tradition," J Am Acad Relig (1998) 66(1): 93–116, available on http://jaar.oxfordjournals.org/content/66/1/93.full.pdf (accessed October 14, 2015).

58. See Lewis, *Glory*, 286–295.

59. B.1:234; 2:577; 4:261; 6:250; etc.

60. The importance of hospitality and honor in Bedouin culture is detailed in Patai, *The Arab Mind*.

61. B.3:641; 8:162.

62. B.1:3.

63. B.3:494.

64. B.1:631.

65. B.3:476; 6:251.

66. B.3:195, 196.

67. B.3:874, 683; 5:496, emphasis mine.

68. B.3:622; 9:83.

69. B.3:891, 683; 5:496.

70. B.2:301.

71. B.4:590.

72. B.4:490.

73. Ibn Ishaq *Sirat,* 240 fn 1.

74. B.7:827, 828.

75. Q.2:154; 3:157, 158; 3:169; 3:195; 4:72; 4:100; 22:58; 47:4–6; 4:66–67.

76. B.1:36; 4:72, 352, 386; 5:318, 377; 9:555, 621.

77. Q.2:154; 3:169.

78. B.3:114.

79. B.5:24, 35, 46, 49.

80. B.1:35; 4:54, 216; 9:332–333.

81. B.4:53, 72.

82. B.6:110.

83. B.4:299, 395; 5:422; 8:403.

84. B.2:427, 428, 431, 436.

85. B.3:580,773; 4:40; 5:383.

86. B.5:405.

87. B.4:680; 7:628–630; 8:616.

88. B.1:624, 688; 4:82–83.

89. B.3:660.

90. B.5:541.

91. B.8:603–604.

92. B.2:336, 381; 5:406.

93. B.2:430–431, 436; 5:406.

94. B.2:431; 5:406, 411.

95. B.4:795; 5:374; 8:434

96. B.1:238; 4:59; 7:441.

97. B.2:468; 4:49, 64; 5:318; 8:558, 572.

98. John 13:1–17.

99. John 18:8.

100. Acts 10:38.

101. John 2:1–10.

102. John 1:1–11, 14; Matt 21:33–46/Mark 12:1–12/Luke 20:9–19.

103. Acts 3:13, as well as fourteen references in the Gospels. In a recognition of divine sovereignty in the death of Christ, Jesus is spoken of as being "handed over to you by God's set purpose and foreknowledge" (Acts 2:23).

104. Parsons, *Unveiling God*, 118.

105. Ibid., 135 n. 84.

106. Acts 2:23–24; 3:13–15; 4:10; 5:30; 10:39–40; 13:28–30.

107. B.5:314.

108. John 14:2–3.

109. This view of the work of Christ has been championed by Aulen, *Christus Victor.*

110. 1 John 3:8.

111. John 12:31.

112. See, for example, Richard Nysse, "Yahweh is a Warrior," in *Word and World* 7/2 (1987). Source: http://www2.luthersem. edu/Word&World/Archives/7-2_Search_for_God/7-2_Nysse. pdf (accessed October 14, 2015). The Christ-as-warrior theme is developed in an eschatological setting in the book of Revelation. He is portrayed as riding on a white horse (Rev 19:11) and making war (Rev 19:11; 17:14), with a double-edged sword issuing from his mouth (Rev 1:16; 2:12, 16; 19:15).

113. Col 2:13–15. Parsons, *Unveiling God*, 119.

114. John 10:11–13.

115. Rev 5:5–6.

116. 2 Tim 1:10.

117. Heb 2:14.

118. 1 Cor 15:55.

119. This view of the atonement, the "Moral Influence" theory, sees Christ's death as an act of obedience which impacts those who hear about it. It was championed by Peter Abelard (AD 1079–1142). See Alister McGrath, "The Moral Theory of the Atonement: An Historical and Theological Critique," *Scottish Journal of Theology*

(1985), 38: 205–220, from http://journals.cambridge.org/action/dis
playAbstract?fromPage=online&aid=3369988 (accessed October 14,
2015).

120. John 15:13.

121. John 10:18.

122. B.4:281; 5:325, 412.

123. Luke 23:34.

124. Q.3:55; 19:33.

125. Mark 16:19; Acts 1:9.

126. Parsons, *Unveiling God*, 119.

127. John 20:28.

15

APPROPRIATING THE CROSS

1. THE TASK OF INTERCESSION

(a) Intercession in Islamic texts

The Qur'an repeatedly denies the possibility of a *shafi'* (mediator or intercessor),[1] particularly for those who did not fulfill all of Islam's requirements.[2] This mediatorial task belongs to God alone.[3] However, there is the possibility of permission from God[4] to one "whose word is acceptable to Him."[5]

The Hadith widen the categories considerably. Angels intercede for those who are praying.[6] People could ask God to forgive the sins of a dead person.[7] The Muslims asked God for rain, through the agency of Muhammad's uncle al-'Abbās.[8]

Muhammad took on the role of intercessor, praying for others to be forgiven.[9] This was extended to the Day of Resurrection, when he claimed that he would intercede for others.[10] Sometimes this process is elaborated, with the people of the earth hastening from one prophet to another. Each prophet describes his inadequacy for this task and sends them to the next prophet. Muhammad is the final link in the chain, and he makes intercession for his people.[11]

However, his intercession would be limited. In the case of his uncle Abū Tālib, who died as an idol worshiper despite the

Prophet's entreaties, Muhammad was uncertain. "Perhaps my intercession will be helpful to him on the Day of Resurrection so that he
may be put in a shallow fire reaching only up to his ankles. His brain
will boil from it."[12] He reported that those who had committed sins
such as illegally taking booty would receive no aid. "When they say
'O Allah's Apostle! Intercede with Allah for me,' . . . I will reply,
'I can't help you, for I have conveyed Allah's Message to you.'"[13]
Muhammad's intercession was limited to deserving Muslims only.
Clearly not every request would be granted: "For every Prophet
there is one invocation which is definitely fulfilled by Allah."[14]

It could be thought that neither Muhammad nor anyone else
has a role in intercession at all. He repeatedly admonished his tribe,
family, wife, and daughter to save themselves because "I cannot save
you from Allah's punishment."[15] One editor notes that "this Hadith
indicates that one can only ask Allah for help directly or through
his performed good deeds. But to ask Allah through dead or absent
prophets, saints, spirits, holy men, angels etc. is absolutely forbidden in Islam and it is a kind of disbelief."[16] The editor's comment
does not accord with the many hadiths above which describe such
an intercession.

There is a clear distinction between human intercession and divine
intercession as the following hadith outlines. Muhammad said:

> Then the prophets and Angels and the believers will inter-
> cede, and (last of all) the Almighty (Allah) will say, "Now
> remains My Intercession." He will then hold a handful of
> the Fire from which He will take out some people whose
> bodies have been burnt, and they will be thrown into a
> river at the entrance of Paradise, called the water of life. . . .
> Those people will come out (of the River of Life) like pearls,
> and they will have (golden) necklaces, and then they will
> enter Paradise whereupon the people of Paradise will say,
> "These are the people emancipated by the Beneficent.
> He has admitted them into Paradise *without them having
> done any good deeds and without sending forth any good (for
> themselves).*"[17]

This is pure salvation by grace. Good works have played no part—it all depends on the action of God. However, it presents Allah's intercession as a last resort. It is much like a final plea for clemency before execution, as practiced in many Muslim countries, to the president or king when all the legal avenues have failed. Allah comes into play only at the end of the day, when all the heavy lifting of a lifetime of personal good works and the post-death intercession by others have proved insufficient. This is quite different from the biblical view of God, who takes the initiative from the very beginning. For Christians, salvation is a plan "that God had destined for our glory before time began."[18] Paul writes of the God "who has saved us and called us to a holy life—not because of anything we have done but because of his own purpose and grace. This grace was given us in Christ Jesus before the beginning of time."[19]

(b) Connections with biblical themes

A significant reference in the Hadith about intercession appears to be inspired by the biblical cry of Jesus for forgiveness for his tormentors:[20] "I saw the Prophet talking about one of the prophets whose nation had beaten him and caused him to bleed, while he was cleaning the blood off his face and saying, 'O Allah! Forgive my nation, for they have no knowledge.'"[21] One of the three efficacious post-death mediatorial roles is "a pious son, who prays for . . . the deceased."[22] The Bible presents Jesus as the perfect Son of God[23] who "always lives to intercede" for those "who come to God through him."[24] Those who sin are comforted with the description of the advocate, the "one who speaks to the Father in our defense—Jesus Christ, the Righteous One."[25] He would be the ideal "interpreter" which every person will desire on the Day of Resurrection, for the Hadith inform us that "there will be none among you but will be talked to by Allah on the Day of Resurrection, without there being an interpreter between him and Him (Allah)."[26] Jesus is uniquely fitted for this role: "For there is one God and there is one mediator between God and men, the man Christ Jesus."[27] In a remarkable convolution and concentration of responsibilities at the grand assize, Jesus is sometimes presented as the defense attorney, main witness, and presiding judge.[28]

2. THE PRIMACY OF FAITH AND LOVE OVER WORKS

(a) Faith and love in the Hadith

According to the above section "the inadequacy of works," human actions, either good or bad, are not a reliable indicator of a person's status before God, nor of one's ultimate destiny.[29] Several hadith propose that this function is performed by faith and love. Some accounts clarify the Muslim definition of *īmān* (faith). Faith is so powerful that even a small amount can save one from hell.[30] After the judgment, Allah will say, "Take out (of the Fire) whoever has got faith equal to a mustard seed in his heart."[31] Faith is described as a complex entity, consisting of more than sixty branches or parts.[32] It is further defined in a statement by Muhammad:

> Whoever possesses the following three qualities will have the sweetness (delight) of faith: (1) The one to whom Allah and His Apostle becomes dearer than anything else. (2) Who loves a person and he loves him only for Allah's sake, (3) Who hates to revert to Atheism (disbelief) as he hates to be thrown into the fire.[33]

(b) Connections with biblical themes

This hadith has three statements, which will be discussed in turn.

(1) The first statement shows that faith requires a basis, although it could be an incorrect basis. People, for example, could attribute natural phenomena such as rain to either Allah or to a star.[34] Yet faith is more than *assensus,* intellectual agreement, for there is generally an affective element involved. Borg states that the Latin roots of the word *credo* "I believe" (i.e., *cre + do*) combine to mean "I give my heart to."[35] Muhammad said, "There is a piece of flesh in the body if it becomes good (reformed) the whole body becomes good but if it gets spoilt the whole body gets spoilt and that is the heart."[36] It may be significant that it was Muhammad's chest, not his head, which was opened and cleaned by the angel Gabriel, before being filled

with wisdom and love.[37] "The heart is the self at its deepest level, a level below the intellect. . . . Prior to the seventeenth century, the word "believe" did not mean believing in the truth of statements or propositions. . . . Grammatically, the object of believing was not statements but a person."[38] This is captured somewhat in the first statement: to hold Allah and His apostle as "dearer than anything else." When a man was asked what he had prepared for the Day of Judgment, he said, "Nothing, except that I love Allah and His Apostle." The Prophet observed: "You will be with those whom you love."[39] The stress has moved from the performance of good works to a relationship of love. When asked about the greatest commandment, Jesus replied that it was to "love the Lord your God with all your heart, . . . soul, . . . mind, . . . and . . . strength."[40] Yet the suggestion of placing Muhammad, a mere man, alongside God as the object of undivided love would seem to negate the Islamic concept of *tawhīd*. Jesus Christ, "being in very nature God,"[41] would seem to be a better alternative.

(2) The second statement, about the one "who loves a person and he loves him only for Allah's sake," hints at a kind of love approaching the biblical *agape*. It is not based on physical attraction *(eros)*, friendship *(philia)*, or affection *(storge)*.[42] The love described in this hadith is simply "for Allah's sake." It suggests a dispassionate commitment for a higher reason. Jesus challenged his hearers about who and how they should love: "But if you love those who love you, what credit is that to you? For even sinners love those who love them."[43] This hadith suggests an undeserved and even unrequited love. It opens the possibility for a redeeming love that extends even to its enemies—a love which is at the heart of the gospel (Rom 5:8).[44] Faith is not, like fatalism, a weak and passive response in the face of uncertainty, but a strong, active expression of love.[45]

(3) The third statement describes a person "who hates to revert to Atheism (disbelief) as he hates to be thrown into the fire." This presents faith as a commitment that will not be turned aside. The believer will not look back.[46] This is faith as *fidelitas*, a single-minded dedication. It requires a turning away from other possible contenders. Jesus declared that His followers' adherence to His teaching superseded obedience to their parents and attachment to their own families.[47]

Borg describes it thus: "Christian faith means loyalty to Jesus as Lord, and not to the seductive would-be lords of our lives, whether the nation, or affluence, or achievement, or family, or desire."[48] Likewise, Muhammad stated: "None of you will have faith till he loves me more than his father and his children . . . and all mankind."[49] When 'Umar, after some prompting, declared to Muhammad, "You are dearer to me than my own self," the Prophet affirmed him with the statement, "Now you are a believer."[50] This is deep personal faith focused on an individual, not on an idea.

3. THE TRANSFORMED LIFE

Both the Hadith and the gospel expect that a life lived in faith will result in a change. It may be expressed in several ways.

(a) A new nature

Accompanying true faith is repentance, a theme referred to several times in the Qur'an.[51] The Hadith reiterates this: the recipient of forgiveness is "the one who regrets (his crime)."[52] The result is a faith which seems to impart a new nature, for "a believer never becomes impure."[53] A transformation, which moves one to a different level of existence, has taken place, resulting in total and permanent purity.

(b) Being born anew—the offer of a clean start

Muhammad said, "Whoever performs *Hajj* for Allah's pleasure and does not have sexual relations with his wife, and does not do evil or sins then he will return (after *Hajj* free from all sins) *as if he were born anew.*"[54]

(c) Close connection with God

One passage describes a close and intimate connection with God attained through devotional exercises. "And the most beloved things with which My slave comes nearer to Me, is what I have enjoined upon him; and My slave keeps on coming closer to Me through performing *Nawāfil* (praying or doing extra deeds besides what is obligatory) till I love him, so *I become his sense of hearing with which he hears, and his sense of sight with which he sees, and his hand with which he grips, and his leg with which he walks*; and if he asks Me, I will give him, and if he asks My protection (Refuge), I will protect him; (i.e. give him My Refuge)."[55]

(d) Remade in a new image

Muhammad said: "Whoever will enter Paradise will be of the shape and image of Adam,"[56] for Adam was made in the image of God. To Muslims, this transformation is an eschatological aspiration—something to be hoped for.

(e) Connections with biblical themes

The Bible provides more detail or moves along from these statements found in the Hadith. There is the promise of a new nature, a clean start, and personal transformation leading to a deeper connection with God.

It is said of a follower of Christ that "he has been cleansed from his past sins."[57] Jesus told his disciples: "You are already clean because of the word I have spoken to you."[58] Baptism symbolizes this cleansing, but it is more than that. "This water symbolizes baptism that now saves you also—not the removal of dirt from the body but the pledge of a good conscience toward God. It saves you by the resurrection of Jesus Christ."[59] From a Christian perspective, the death and resurrection of Christ is key in this process, for "by one sacrifice he has made perfect forever those who are being made holy."[60] His sacrifice has initiated this radical cleansing process. "The law requires that nearly everything be cleansed with blood, and without the shedding of blood there is no forgiveness."[61] The Bible affirms this as the transforming work of the Holy Spirit, both in the Old[62] and New[63] Testaments. In Christian teaching, the physical departure of Christ from the earth was antecedent to the coming of the Holy Spirit.[64]

A new birth is, for Christians, a soteriological necessity. Jesus declared: "I tell you the truth, no one can see the kingdom of God unless he is born again."[65] However, it is not achieved by the performance of commendable deeds or by avoiding iniquity; it remains a sovereign act of God. A later generation of Christians was assured, "You have been born again, not of perishable seed, but of imperishable, through the living and enduring word of God."[66]

Biblical teaching also describes God acting and working through His people. Isaiah describes Israel as attributing her entire good work to her Lord: "all that we have accomplished, You have done for us."[67] Christians are spoken of as "fellow workers with God,"[68] sharing the same yoke and burden.[69] They can accomplish God-appointed tasks by His "power that is at work within us,"[70] "for it is God who works in you to will and to act according to his good purpose."[71] More than this, they can become "partakers of the divine nature."[72] Jesus speaks of Himself as the vine, with His followers as the branches. He tells them: "Apart from me, you can do nothing."[73]

For Christians, this transformation is a process which can begin now. Paul assures his readers that we "with unveiled faces all reflect the Lord's glory, [and] are being transformed into his likeness with ever-increasing glory, which comes from the Lord, who is the Spirit"[74] because we "have put on the new self, which is being renewed in knowledge in the image of its Creator."[75]

For Muslims, the ultimate goal seems to be to fulfill the law, and so please Allah, encouraged by a system of punishments and rewards. For Christians, the goal is communion with God, encouraged by God's enabling grace, which results in personal transformation. As one writer puts it: "my inability to keep God's commandments is where my faith starts, not where it ends."[76]

4. ASSURANCE OF THE BELIEVER

(a) Islamic teaching

Although Muhammad was unable to have any assurance for himself to enter paradise,[77] he pronounced it to Abū Bakr, Umar, Uthman,[78] and others. Some Muslims would deny this possibility. Ismail Faruqi states that "unlike Christianity, Islamicity is never a fait accompli. Islamicity is a process. It grows, and it is sometimes reduced. There is no time at which the Muslim may carry his title to paradise, as it were, in his pocket. Instead of 'salvation,' the Muslim is to achieve felicity through unceasing effort."[79]

(b) Connection with biblical themes

This assurance is an end point of Christian faith, the logical finale of a Christ-based trajectory. It is therefore not surprising that Islamic teaching based on the Qur'an and the Hadith should not arrive at this conclusion. This is one of the areas of greatest disconnect between Muslim and Christian theology. For Christians, assurance of eternity with God is an outcome of Christ's work on their behalf rather than of their own effort. Jesus asserted that "whoever has my word and believes in him who sent me has eternal life and will not be condemned; he has crossed over from death to life."[80] Jesus' follower John affirmed this: "I write these things to you who believe in the name of the Son of God that you may know that you have eternal life."[81]

NOTES

1. Q.6:51, 70, 94; 31:13; 40:18; 74:48.
2. Q.74:48.
3. Q.6:70; 32:7; 83:19.
4. Q.10:3.
5. Q.20:109.
6. B.1:620, as long as the person praying does not break wind! B.1:466.
7. B.1:55.
8. B.5:59.
9. E.g., B.4:135.
10. B.1:331, 429; 2:553; 6:242–243.
11. B.6:3, 236; 8:570; 9:507, 601.
12. B.5:224; 8:569.
13. B.2:485; 4:307.
14. B.9:566.
15. B.4:16; 6:294.
16. B.4:671.

17. B.9:532.2 (emphasis mine).

18. 1 Cor 2:7.

19. 2 Tim 1:9.

20. Luke 23:34.

21. B.4:683.

22. Sahih Muslim 13:4005, as related by Abū Huraira. http://sunnah. com/muslim/25/20 (accessed October 14, 2015).

23. Heb 2:10; 5:9; 7:28.

24. Heb 7:25.

25. 1 John 2:1.

26. B.8:547.

27. 1 Tim 2:5.

28. Jesus as advocate: 1 John 2:1; Jesus as witness: Matt 10:32; Jesus as judge: John 5:27; Matt 25:31–46.

29. B.4:430, 549; 8:593–594; 9:546.

30. B.1:21, 42.

31. B.8:565; 9:660, 601.

32. B.1:8.

33. B.1:15.

34. B.2:148.

35. Borg, *The Heart of Christianity*, 40. However, this claim has been disputed and labeled as a "folk etymology." Source: http://creedal-christian.blogspot.com/2010/11/what-credo-means.html (accessed October 14, 2015).

36. B.1:49.

37. B.1:345. However, Yusuf Ali conflates the two with his comment: "The breast is symbolically the seat of knowledge and of the highest feeling of love and affection." Yusuf Ali, *The Holy Qur-an: Text, Translation and Commentary*, 1755, n. 6188.

38. Borg, *The Heart of Christianity*, 40.

39. B.5:37; 8:192.

40. Mark 12:30/Luke 10:27/Matt 22:37.

41. Phil 2:6.

42. Lewis, *The Four Loves*.

43. Luke 6:32.

44. More extensive treatments of the love of God in the Qur'an can be found in Zwemer, *The Moslem Doctrine of God,* and Farid Mahally, "A study of the word 'love' in the Qur'an," *Hubb Allah fi al-Qur'an,* from http://www.answering-islam.de/Main/Quran/Themes/love.htm (accessed on October 14, 2015).

45. Gal 5:6.

46. Luke 9:62.

47. Matt 10:37/Luke 14:26; Matt 12:50/Mark 3:35/Luke 8:21.

48. Borg, *The Heart of Christianity,* 33.

49. B.1:13–14.

50. B.8:628.

51. Q.2:160; 3:89; 19:60; 20:82; 25:70.

52. B.5:194.

53. B.1:283.

54. B.2:596; 3:45–46 (emphasis mine).

55. B.8:509 (emphasis mine).

56. B.8:246.

57. 2 Pet 1:9.

58. John 15:3.

59. 1 Pet 3:21.

60. Heb 10:14.

61. Heb 9:22.

62. Ezek 36:26.

63. 2 Cor 3:18.

64. John 16:7.

65. John 3:3.

66. 1 Pet 1:23.

67. Isa 26:12.

68. 1 Cor 3:9; 2 Cor 6:1.

69. Matt 11:28–30.

70. Eph 3:20.

71. Phil 2:12–13.

72. 2 Pet 1:3–4.

73. John 15:5.

74. 2 Cor 3:18.

75. Col 3:10.
76. Dalby, *Healing the Masculine Soul,* 99.
77. See chapter 11, part 2.
78. B.8:235; 9:217, 367.
79. Al-Faruqi, "Christian Mission and Islamic Da'wa," 391.
80. John 5:24.
81. 1 John 5:13.

IV

USING THE HADITH
IN CHRISTIAN MINISTRY:
PRACTICAL IMPLICATIONS

THERE IS MUCH OUTLINED in the Hadith which intersects with Christian teaching. A careful practitioner could use these to raise significant issues with Muslims. In the context of Muslim-Christian engagement, the Hadith can be a valuable set of tools to be utilized in a variety of ways. They can be used to promote Muslim-Christian dialogue by emphasizing the elements of concord. They can also establish connections by allowing the good news of Jesus Christ to be presented through the medium of the Hadith. Each of these will be dealt with in turn.

16

DIALOGUE WITH MUSLIMS

DIALOGUE ESTABLISHES A TWO-WAY DISCUSSION between proponents of different viewpoints. This involves willingness to both speak and to pay attention to what others are saying. When the child Jesus was found in the temple, he was "sitting among the teachers, listening to them, and asking them questions."[1] New opportunities for such listening and asking questions are now arising. The 2007 Common Word initiative[2] marks a significant development in Muslim-Christian relations and a noteworthy mind shift. John Esposito brands it as "a historic event," stating that "if you look at the history of Islam and the Muslim world, this is really the first time that we have an initiative where Muslims have collectively come together and agreed to what binds them to Christians."[3] Many Christians have responded positively to these overtures, as is shown in statements on the Common Word website.[4] Others, such as John Piper, have stood against this initiative, noting that some public responses have lacked clarity on what Christians believe.[5] Christians will need to be clear about their goals before entering into such dialogue.

The Mini-Consultation on Reaching Muslims, held in Pattaya, Thailand (1980), under the auspices of the Lausanne movement, divided dialogue into three types based on its goals.

(a) Discursive dialogue is "a conversation conducted to convince another party of the truth (e.g., Acts 17:2; 18:4)."

(b) In "dialogue on religious experience . . . members of
different faiths seek to share their particular religious
experiences with one another."

(c) "Secular dialogue" discusses "ways in which greater
communal understanding can be developed, how common action can be taken to correct various social evils,
and how followers of different faiths can co-operate
in the task of community development and national
reconstruction."[6]

Each method has a different focus: objective truth, personal
experience, or combined action. Dialogue, then, may have three
objectives: to convince others of one's own beliefs, to comprehend
their understanding of the truth, or to cooperate with them in
implementing the truth in practical ways (see Table 20).

TYPE OF DIALOGUE	AIM	FOCUS
Discursive	Convince	Belief
Religious experience	Comprehend	Experience
Secular dialogue	Cooperate	Action

TABLE 20: Varieties of dialogue

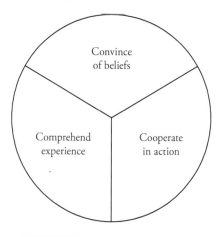

ILLUSTRATION 18: Goals of dialogue

These three elements can be represented diagrammatically (see Illustration 18). We will look at these three in detail.

1. DISCURSIVE DIALOGUE

Dialogue between Muslims and others took place early in the establishment of Islam. The Hadith describe the interaction between Muhammad and the Christian delegation that came from Najran.[7] Much more detail of this meeting is given in the earliest biography, the *Sirat Rasūl Allah*, which was compiled by Ibn Ishaq and edited by Ibn Hisham. From this text we learn that sixty riders came, that the conversation lasted several days, and that serious theological discussions took place. Each side sought to present its own point of view and to listen to the replies of the other.[8] However, there are several factors which need to be taken into account as we engage in dialogue. Some of these are potential pitfalls, while others are possible stepping-stones to enhance the discussion.

(a) Evangelism and da'wa should not be confused with "proselytization"

Islam, like Christianity, began with public proclamation. Just as Jesus announced the coming of the kingdom of God to the Jews,[9] Muhammad preached to the Arabs in the marketplaces of Mecca.[10] The Hadith is clear that the sermons of Islam's Prophet concealed nothing of what was revealed to him,[11] and Jesus told His disciples that "everything that I learned from my Father I have made known to you."[12] Just as Jesus sent out the Twelve[13] and the seventy-two,[14] so Muhammad designated twelve men to lead in Medina[15] and sent seventy reciters of the Qur'an from the tribe of Bani Salim to the tribe of Bani Amir at Najd to proclaim Islam to them.[16]

Proclamation of one's faith as a part of dialogue, however, can be controversial. The WCC Muslim-Christian encounter at Chambesy, Switzerland, in 1979 insisted that dialogue should never be used for "proselytization."[17] Significantly, they did not use the term "evangelism," the normal Christian term for sharing one's faith, nor 'da'wa', the Muslim equivalent, but opted for the pejorative term "proselytization." One writer contrasts the "proper

invitation to share one's faith" over against the "exploitative or sub-
tly coercive techniques or proselytism,"[18] and another announces
that "we do not support proselytism or any other form of coercion
or inducement."[19] Kerr refers to "the distorting malpractice of proselytism," where the "Arabic *igtinas* implies 'snaring' as of an animal
in a hunt."[20] If proselytization is defined as the use of deception,
duress, or incentive to cause people to change their religion, then
all reasonable Christians and Muslims would agree that it is never
appropriate. Any declaration of faith should take place in an open
atmosphere of "gentleness and respect."[21] People should have the
freedom to accept the views of others without expecting favor, or to
reject them without experiencing fear.

(b) The use of Islamic sources indicates respect

The use of the Hadith as a connection to the gospel can convey the
importance which the Christian evangelist places on the Muslim
hearer. Islamic tradition is taken seriously and valued, and the
gospel is presented in terms which imply dignity, esteem, and an
attitude of acceptance of Muslim people. This is in stark contrast to
an approach which ignores Islamic beliefs and traditions, and seeks
to engage Muslims based on Christian-only terminology and para-
digms, deeming all Muslim sources as worthless.

(c) The Hadith can be an aid in understanding biblical inspiration

As an example of this approach, we can consider a way in which the
Hadith may be used to help Muslims understand the Christian concept of biblical inspiration. When Muslims begin to read the Bible,
they are often perplexed. They encounter a text which may have variant
readings listed in the footnotes, and multiple and differing accounts of
the same event, e.g., the creation of man (Gen 1 and Gen 2).[22] "How
could this book be from God?" they ask. The New Testament seems
even more confusing. Instead of the one *Injeel* (gospel) mentioned
in the Qur'an, they find four Gospels attributed to Matthew, Mark,
Luke, and John. "Which one is the real Gospel?" they ask. Part of the
problem arises from their perception of revelation.

Most Muslims (and many Christians, as well) think in terms of
Jesus as equivalent to Muhammad, since both are seen as the founders,

spokesmen, and prophets for their religions. The Muslim writer Charles Le Gai Eaton questions this: "The Christian, if he wishes to understand Islam, must resist the temptation to compare Muhammad with Jesus, for these two had entirely different roles in the scheme of things."[23] Moreover, the Bible is equated with the Qur'an, for both are holy books. Wilfred Cantwell-Smith has suggested that a better parallel would be Jesus as corresponding to the Qur'an.

> Muslims and Christians have been alienated partly by the fact that both have misunderstood each other's faith by trying to fit it into their own pattern. The most usual error is to suppose (on both sides) that the roles of Jesus Christ in Christianity and of Muhammad in Islam are comparable. . . . If one is drawing parallels in terms of the structure of the two religions, what corresponds in the Christian scheme to the Quran is not the Bible but the person of Christ—it is Christ who is for Christians the revelation of (from) God.[24]

Interestingly, Nasr refers to the Qur'an as "the central theophany (divine manifestation) of Islam."[25]

Davis moves beyond this to present further equivalents: "The (central) place occupied by Christ in the Christian religion belongs in Islam to the Qur'an as the very Word of God. Muhammad's position is roughly parallel to that of Paul or the Apostles, and the nearest equivalent to the New Testament is not the Qur'an, but the Hadith."[26] This can be depicted in a table:

	CHRISTIAN VIEW	MUSLIM VIEW
Primary revelation is . . .	Jesus Christ	the Qur'an
Witnesses to the revelation are . . .	the apostles (including Paul)	Muhammad
Record or explanation of the revelation is in . . .	the Bible	the Hadith

TABLE 21: Contrasting views of revelation

(d) Comparing Jesus and the Qur'an

Several factors support this point of view. Both Jesus and the Qur'an are seen by their respective religious communities as "the word of God" coming down from heaven, directly from God.[27] To take their physical forms on earth, they were temporarily "hosted" by human intermediaries (Mary and Muhammad), who were simply means of transmission, and did not have any impact on the divine nature or essence of Jesus or the Qur'an. Just as Jesus is described as "the word cast into Mary,"[28] so the Qur'an could be seen as the word cast into Muhammad. Both Jesus and the Qur'an (in the form of the "preserved Tablet" which is believed to be in heaven) are seen as eternally pre-existent.[29] Both proclaim their perfection.[30] Both are presented as the final divine revelation.[31] Both testify to transmitting the very words of God[32] and are preserved and protected by God.[33] Both are seen as unique to their religions—Jesus is the only begotten Son,[34] while the Qur'an is described as "inimitable,"[35] for its detractors are challenged to produce a comparable *sura*. When asked to perform a miracle, Muhammad could point only to the Qur'an.[36]

(e) Comparing the Bible and the Hadith

A comparison of the Bible and the Hadith likewise finds many parallels. Each record has multiple accounts of certain events, yet with some differences. These discrepancies may involve slight changes in the order of events, or minor details may be included or omitted. Clearly the various elements of the content have come through different channels of transmission. The science of transmission is claimed to be highly developed within Islam, and the Gospel writer Luke admits to accessing a multiplicity of sources.[37] Some details reflect the character and background of the transmitter. Luke the physician includes clinical history details of those Jesus healed,[38] but diplomatically omits information which was critical of the medical profession.[39] Aisha, the young wife of Muhammad, provides particulars from their bedroom,[40] as well as criticism of his anti-women comments.

Whereas the Qur'an is seen a direct *wahi* (revelation) from God in the manner of a typewriter or fax transmission, both the Bible and the Hadith sanction some human involvement in their collation. Ali ibn Mohammed Al-Jurjani (d.816/1413) describes it as follows: "A Sacred Hadith is, as to the meaning, from Allah the Almighty; as to the wording, it is from the Messenger of Allah." Ali Ibn Sultan Muhammad Al-Qari, the Hanifi jurisprudent (d.1016/1605) spoke of Muhammad's role in the following terms: "Allah . . . entrusted to him the expressing of it in such words as he wished."[41]

(f) Criticism of this view

Although the list of correlations between Jesus and the Qur'an, the apostles and Muhammad, and the Bible and the Hadith has much to commend it, it also suffers from difficulties. It is true that the primary revelation is Jesus Christ, but the apostles were more than simply witnesses. They were the recipients of revelation, and some of them went on to become writers of Gospels and epistles. The biblical concept of inspiration is of "men [who] spoke from God as they were carried along by the Holy Spirit."[42] Each of the New Testament writers has a personal style and unique vocabulary which distinguishes them from the others. There is clearly more personal input involved in this than was allowed to Muhammad with his mechanical "typewriter-like" transmission of the words of the Qur'an. Similarly, Mary was more than just a "means of entry" of the Son of God into the world, since Jesus took His humanity from her. The comparison between the Bible and the Hadith has been criticized by Temple Gairdner, who found more differences between the textual histories of the Hadith and Gospels than he found similarities.[43] The Hadith, as important as they are to Muslims, are still considered a "second-class" revelation, whereas Christians consider the Bible to be the inspired Word of God. Moreover, it is inevitable that Jesus and Muhammad should be compared, since both are seen as the founders of major religions. Consequently, both are seen by their respective traditions as the epitome of human existence and have become the objects of devotion and piety.

2. RELIGIOUS EXPERIENCE DIALOGUE

In this form of dialogue, the focus is on how one's faith impacts oneself in an existential way. The goal is to identify faith's effects on feelings and responses. Muhammad, in an act of emotion and understanding, once announced to his followers: "Today a pious man from Ethiopia has expired. Come on to offer the funeral prayer."[44] The "pious man" was the Christian Abyssinian king, bearing the title "Najashi," who had provided refuge for the persecuted Muslims.[45] He was "a king who would not tolerate injustice,"[46] so Muhammad felt that his people would be safe there. Here it was Muhammad's positive feelings about the Ethiopian ruler that came to the fore, allowing him to bridge the theological differences between them.

A number of key issues need to be kept in mind to enhance this kind of dialogue.

(a) Interfaith dialogue

The Hadith can be a helpful starting place for dialogue, since they identify some common ground that exists between Islamic and Christian worldviews. This can be a useful tool to build understanding of the other's faith journey. Nazir-Ali calls this "interior dialogue, [where] each partner will need to understand the ways in which spiritual experiences are interpreted by the other."[47] This could happen through a series of interfaith discussions. A comparison of similar events in the lives of Muhammad and Moses and other prophets[48] could be a good starting point for members of Christian and Muslim communities to evaluate their own modern-day similarities. The use of personal narrative is a key methodology in this approach. It is at the level of lived experience that hearts can meet and relationships be built.

Interfaith dialogue may also delve into issues such as the ultimate fate and eternal destiny of the human race. The Hadith passages which discuss eschatology[49] and heaven and hell[50] could be applied in this context.

(b) Interfaith worship

For some, the common ground discovered in "religious experience dialogue" can be expressed in interfaith worship. The Hadith present a picture of God which has some compatibility with a Christian understanding of the divine, and these commonalities may be recognized. These include the view of divine omniscience, divine emotions, and the desire for repentance.[51]

Likewise, many of the supplications of Muhammad could be included as part of interfaith worship, alongside Christian prayers.[52] Other prayers which could also be used in this context have been identified.[53]

One should not suppose that the existence of such parallels indicates that interfaith worship should be entered into without serious thought. Vinay Samuel and Chris Sugden define dialogue as "being open to other religions, to recognize God's activity in them, and to see how they are related to God's unique revelation in Christ."[54] They do not infer that this openness should lead to syncretism; rather, "the goal of dialogue is to affirm the Lordship of Christ over all life in such a way that people within their own context may recognize the relevance of that Lordship to them and discover it for themselves."[55] For many evangelical Christians, involvement in interfaith worship would be seen as the first step onto a dangerous and slippery slope. It is not possible to ignore the significant differences that exist between Islam and Christianity.

3. SECULAR DIALOGUE

The ethical teachings of the Hadith lend themselves to a third approach, "secular dialogue," which Zebiri has called "the dialogue of needs." She sees it as focusing on "areas of practical co-operation such as social justice and ecological issues."[56] The Catholic Church envisages this possibility with its statement during the Vatican Council in 1964:

Although in the course of the centuries many quarrels and hostilities have arisen between Christians and Muslims, this

Council urges all to forget the past and to strive sincerely for mutual understanding. On behalf of all mankind, let them make common cause of safeguarding and fostering social justice, moral values, peace and freedom.[57]

Anglican bishop Nazir-Ali speaks of such collaboration in Pakistan when Christian medical teams implemented an immunization program for Christian and Muslim children in *busti* (slum) areas. The team's arrival was announced to the public through the loud-speakers of local mosques.[58] Chapman points out that "Muslims and Christians have been able to work side by side in South Africa in their opposition to apartheid."[59] There is a call for such team-work from the Muslim side by Sardar in an article entitled "The Ethical Connection: Christian-Muslim Relations in the Postmodern Age,"[60] where he calls for "a joint ethical endeavour by Muslims and Christians" in the face of "the forces of atheism, secularism and materialism, resulting in a desire to join ranks and co-operate constructively with Christians as fellow theists."[61]

(a) Bases and activities for secular dialogue

The shared bases for such cooperation are summarized below in Table 22. Activities which could be undertaken by Muslims and Christians at organizational, communal, and/or individual levels are outlined.

THEOLOGICAL AND PHILOSOPHICAL BASES		
God is merciful to those who are merciful to others	B.2:373; 7:559; 8:26	Matt 5:7
Wish for others what you want for yourself	B.1:12	Matt 7:12
Giving is better than receiving	B.4:13, 371	Acts 20:35; Matt 5:42

TABLE 22: Bases for secular dialogue

Both Islam and Christianity set high standards of individual and communal behavior for their adherents. According to the Hadith, Muhammad made the statement, "The most beloved to me amongst you is the one who has the best character and manners."[62]

Jesus advised his followers, "Let your light so shine before men that they give glory to your Father who is in heaven."[63] Muslims and Christians can stand together on many public and private morality issues, to raise the general standards of social behavior, with a particular emphasis on how one's actions affect others. These could be undertaken through joint advertising or awareness-raising campaigns, such as conferences.

PUBLIC AND PRIVATE MORALITY ISSUES		
Truth-telling	B.1:17; 8:116	Eph 4:15
Respect for others' reputations	B.1:17	Rom 13:7
Respect for others' property	B.1:17	Matt 25:14–30
Returning lost property	B.1:91	Ex 23:4
Care of children	B.1:17	Matt 18:6/Mark 9:42/Luke 17:2
Sexual purity	B.1:17	Matt 5:28; Heb 13:4
Obedience to leaders	B.4:203	Heb 13:17; 1 Pet 2:13–14

TABLE 23: Examples of moral issues

Zebiri notes that it is in the area of public morality that Islam can find a relationship with other faiths. She suggests that the Qur'an appears to "offer a rationale for competing religions: 'For each We have appointed a divine law and traced-out way. Had God willed He could have made you one community. But [He wished] to try you by that which he has given you; so vie with one another in good works' (5:48)."[64] This accords with the biblical command: "Outdo one another in showing honour."[65]

There are also bases for common action in certain areas. Social needs affect all communities: cooperation, rather than competition, is the best way forward. The Hadith and the Bible enumerate some areas where such collaboration could take place.

Other Christians would see such cooperation on a theological basis as a betrayal of both religious traditions, for it ignores what they see as significant differences between Islam and Christianity. Instead they would prefer any collaboration to take place on the basis of shared humanity without any reference to spiritual values; otherwise confusion may result.[66]

POSSIBLE SOCIAL JUSTICE ACTIVITIES		
Feeding the poor	B.1.11, 17	Matt 25:35,36
Caring for the oppressed	B.7:104	Matt 25:35,36
Freeing the captives –legal advocacy	B.4:282	Luke 4:18
Visiting the sick	B.7:103	Matt 25:35,36
Forgiving the debts	B.4:687	Matt 6:12
Care of orphans	B.2:544	Jas 1:27
Treatment of women	B.4:642; 5:163	1 Pet 3:7

TABLE 24: Potential areas for action

(b) Contentious issues raised in dialogue

As relationships between Christians and Muslims deepen through contact and combined activities, a space is constructed to discuss more difficult matters. Issues of painful contention between Muslims and Christians, particularly in the way that each group treats the other, can be raised. A pressing matter is religious freedom for Christians in Islamic contexts. Although Muslims are allowed to congregate openly, build mosques, propagate their religion, and even receive government funding for Islamic programs and institutions in Western countries which have a Christian majority and heritage, these same rights are rarely extended to Christian communities in Muslim-majority countries. No Christian churches, for example, are currently allowed in Saudi Arabia or Yemen.[67] This is based on Muhammad's command in the Hadith to "expel the pagans from the Arabian peninsula."[68] Before putting this into action, the second Caliph checked the source of the saying. "'Umar ibn al-Khattab searched for information about that until he was absolutely convinced that [Muhammad] had said, 'Two deens [religions] shall not co-exist in the Arabian Peninsula,' and he therefore expelled the Jews from Khaybar."[69] Christian freedom to propagate their religion among Muslims is severely limited by the Hadith's prohibition on conversion. Muhammad had commanded, "Whoever changed his Islamic religion, then kill him."[70] Thus freedom of choice in the matter of faith is not allowed to Muslims.

Many Muslims in the West and elsewhere suffer from stereotyping and racism, following the events of September 11, 2001. They feel that they bear the burden of collective guilt for the actions of some of their members. Dialogue with Christians and others is an appropriate place to air these concerns. Muslim women, particularly if they wear a *hijab*, are often seen as oppressed or even unintelligent. Some of the material outlined under Chapter 5, "The Positive Depiction and Treatment of Women," could form a good basis for discussion about these matters. It is important that both Muslims and Christians have an opportunity to speak with others about the matters that are affecting their communities.

NOTES

1. Luke 2:46.
2. A Common Word, http://www.acommonword.com/.
3. Source: http://www.commongroundnews.org/article. php?id=21957&lan=en&sid=1&sp=0 (accessed October 14, 2015).
4. Source: http://www.acommonword.com/index. php?lang=en&page=responses (accessed October 14, 2015).
5. Source: http://www.youtube.com/watch?v=rTY-9FY13kw (accessed October 14, 2015). Another response from the Uniting Church of Australia can be found at http://assembly.uca.org.au/rof/images/stories/resources/acommonwordresponse.pdf (accessed October 14, 2015).
6. Lausanne Occasional Papers, "Christian Witness to Muslims," no. 13, Thailand Report, 22.
7. B.5:663, 664; 9:360.
8. Ibn Ishaq, *Sirat*, 270–277.
9. E.g., Mark 1:15.
10. B.4:724; 5:201.
11. B.6:136; 9:622, explaining Q.5:67.
12. John 15:15.
13. Matt 10:5/Mark 3:13/Luke 9:1.
14. Luke 10:1.
15. Ibn Ishaq, *Sirat*, 204.

16. B.2:116; 4:57, 299; 5:414, 416, 417, 422.

17. Nazir-Ali, *Islam: A Christian Perspective*, 148.

18. T. Michel, "Rights of Non-Muslims in Islam: An Opening
     Statement," cited in Siddiqui, *Christian-Muslim Dialogue*, 61.

19. Swartley, "Course Introduction," xxvi.

20. Kerr, "Islamic *da'wa* and Christian Mission," 163.

21. 1 Pet 3:15.

22. The Qur'an, of course, contains many parallel accounts, including the
     creation (Q.7:54 [in six days] and Q.41:9–12 [in eight days]), Satan's
     fall (Q.2:34; 7:11–18; 17:61; 18:50; and 20:116), the sin of Adam
     and his wife (Q.2:35–39; Q.7:19–25; and Q.20:120–123), the story
     of Noah (Q.7:59–64; and 11:25–49), the birth of John the Baptist
     (Q.3:38–41 and Q.19:1–15), and the birth of Jesus (Q.3:42–48 and
     19:16–34). There are some differences between the various accounts.

23. Eaton, *Islam and the Destiny of Man*, 96.

24. Smith, *Islam in Modern History*, 17–18.

25. Source: http://www.britannica.com/EBchecked/topic/487666/Quran
     (accessed October 14, 2015).

26. Davis, *Christ and the World Religions*, 104.

27. John 6:51; Q.20:113.

28. Q.4:171.

29. John 1:1; Q.85:22.

30. John 8:46; Q.18:1.

31. Heb 1:3; Q.5:3.

32. John 8:28; Q.55:2.

33. John 7:30; Q:15:9.

34. John 1:18.

35. Q.2:23.

36. Q.21.3, 5, 10.

37. Luke 1:3.

38. E.g., Luke 8:42.

39. Mark 5:26, cf. Luke 8:43.

40. B.3:247.

41. Ibrahim and Johnson-Davies, *Forty Hadith Qudsi*, 8.

42. 2 Pet 2:21.

43. Gairdner, "Moslem Tradition and the Gospel Record. The Hadith
     and the Injil."

44. B.2:406, 412; 5:220.

45. B.3:494; 4:364; 5:212, 215, 216, 245, 539; 7:698.

46. Ibn Ishaq, *Sirat,* 146.

47. Nazir-Ali, *Islam: A Christian Perspective*, 145.

48. See chapter 4, parts 1 and 2.

49. See chapter 6, part 3 (a).

50. See chapter 6, part 3 (b).

51. See chapter 8.

52. See chapter 6, part 2.

53. For an analysis of Muslim prayers, see Padwick, *Muslim Devotions,* and Padwick, "The Language of Muslim Devotion," 5–21, 98–110, 194–209, as well as the anthology by Cragg, *Alive to God.*

54. Samuel and Sugden, "Dialogue," 122. This is dialogue for the purpose of more effectively proclaiming Christ, rather than dialogue to enable Christians to discern truth which is lacking in what has been revealed to them.

55. Samuel and Sugden, *Dialogue with Other Religions,* 122.

56. Zebiri, *Muslims and Christians Face to Face,* 33–34.

57. *Nostra Aetate,* quote from Speight, *God Is One: The Way of Islam,* 101–102.

58. Nazir-Ali, *Frontiers,* 86.

59. Chapman "Christian Perceptions of Islam," 103.

60. Sardar, "The Ethical Connection: Christian-Muslim Relations in the Postmodern Age."

61. Zebiri, *Muslims and Christians,* 173, 181.

62. B.5:104.

63. Matt 5:16.

64. Zebiri, *Muslims and Christians,* 16.

65. Rom 12:10.

66. I am grateful to Mark Durie for this insight. See http://www.jmm.org.au/articles/32061.htm (accessed October 14, 2015).

67. Apart from the pre-existing churches built by the British in Aden.

68. B.4:288, also 4:393; 5:716.

69. Hadith Muwatta 45:1618. See Sunnah.com/malik/45

70. B.9:57; also 4:260; 9:17, 271.

17

DISCUSSION WITH MUSLIMS

THE BIBLE IS CONCERNED with engaging other worldviews as much as possible. The Genesis writer, for example, "employs certain terms and motifs, partly taken from his ideologically incompatible predecessors and partly chosen in contrast to comparable concepts in ancient Near Eastern cosmogonies, and fills them in his own usage with new meaning consonant with his aim and world-view."[1]

In the Hadith, we find similar links which may be used.

1. THE NATURE OF GOD

The Hadith speak of a God who is good, holy, and active, who desires to be near His people.[2] Allah is not simply a distant and invisible being who is pure power. He is portrayed as benevolent, bringing good out of evil, yet with a strong sense of anger against sin. The possibility of a divine enfleshment is hinted at. He comes down nightly to seek those who desire him. He runs toward those who walk toward him, and is joyful at their repentance. Allah is depicted as very near, especially at times of prayer.[3] These passages are laden with potential springboards for discussion about the nature and action of God. They move beyond a divine aloofness suggested by the Qur'an and toward the Bible's depiction of

God's proximity, beneficence, and initiative. More importantly, they present an almost physical image of the God who comes down toward the earth, calling—virtually pleading—for people to turn to Him, seeking them out like a man who found a lost camel in the desert, and running full of joy toward the lost and repentant soul. This connects with the biblical idea of the good shepherd looking for the lost sheep, or the loving father running out to welcome the prodigal son. There is the suggestion that God "can locally manifest his presence," an important precursor to consideration of the incarnation.[4] The use of such direct and active descriptions reminds us of Kenneth Cragg's call to the church to "break free of 'substance' metaphors that set Christology/theology in the realm of abstract metaphysics, and bring it firmly into the concrete 'operation' of divine energy to save."[5]

There is a progression in divine involvement with humanity as detailed in Table 25:

QUR'ANIC VIEW	HADITH VIEW	OLD TESTAMENT VIEW	NEW TESTAMENT VIEW
God never appears physically	God will be visible in Paradise	God appears from time to time	God appears in the flesh
No theophany	Eschatological theophany	Occasional theophany	Incarnation

TABLE 25: Progression through the various texts

The Bible is also clear that "without holiness no one will see the Lord."[6] This raises the question of human nature and the eschatological imperative of how such holiness may be attained.

2. THE NATURE OF HUMANITY

Although the Islamic view of humanity as expressed through the Qur'an and the Hadith reaches neither the heights nor the depths of the Christian understanding, there is common teaching about human origins which define human nature. People are described as created in the image of God, and Muslim scholars differ about the meaning of this phrase. These scholars may deny the concept of a "Fall" in Islam, but the Hadith outline some serious problems within human nature.[7] People are simultaneously magnificent, created in God's image,[8] yet miserable, burdened by their sin.[9] They are constituted of the dust of the earth, indicating a downward gravitational pull in a moral sense. Yet they are enlivened by the divine afflatus, the very breath of God Himself, indicating the heights from which they have come, and to which they could return. This makes humans capable of standing before God, but at the same time their sin excludes them from His presence. Humans are treated at times individually and at times corporately, but always bearing some resemblance to their forbear Adam.[10] Adam's sin affected future generations in various ways, including a propensity toward sin.[11]

3. THE NEED FOR FORGIVENESS

In the Hadith, sin is serious in God's sight, for it separates people from God. All sins will incur debts or penalties which must be paid, hence the frequent use of commercial analogies.[12] Although there are many actions that can earn forgiveness for one's sins, the chances of achieving an ultimate positive balance do not look encouraging. Every Muslim, according to the Hadith, totters between the promise of forgiveness and reward, based on his or her good works, and the threat of condemnation, due to his or her sins. Muslims are given a variety of ways of expiating their sins, but the definition of the "unforgivable sin" grows wider. This is combined with the news that believers lose their status as believers when they sin, suggesting an unstable identity. The result is an uncertain outcome for those who sin.[13]

Fortunately, there are some positive biblical connections associated with the ideas in the Hadith, and this leads to some missiological implications about how to view Muslims on the path to faith in Christ.[14] The Hadith hint, and the Bible affirms, that good works are questionable in their efficacy and not sufficient to assure one's eternal destiny in Paradise. Even the Prophet himself admitted this.[15] Clearly some other means of approach to God are needed. God's unmerited mercy becomes crucial, and this strongly connects with some biblical themes.

4. ISSUES OF ATONEMENT

Although the Qur'an appears to endorse a simple equation of reward or punishment for doing good or evil,[16] the Hadith give teaching and examples which challenge such black-and-white categories. However, the Hadith show that there is not a simple one-to-one correspondence between bad deeds and punishment, because

- sins may be overlooked completely.
- an alternative punishment may be designated.
- the sin may be allocated to someone else.
- someone may choose to pay the penalty for another's sin.
- there is no penalty in the next life if a sin is paid for in this life.[17]

Similarly there is no simple correspondence between good deeds and reward, because

- a good work may not be completed, yet it still gains a reward.
- a person may receive a reward from the good actions of someone else.
- a living person may perform a good work to the benefit of a dead person.
- a single good act may have positive outcomes for many people with eternal results.
- a solitary action by one person could have everlasting consequences for many others.[18]

Moreover, the rewards and punishments could cross the life/death boundary—they are not chronologically determined.[19] The Hadith contain many references to sacrifice, where the death of a living being profits the person on whose behalf the offering was made.[20] Similarly, the idea of ransom or redemption, where another person pays the price for a captive to be released, is found in the Hadith.[21]

While Islam in theory denies the possibility of someone paying for the deeds of another, in actual fact this is presented as a reality. But more than this, Islamic teaching recognizes the inadequacy of human actions actually fulfilling the divine requirements, for "every soul will come pleading for itself on that Day."[22] Obviously some external help is being sought.

It is clear from the above references that people could receive the benefits of some act which they had not performed, or avoid the disadvantages normally due to non-completion of a requirement. However, something else must be provided in exchange, or the required action carried out on their behalf by someone else. This concept is mentioned seventy-nine times in the Bible, both in the Old Testament[23] and the New Testament.[24] This has great implications for explaining the death of Christ as a substitutionary atonement.

5. CONNECTIONS WITH BIBLICAL THEMES

The Qur'an proclaims: "And whoever earns a fault or a sin and then throws it on to someone innocent, he has indeed burdened himself with falsehood and a manifest sin."[25] This would seem to "cut the nerve" of the substitutionary atonement: a guilty person cannot cast his sins onto someone innocent. However, as outlined above, the "substitutionary principle" is applied every time a person makes expiation for his or her sins. Instead of receiving the penalty prescribed for that sin, the guilty person is able to avoid the penalty by doing something else. In every case, this requires some kind of sacrifice, either of wealth (feeding a certain number of poor persons, freeing a slave)[26] or of blood (killing an innocent sheep, goat, cow, or camel).[27] In the latter case, the innocent and unwilling sacrifice victim pays for the guilty person's sin. The difference is that Christ willingly took it upon Himself: "I lay down my life—only to take it up again. No one takes it from me, but I lay it down of my own accord. I have authority to lay it down and authority to take it up again."[28]

William St. Clair Tisdall suggests that the one who acted on behalf of humanity would need to be free of any burden of his own. "God's law teaches that man owes him a duty of perfect devotion and man's failure to attain this results in him being in debt to God. However, as every creature owes a duty of absolute obedience to its creator, no creature can have any surplus merit, to pay the debt of another creature. Therefore only God can be the saviour, for only he can pay another's debt."[29] Significantly, both Islamic teachings and the Bible point toward only one man who carried no debt of sin.[30]

6. OTHER PICTURES OF THE CROSS

Sacrifice, atonement, and redemption are not the only representations which can be applied to the cross of Christ. The Hadith outline the responsibility of the host who must provide asylum for his guests when they are under threat. Jesus can be depicted as the guest who should have received sanctuary, yet was betrayed to His enemies and then killed. This may be a potent depiction in Middle Eastern and other cultures where corporate shame has more cogency than individual guilt.[31] For the truculent Arabs, a battle scenario could be described with the Warrior Christ going out to face the spiritual enemies of Satan and death, and being vindicated by His final victory.[32] But in the process, Christ loses His life as a martyr on the cross. He is a willing victim who lays down His life for a noble cause—the salvation of humanity—for "Christ Jesus came into the world to save sinners."[33] Christ's betrayal and martyrdom becomes even more tragic in the context of His sinlessness—He was pure and spotless for all of His life.[34] All of these elements are, in their own way, keys to understanding the deeper meanings of the death of Christ.

7. CHRIST AS MEDIATOR AND INTERCESSOR

The Qur'an is somewhat equivocal about the role of a mediator or intercessor. However, the Hadith provide much more detail and open up new categories. Sometimes Muhammad claimed this function for himself, but at other times he appeared to deny it. Yet there is a clear and definitive divine intercession, where God Himself acts positively and powerfully on behalf of those who have no basis to commend themselves—this is a sign of pure grace. In the Bible Jesus is presented as the ideal mediator who intercedes to His heavenly Father for those who come to Him.[35]

8. THE PRIMACY OF FAITH AND LOVE OVER WORKS

Faith and love can be shown to be more important than works, which are task-oriented and goal-centered. Scientific "belief" may be seen as impersonal, focused on theories, data, and facts. It is cerebral and impassive, and attempts to be entirely objective.[36] True faith involves the whole person—heart, mind, and will. Faith can be *assensus* or belief, but it is focused on relationships, where meaning and significance is drawn from and attached to the other. Some of the hadith bring out this emphasis. This is particularly important from a Christian consideration which posits that "God is love."[37] Biblical faith is a response to that love. Consequently, "the only thing that counts is faith expressing itself through love."[38] Faith can also be *fidelitas*, commitment, or dedication, for it places its object far above all other contenders.[39]

9. THE TRANSFORMED LIFE

The result of this dedicated faith is a transformed life, characterized by cleansing, purity, and holiness. It is like the imparting of a new nature, resulting from a second birth. God Himself seems to be acting within the person, and each one starts to take on the shape and image of Adam. For each of these concepts found in the Hadith, there is a more definite and stronger biblical parallel which can be propounded. Rather than being an eschatological possibility, the Christian Scriptures present them as a current reality. This new start, or second birth, brings a closer connection with God, with a divine working within and the outward expression of God's character.[40]

10. ASSURANCE OF THE BELIEVER

The logical outcome on such a path is an assured place in the presence of God in heaven forever. Neither the Qur'an nor the Hadith are very clear about this—even the Prophet Muhammad expressed uncertainty about his own eternal destiny. For Christians, however, this assurance is explicitly outlined and described.[41]

11. CRITICISM OF THESE USES OF THE HADITH[42]

It could be claimed that this use of the Hadith is reading back into the text that which is not there. This question can be answered in several ways.

First, every text is subject to interpretation, and each interpretation draws a different trajectory from the others, resulting in diverse conclusions. Muslims themselves have found a variety of meanings within their sacred texts. They have not always agreed with each other on how to understand the Qur'an. The verse, "The Hour has drawn near and the moon has been cleft asunder,"[43] for example, has been variously interpreted. It has been seen as a miracle performed by Muhammad when the Meccans asked him for a sign,[44] or as a naturally occurring lunar eclipse in the Prophet's time,[45] or as a scientific prophecy fulfilled when American astronauts landed on the moon in 1969 and dug up soil samples, thereby "clefting" the moon,[46] or as an eschatological sign in the sky at the final judgment.[47] This one verse has been attributed to past, current, and future events. Ironically, Yusuf Ali adds a fifth possible interpretation: "the phrase is metaphorical, meaning that the matter has become clear as the moon."[48]

The Hadith likewise have been interpreted differently by a range of groups, leading to variant conclusions or trajectories (X, Y, Z in Illustration 19).

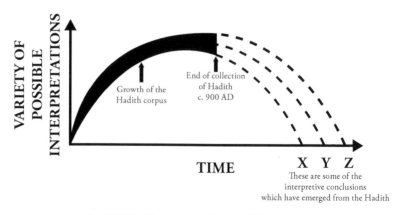

ILLUSTRATION 19: Trajectories of interpretation

Modern Muslim feminists[49] have been able to uncover meanings and provide interpretations which have eluded "patriarchalist" male exegetes for centuries. Using the same materials, Jihadist Muslims[50] draw completely different conclusions from those who proclaim that "Islam means peace."[51] Sufi practitioners have garnered support for their *tariqas* (methods) by using the Hadith.[52]

In the light of these factors, it is likely that new directions of study in the Hadith will continue to emerge, resulting in conclusions which may be mutually exclusive. This study is a further contribution to the field. Some of the lines of exegesis taken in this study may not be acceptable to many Muslims. They will object to the clearly Christian analysis which has been applied to the Hadith. This study seeks connections with Islamic texts for a missional purpose. Such a goal and its methodology may be rejected by many Muslims. This is to be expected. It is also clear that not all of the material in the Hadith will be suitable for this goal. The Hadith contain some aspects which are inimical to a Christian understanding of the world.[53] The Hadith, like the Qur'an, present a range of views on a variety of topics— neither of these documents is univocal. The comments by Muslim journalist Irshad Manji about the Qur'an—that it is "a bundle of contradictions," is "profoundly at war with itself,"[54] and has "wild mood swings"[55]—could just as easily be applied to the Hadith.

This phenomenon allows a commentator to pick up on one stream and follow it to a certain conclusion, while admitting that there are other streams which could lead to completely different outcomes. Sometimes Muslim writers raise potential lines of investigation, such as the comment by Hamidullah that "incarnation would be the best" way of God revealing Himself.[56] Islam itself has identified a possible issue, but does not itself give an answer to this expressed need.

Many of the themes of the Bible can be found in the Hadith. Clearly the Hadith (and Islam in general) do not contain a full-orbed presentation of the good news as found in Christ; otherwise they would be a restatement of Christian teaching, rather than the building blocks of a different religion. However, the Hadith do contain many springboards providing a connection with biblical themes. Kraft points out that we need to "approach [non-Christians] with the Gospel in terms of what their perception of reality is, rather than in terms of our understandings."[57] Some tenets found in the Hadith are like seeds which can flower into a fuller expression of the good news of the gospel. They are a launching pad for further exploration by Muslims and Christians together.

Can such common ground be a fruitful place? Steve Bell tells the story of an Egyptian man. "Even the prophet Muhammad and the Qur'an became stepping stones facilitating Ahmed's journey to Christ. It had become clear to him that Jesus' moral and spiritual authority was total and that what he demanded from Ahmed was not some new external observance alongside his Islam but the redirecting of it."[58]

12. HOW TO USE THIS MATERIAL

There is a variety of ways in which this material may be shared with Muslims and the wider community. The ideas and connections expressed in this study need to be debated at the academic level. Opportunities could be taken for discussion through university colloquia or public forums. They could be written up as journal articles or presented as papers for interfaith seminars. With the increasing number of Islamic chairs in Western universities, often funded from Arab or Muslim-majority countries, new openings have been created for such academic exploration. Yet the material should not remain the reserve of scholarly debate. It is important that it be used in practical applications. Many missionaries and cross-cultural workers are seeking new ways to inject biblical truth into their conversations with Muslims. The Hadith provide an ideal starting point for such discussions. The material in this study finds a place among contextualized approaches.[59] The "insider movement" utilizes indigenous forms and materials as a vehicle for the Christian faith.[60] The Bible, and other materials, have been translated into other languages using a Qur'anic style.[61] The Qur'an has been used in dialogue with and outreach to Muslims,[62] as have the Camel Method[63] and the Five Pillars of Islam.[64] The Hadith could have a similar application.

Nor need its application be restricted to literary methods. The rate of illiteracy is very high in Arab countries,[65] as well as other Muslim-majority countries. The result is that a significant proportion of the Muslim world consists of oral, rather than literate, communicators. "Information must come to oral communicators through stories, parables, poems, ballads, and similar types of formats. Format is the key for them."[66] The Hadith are mostly in narrative form, which is ideal for oral communicators. Significantly, 75 percent of the Bible is also in narrative form,[67] allowing important linkages between the Hadith and the Bible to be constructed.

NOTES

1. Hasel, "The Significance of the Cosmology in Genesis 1 in relation to Ancient Near Eastern Parallels," 20.
2. See chapter 8, parts 1 and 2.
3. See chapter 8, part 4.
4. Parsons, *Unveiling God*, 191.
5. Cragg, *Jesus and the Muslim*, 166.
6. Heb 12:14.
7. Gen 2:7; Q.15:28–29.
8. See chapter 9, part 1.
9. See chapter 9, part 2.
10. See chapter 9, part 6.
11. See chapter 9, part 3.
12. See chapter 10, part 3.
13. See chapter 10, part 6.
14. See chapter 10, part 7.
15. See chapter 11, part 3.
16. See chapter 12, part 1.
17. See chapter 12.
18. See chapter 13, parts 1-5.
19. See chapter 13, part 6.
20. See chapter 14, part 2, section (a).
21. See chapter 14, part 2, section (b).

22. Q.16:111.

23. E.g., Gen 22; Deut 0:16; Lev 4:21–35; 17:11.

24. E.g., Matt 20:28; 26:28; Mark 14:24; Luke 22:19-20; John 6:51; 10:11.

25. Q.4:112.

26. E.g., B.5:478.

27. E.g., B.1:293.

28. John 10:17–18.

29. As summarized by Parsons, *Unveiling God*, 12.

30. See chapter 14, part 1.

31. See chapter 14, part 3, section (a).

32. See chapter 14, part 3, section (b).

33. 1 Tim 1:15.

34. See chapter 14, part 1.

35. See chapter 15, part 1.

36. In fact, science is not totally objective, for "scientific theories are [not] a mere description of experimental facts. . . . Facts are theory laden and theories are formulated on the basis of certain philosophical assumptions." Iqbal, *Islam and Science*, 296.

37. 1 John 4:8, 16.

38. Gal 5:6.

39. See chapter 15, part 2.

40. See chapter 15, part 3.

41. See chapter 15, part 4.

42. See the earlier discussion in Chapter 3

43. Q.54:1.

44. B.6:390 cited in Al-Hilali and Khan, *Translation of the meanings of the Noble Qur'an*, 725.

45. See http://muslimvilla.smfforfree.com/index.php?topic=1082.0;wap2 (accessed October 14, 2015). This could be based on the forty references to eclipses in al-Bukhāri's Hadith.

46. Source: http://www.harunyahya.com/books/faith/Allahs_miracles_of_the_quran/Allahs_miracles_of_the_quran4.php (accessed October 14, 2015).

47. Muhammad Asad writes: "It is practically certain that the above Qur'an-verse does not refer to [a miracle in the Prophet's time] but, rather, to a future event: namely, to what will happen when the Last

Hour approaches." Source: http://muslimvilla.smfforfree.com/index.
php?topic=1082.0;wap2 (accessed October 14, 2015).

48. Ali, *The Holy Qur'ān: text, translation and commentary*, 1454.

49. See, for example, Mernissi, "Women's Rights in Islam," 112–126.

50. See Mustafa Mashhur, "Jihad is the way," in *The Laws of Dawa,* vol.
5, trans. Itamar Marcus and Nan Jacques Zilberdick, http://palwatch.
org/STORAGE/special%20reports/Jihad_is_the_way_by_Mustafa_
Mashhur.pdf (accessed October 14, 2015).

51. See Afroz Ali, *Jihad—the Australian Context,* http://alghazzali.org/
resources/articles/jihad2.pdf (accessed October 14, 2015).

52. Based on B.1:110, in which Muhammad stated that Satan cannot
impersonate him in a dream, all of the fifteenth century Sufi masters
claimed that Muhammad had appeared to them in a dream and
commanded them to start a new Method or *tariqa.* Trimingham, *Sufi
Orders,* 190.

53. This is outlined in my other book, *Challenging Islamic Traditions.*

54. Manji, *The Trouble with Islam Today*, 36.

55. Ibid., 51.

56. See chapter 8, part 6.

57. Kraft, *Anthropology for Christian Witness,* 5.

58. Bell, *Grace for Muslims?*, 37.

59. Trotter, *Sevenfold Secret*; Bible passages in Chapman, *The Pillars of
Religion in the Light of the Tawrat, Zabur and Injil*; Malek, "Allah-u
Akbar Bible Lessons: Aspects of Their Effectiveness in Evangelizing
Muslims."

60. Travis and Travis, "Contextualisation among Muslims, Hindus and
Buddhists."

61. Goble and Munayer, *New Creation Book for Muslims* and the life
of Christ in Qur'anic style in *Sirat al-Masih bi-Lisan Arabi Fasih.*
For a comparison of this style with existing Arabic Bible transla-
tions, see Owen, "A Classification System for Styles of Arabic Bible
Translations," 8–10. For reactions to it, see Schlorff, "Feedback on
Project Sunrise (Sira)," 22–32.

62. Accad, *Building Bridges.*

63. Greeson, *The Camel: How Muslims are coming to Christ.*

64. Woodberry, "Contextualisation among Muslims: Reusing Common
Pillars."

65. *The Arab Development Report 2003.*

66. James B. Slack, *The Ways People Learn,* http://media1.imbresources. org/files/83/8361/8361-46134.pdf (accessed October 14, 2015).

67. Tom Steffen cited by Brown, "Communicating God's message in an Oral Culture," 126.

18

CONCLUSION

THE QUR'AN HAS ONLY 6,200 verses and remarkably little legal or practical detail. If Islam is to fulfill its claim to be an all-emcompassing rule of life for all Muslims at all times, a significant volume of extra material is needed to cover every possible situation and contingency that might arise. The Hadith provide this service, making it a necessary provision for Muslims to enable them to structure their lives.

Moreover, a discourse can be found in the Qur'an and the Hadith which justifies its existence and application. In general, these documents are still widely accepted as authoritative within the house of Islam. In the *madrasas* of Asia, North Africa, and the Middle East, and in mosques and prayer rooms throughout the world, these stories of the actions and sayings of the Prophet Muhammad and his companions are recounted on a weekly basis. They inform the minds, dictate the habits, and inspire the lives of the vast majority of the followers of Islam. It is unlikely that the Hadith will lose its popularity and power in the near future. Muhammad remains for most Muslims the supreme example for emulation. Riots and killings by Muslims as a result of the 2005/6 "Muhammad cartoons"[1] and the 2011 movie clip "Innocence of Muslims"[2] show that Islam's founder is still able to rally much support on the Muslim street.

Islam, for its part, is on the march. A high population growth, making it the fastest growing major religion in the world, the wealth flowing in from Middle Eastern oil, along with widespread migration to the West for education and employment, have given Muslims an increasing confidence and opportunity to proclaim their religion. Much of their inspiration comes from the *diktats* and methods found in the Hadith.

However, Christian mission also continues to expand, with increasing contact with Muslims in Africa, Asia, and the Middle East, as well as in the West. The relative lack of success of mission *vis-à-vis* the house of Islam in the past suggests a need for new approaches. This situation calls for courage and creativity. The Hadith can be a culturally appropriate tool for followers of Jesus Christ to employ in the encounter with Muslims. The Hadith lend themselves to a variety of applications, depending on the context. When looking at the Hadith through the lenses of concord and connections, many links with biblical truth can be discerned.

Through dialogue with Muslims, Christians can find material in the Hadith with which they agree. There are elements of theology, devotion, ethics, and history which could produce topics for fruitful discussion. In these post-9/11 days of the purported clash of civilizations, it is important to recognize those issues which constitute common ground. The shared humanity of Muslims and Christians requires that these be taken seriously. A positive Muslim analysis of the life of Muhammad, taken from the Hadith, provides material for an analysis of values and areas of further discussion. Some Christians would feel comfortable to move beyond this to shared worship or devotional exercises based on a mutual understanding of God. Others may want to limit this to discussions about personal religious experience. The devotional material within the Hadith provides a good starting point. Christians seeking partners to bring change in their community can find among Muslims some who will cooperate in political and social campaigns based on shared concerns and values outlined in the Hadith.

Yet this should not lead to a naive dismissal of the differences between Muslim and Christian belief. Some of the Hadith reveal significant gaps between Islam and Christianity. These are not to be ignored—they should be admitted and addressed. The possibility of critical approaches to Islam, such as have been practiced throughout history, is opened up. However such a debate can and must be carried out in a non-destructive way that both illustrates and commends the gospel. This calls for both frankness and maturity.

Islam, like any religious or philosophical system, contains echoes of the truth. A shared geography and history means that many vestiges of Judaism and Christianity remain embedded within Islam. These are to be sought out and explored. The Hadith's view of the dignity of humankind (made in the image of God), as well as human weakness and sin, forms a basis for fruitful anthropological conversations. In this, as in many other topics, the Hadith seems to present a development beyond the Qur'an's representation of these matters. Likewise the Hadith's appraisal of the primacy of faith, the forgiveness of sins, and the inadequacy of works challenge some traditional and widespread Islamic works-based views of salvation. It is important that the cross, God's solution to human sin, be presented to Muslims.

Issues such as the mediatorial principle, substitution, sacrifice, and ransom, as well as the sinlessness of Christ, are found in the Hadith. They can

ILLUSTRATION 20: A protester displaying the cross and the crescent in Tahrir Square, Cairo. The sign reads: "Pay attention!!! One blood, one nation."[a]

---

a. Source: "The Friday of One Demand," Al Jazeera English, November 18, 2011. Made available under an Attribution ShareAlike 2.0 Generic license. https://www.flickr.com/photos/aljazeeraenglish/6359347781/ (accessed on January 22, 2015).

serve as launching pads which cause us to look beyond the Hadith to the One who is the Way, the Truth, and the Life. There are other pictures of the atonement hinted at in these documents, such as recognizing the shame of betrayed hospitality, and rejoicing in the victory of a brave warrior who is tragically killed in battle as a martyr, yet later miraculously raised from the dead. The new life that results from the transforming work of the Holy Spirit in the believer's life can arise out of these discussions from the Hadith.

Both of these approaches, dialogue and development, will require different expressions of Christian character. Dialogue calls for humility, in being willing to accept the truths that others might bring. Development calls for discernment, in determining the ways that God's message can be contextualized for a new situation.

In February 2011, as Christians and Muslims stood together in Tahrir Square in Cairo calling for then President Hosni Mubarak to resign, flags and other symbols with the cross and the crescent together were often displayed. The photograph featured in Illustration 20 was taken on November 18, 2011, during further demonstrations in the aftermath of revolution.

This was not the first time that such symbolism has been used.

Early last century, Egyptian Muslims and Christians combined to oppose the British occupation of their land. In the flag used by these nationalistic Egyptians, US missiologist Dudley Woodberry finds a parable of the relationship between Islam and Christianity. "The

ILLUSTRATION 21:
The Cross and
Crescent flag used
in Egypt in 1919[b]

cross within the crescent on the flag of the Egyptian independence movement of 1919 was emblazoned on a black background much as the crescent moon stands against the dark night sky. The crescent moon reflects light and beauty but not at the center where it is empty and dark. In the emblem the cross fills that void" (see Illustration 21).

---

b.   Dudley Woodberry, "Missiological Issues in the Encounter with Emerging Islam," *Missiology: An International Review* 28 (January 2000): 19-34.

Through this analogy, Woodberry suggests that, just as the moon dimly reflects the light of the sun, Islam bears a reflection of Christ, the Light of the World. Just as the center of the crescent moon is dark, it is the cross of Christ that can fill Islam's empty void.[3]

Is it possible that the Hadith might yet prove to be one of the keys in facilitating such a process?

NOTES

1. Source: http://www.bbc.co.uk/news/world-europe-11236158 (accessed October 15, 2015).

2. Source: http://www.ibtimes.com/%E2%80%98innocence-muslims%E2%80%99-protests-death-toll-rising-pakistan-794296 (accessed October 15, 2015).

3. Woodberry, "Missiological Issues in the Encounter of Emerging Islam."

APPENDIX
List of Topics in al-Bukhari's Hadith with Volume, Book, and Account Numbers

TOPIC	LOCATION	NUMBER OF ACCOUNTS IN EACH BOOK	CUMULATIVE NUMBER OF ACCOUNTS
Revelation	Vol 1 Bk 1 nos 1–6	6	6
Belief	Vol 1 Bk 2 nos 7–55	43	49
Knowledge	Vol 1 Bk 3 nos 56–136	61	110
Ablutions (*Wudū'*)	Vol 1 Bk 4 nos 137–247	111	221
Bathing (*Ghusl*)	Vol 1 Bk 5 nos 248–292	45	266
Menstrual Periods	Vol 1 Bk 6 nos 293–329	37	303
Rubbing Hands and Feet with Dust (*Tayammum*)	Vol 1 Bk 7 nos 330–344	15	318
Prayers (*Salāt*)	Vol 1 Bk 8 nos 345–471	127	445
Virtues of the Prayer Hall (*Sutra* of the *Musalla*)	Vol 1 Bk 9 nos 472–499	28	473
Times of the Prayers	Vol 1 Bk 10 nos 500–576	77	550
Call to Prayers (*Adhān*)	Vol 1 Bk 11 nos 577–698	122	572
Characteristics of Prayer	Vol 1 Bk 12 nos 699–832	134	608
Friday Prayer	Vol 2 Bk 13 nos 1–63	63	671
Fear Prayer	Vol 2 Bk 14 nos 64–68	5	676
The Two Festivals (*'ayd*)	Vol 2 Bk 15 nos 69–104	36	712
Witr Prayer	Vol 2 Bk 16 nos 105–118	14	726
Invoking Allah for Rain (*Istisqā'*)	Vol 2 Bk 17 nos 119–149	31	757

TOPIC	LOCATION	NUMBER OF ACCOUNTS IN EACH BOOK	CUMULATIVE NUMBER OF ACCOUNTS
Eclipses	Vol 2 Bk 18 nos 150–172	23	780
Prostration during Recital of Qur'an	Vol 2 Bk 19 nos 173–185	13	793
Shortening the Prayers (*At-Taqsīr*)	Vol 2 Bk 20 nos 186–220	35	828
Prayer at Night (*Tahajjud*)	Vol 2 Bk 21 nos 221–288	68	896
Actions while Praying	Vol 2 Bk 22 nos 289–328	40	936
Funerals (*Al-Janā'iz*)	Vol 2 Bk 23 nos 329–483	155	1091
Obligatory Charity Tax (*Zakāt*)	Vol 2 Bk 24 nos 484–578	95	1286
Obligatory Charity Tax after Ramadaan (*Zakāt ul Fitr*)	Vol 2 Bk 25 nos 579–588	10	1287
Pilgrimage (*Hajj*)	Vol 2 Bk 26 nos 589–823	235	1522
Minor Pilgrimage (*'umra*)	Vol 3 Bk 27 nos 1–32	32	1584
Pilgrims Prevented from Completing the Pilgrimage	Vol 3 Bk 28 nos 33–46	14	1598
Penalty of Hunting while on Pilgrimage	Vol 3 Bk 29 nos 47–90	44	1642
Virtues of Madinah	Vol 3 Bk 30 nos 91–114	24	1666
Fasting	Vol 3 Bk 31 nos 115–225	111	1777
Praying at Night in Ramadaan (*Tarawīh*)	Vol 3 Bk 32 nos 226–241	16	1793
Retiring to a Mosque for Remembrance of Allah (*I'tikāf*)	Vol 3 Bk 33 nos 242–262	21	1814
Sales and Trade	Vol 3 Bk 34 nos 263–440	178	1992
Sales in which a Price Is Paid for Goods to Be Delivered Later (*As-Salam*)	Vol 3 Bk 35 nos 441–460	20	2012
Hiring	Vol 3 Bk 36 nos 461–485	25	2037

TOPIC	LOCATION	NUMBER OF ACCOUNTS IN EACH BOOK	CUMULATIVE NUMBER OF ACCOUNTS
Transferance of a Debt from One Person to Another (*Al-Hawāla*)	Vol 3 Bk 37 nos 486–495	10	2047
Representation, Authorization, Business by Proxy	Vol 3 Bk 38 nos 496–512	17	2064
Agriculture	Vol 3 Bk 39 nos 513–540	28	2092
Distribution of Water	Vol 3 Bk 40 nos 541–569	29	2131
Loans, Payment of Loans, Freezing of Property, Bankruptcy	Vol 3 Bk 41 nos 570–607	38	2169
Lost Things Picked up by Someone (*Luqata*)	Vol 3 Bk 42 nos 608–619	12	2181
Oppressions	Vol 3 Bk 43 nos 620–662	43	2224
Partnership	Vol 3 Bk 44 nos 663–684	22	2246
Mortgaging	Vol 3 Bk 45 nos 685–692	8	2254
Manumission of Slaves	Vol 3 Bk 46 nos 693–739	47	2301
Gifts	Vol 3 Bk 47 nos 740–804	65	2366
Witnesses	Vol 3 Bk 48 nos 805–854	50	2416
Peacemaking	Vol 3 Bk 49 nos 855–873	19	2435
Conditions	Vol 3 Bk 50 nos 874–895	22	2457
Wills and Testaments (*Wasāyā*)	Vol 4 Bk 51 nos 1–40	40	2496
Fighting for the Cause of Allah (*Jihād*)	Vol 4 Bk 52 nos 41–323	283	2879
One-fifth of Booty to the Cause of Allah (*Khums*)	Vol 4 Bk 53 nos 324–412	89	2968
Beginning of Creation	Vol 4 Bk 54 nos 413–542	130	3108
Prophets	Vol 4 Bk 55 nos 543–658	116	3224
Virtues and Merits of the Prophet and His Companions	Vol 4 Bk 56 nos 659–841	183	3407

TOPIC	LOCATION	NUMBER OF ACCOUNTS IN EACH BOOK	CUMULATIVE NUMBER OF ACCOUNTS
Companions of the Prophet	Vol 5 Bk 57 nos 1–119	119	3526
Merits of the Helpers in Madinah (*Ansār*)	Vol 5 Bk 58 nos 120–284	164	3691
Military Expeditions Led by the Prophet (*Al-Maghāzi*)	Vol 5 Bk 59 nos 285–749	465	4156
Prophetic Commentary on the Qur'an (*Tafsīr* of the Prophet)	Vol 6 Bk 60 nos1–501	501	4657
Virtues of the Qur'an	Vol 6 Bk 61 nos 502–582	81	4738
Wedlock, Marriage (*Nikāh*)	Vol 7 Bk 62 nos 1–62	62	4800
Divorce (*Talāq*)	Vol 7 Bk 63 nos 63–262	200	5000
Supporting the Family	Vol 7 Bk 64 nos 263–285	23	5023
Food, Meals	Vol 7 Bk 65 nos 286–375	90	5113
Sacrifice on Occasion of Birth (*'Aqīqa*)	Vol 7 Bk 66 nos 376–383	8	5121
Hunting, Slaughtering	Vol 7 Bk 67 nos 384–451	68	5189
Al-Adha Festival Sacrifice (*Adāhi*)	Vol 7 Bk 68 nos 452–480	29	5218
Drinks	Vol 7 Bk 69 nos 481–543	63	5281
Patients	Vol 7 Bk 70 nos 544–581	38	5319
Medicine	Vol 7 Bk 71 nos 582–673	92	5411
Dress (*al-libās*)	Vol 7 Bk 72 nos 674–852	179	5590
Good Manners and Form (*Al-Adab*)	Vol 8 Bk 73 nos 1–245	245	5835
Asking Permission (*al-ista'idhān*)	Vol 8 Bk 74 nos 246–316	71	5906
Invocations (*ad-Du'wāt*)	Vol 8 Bk 75 nos 317–420	104	6010
To Make the Heart Tender (*Ar-Riqāq*)	Vol 8 Bk 76 nos 421–592	172	6182
Divine Will (*Al-Qadar*)	Vol 8 Bk 77 nos 593–617	25	6207

TOPIC	LOCATION	NUMBER OF ACCOUNTS IN EACH BOOK	CUMULATIVE NUMBER OF ACCOUNTS
Oaths and Vows	Vol 8 Bk 78 nos 618–698	91	6298
Expiation for Unfulfilled Oaths	Vol 8 Bk 79 nos 699–715	17	6315
Laws of Inheritance (*Al-Farā'id*)	Vol 8 Bk 80 nos 716–762	47	6362
Limits and Punishments Set by Allah (*Hudūd*)	Vol 8 Bk 81 nos 763–793	31	6393
Punishment of Disbelievers at War with Allah and His Apostle	Vol 8 Bk 82 nos 794–842	49	6442
Blood Money (*Ad-Diyat*)	Vol 9 Bk 83 nos 1–52	52	6494
Dealing with Apostates	Vol 9 Bk 84 nos 53–72	20	6514
Saying Something under Compulsion (*Ikrāh*)	Vol 9 Bk 85 nos 73–84	12	6526
Tricks	Vol 9 Bk 86 nos 85–110	26	6552
Interpretation of Dreams	Vol 9 Bk 87 nos 111–171	70	6622
Afflictions and the End of the World	Vol 9 Bk 88 nos 172–250	79	6701
Judgments (*Ahkām*)	Vol 9 Bk 89 nos 251–331	81	6782
Wishes	Vol 9 Bk 90 nos 332–351	20	6802
Accepting Information Given by a Truthful Person	Vol 9 Bk 91 nos 352–372	21	6823
Holding Fast to the Qur'an and *Sunnah*	Vol 9 Bk 92 nos 373–468	96	6919
Oneness, Uniqueness of Allah (*Tawhīd*)	Vol 9 Bk 93 nos 469–652	184	7103

BIBLIOGRAPHY

PRIMARY SOURCES

Ali, Abdulla Yusuf. *The Holy Qur-an: Text, Translation and Commentary.* Leicester: The Islamic Foundation, 1975.

———. *The Holy Qur'ān: English translation of the meanings and Commentary.* Al-Madinah: King Fahd Complex for the Printing of the Holy Qur'ān, AH 1413 (AD 1992).

Hilali, Muhammad Taqi-ud-Din, al- and Muhammad Muhsin Khan. *Translation of the meanings of the Noble Qur'an in the English language.* Madinah, K.S.A.: King Fahd Complex for the Printing of the Holy Qur'an, AH 1427 (AD 2006).

Ishaq, Ibn. *Sirat Rasul Allah.* Translated by A. Guillaume as *The Life of Muhammad.* Karachi: Oxford University Press, 1998.

Khan, Muhammad Muhsin, trans. *The Translation of the Meanings of Sahīh Al-Bukhari* Arabic/English, 9 vols. Riyadh: Darussalam Publishers and Printers, 1997.

BOOKS AND ARTICLES

Abdalati, Hammudah. *Islam in Focus,* Beltsville, MD: Amana Publications, 1998.

Accad, Fouad. *Building Bridges: Christianity and Islam.* Colorado Springs: NavPress, 1997.

Adam, Peter. *Hearing God's Words: Exploring Biblical Spirituality.* Downers Grove, IL: InterVarsity Press, 2004.

Akhtar, Shabbir. *A Faith for All Seasons: Islam and Western Modernity.* London: Bellew Publishing, 1990.

Anderson, J. N. D. *Christianity and Comparative Religion.* London: Tyndale, 1970.

Anderson, Norman. *Islam in the Modern World: A Christian Perspective.* Leicester: IVP, 1990.

The Arab Development Report 2003. Amman: UNDP, 2003.

Armstrong, Karen. *Muhammad: Prophet for Our Time.* London: Harper, 2006.

Association of Evangelicals in Africa, Lausanne Committee for World Evangelization, Servants Fellowship International, and International Institute for the Study of Islam and Christianity. *Ministry in Islamic Contexts: Report of a Consultation Sponsored by Association of Evangelicals of Africa, Lausanne Committee for World Evangelization, Servants Fellowship Internationl (IISIC): 3–8 December 1995, Nicosia, Cyprus.* Oslo: Lausanne Committee for World Evangelisation, 1996.

Aulen, Gustaf. *Christus Victor: An Historical Study of the Three Main Types of the Idea of the Atonement.* Translated by A. G. Herbert. New York: MacMillan, 1977. Reprinted Wipf and Stock 2003.

Azami, Habib Ur Rahman. *The Sunnah in Islam.* London: U.K. Islamic Academy, 1995.

Azami, M. M. *Studies in Hadith Methodology and Literature.* Kuala Lumpur: Islamic Book Trust, 1977.

Baidawi, Nasr ud-din Abi Saeed, al-. *Anwār al-tanzīl wa Asrār al-ta'wīl,* 5 vols. Beirut: Dar al-Fikr, 1996.

Barlas, Asma. *"Women's Readings of the Qur'ān."* In *The Cambridge Companion to the Qur'an,* edited by Jane Dammen McAuliffe. Cambridge: Cambridge University Press, 2006.

Bell, Steve. *Grace for Muslims?* Milton Keynes: Authentic, 2006.

Bennett, Clinton. *In Search of Muhammad.* London: Cassell, 1998.

———. *Muslims and Modernity: An Introduction to the Issues.* London: Continuum, 2005.

Borg, Marcus. *The Heart of Christianity.* San Francisco: HarperCollins, 2003.

Boyce, Mary. "Organisational Story and Storytelling: A Critical Review." *Journal of Organisational Change Management* 9 no. 5 (1996): 5-23.

Brooks, Geraldine. *Nine Parts of Desire: The Hidden World of Islamic Women.* New York: Anchor, 1995. Republished by Bantam Books, 2008.

Brown, Daniel W. *Rethinking Tradition in Modern Islamic Thought.* Cambridge: Cambridge University Press, 1996.

Brown, Jonathon A. C. *Hadith: Muhammad's Legacy in the Medieval and Modern World.* Oxford: OneWorld, 2009.

Brown, Rick. "Communicating God's Message in an Oral Culture." *International Journal of Frontier Missions* 21, no. 3 (Fall 2004): 122–27.

Burton, John. *An Introduction to the Hadith.* Edinburgh: Edinburgh University Press, 1994.

Caner, Ergun Mehmet and Emir Fethi Caner. *Unveiling Islam.* Grand Rapids, MI: Kregel Publications, 2002.

Chapman, Colin. *The Bible Through Muslim Eyes.* Cambridge: Grove, 2008.

———. "Christian Perceptions of Islam: Threat, Challenge or Misunderstood Ally?" *Evangelical Review of Theology* 20, no. 2 (April 1996): 100–05

———. *The Cross and the Crescent: Responding to the Challenge of Islam.* London: IVP, 1995. Revised 2007.

———. *The Pillars of Religion in the Light of the Tawrat, Zabur and Injil.* Beirut: The Bible Society, 1984.

Childs, Brevard. *Introduction to the Old Testament as Scripture.* Philadelphia: Fortress, 1979. Reprinted by Augsburg Books, 2010.

Clark, Charles. *Islam.* Religions of the World. San Diego: Lucent Books, 2002.

Collins, Francis. *The Language of God.* New York: Free Press, 2006.

Cragg, Kenneth. *Alive to God: Muslim and Christian Prayer.* London: Oxford University Press, 1970.

———. "Islamic Theology: Limits and Bridges," In *The Gospel and Islam: A Compendium,* edited by Don McCurry, 196-207. Monrovia, CA: MARC, 1978.

———. *Jesus and the Muslim.* London: George Allen & Unwin, 1985. Reprinted by OneWorld Publications, 1999.

———. *Muhammad and the Christian: A Question of Response.* London: Dalton, Longman and Todd, 1984. Reprinted by OneWorld Publications, 1999.

Dalby, Gordon. *Healing the Masculine Soul.* Nashville: Thomas Nelson, 2003.

Davis, C. *Christ and the World Religions.* London: Hodder & Stoughton, 1970.

Davis, John J. *Moses and the Gods of Egypt.* 2nd ed. Grand Rapids: Baker Books, 1986.

Dickinson, Eerik. "Ibn al-Salāh al-Shahrazūrī and the Isnād." *Journal of the American Oriental Society* 122, no. 3 (2002): 481-505.

Durie, Mark. *The Third Choice: Islam, Dhimmitude and Freedom.* Melbourne: Deror Books, 2010.

Eaton, Charles Le Gai. *Islam and the Destiny of Man.* London: George Allen & Unwin, 1985.

Elder, E. E. "The Crucifixion in the Koran." *The Muslim World* 13, issue 3 (July 1923): 242–258.

Eliade, Mircea. *From Primitives to Zen.* London: Collins, 1967. Reprinted Harper and Row, 1977.

Fadi, Abd, al-. *The Person of Christ in the Gospel and the Koran.* Rikon, Switzerland: The Good Way, 1975.

Faruqi, Ismail R., al-. *Christian Ethics: A Historical and Systematic Analysis of Its Dominant Ideas.* Montreal: McGill University Press 1967.

———. "Christian Mission and Islamic Da'wa" in *International Review of Mission*, volume LXV, no. 260 (October 1976), 391-409.

———. *Islam.* Beltsville, MD: Amana Publications, 1998.

Firestone, Reuven. *Jihad: The Origin of Holy War in Islam.* Oxford: Oxford University Press, 1999.

———. *Journeys in Holy Lands: The Evolution of the Abraham-Ishmael Legends in Islamic Exegesis.* New York: State University of New York Press, 1990.

Gairdner, William Temple. "Moslem Tradition and the Gospel Record. The Hadith and the Injil," *Moslem World* 5 (1915): 349-379.

Goble, Phil and Salim Munayer. *New Creation Book for Muslims.* Pasadena: Mandate Press, 1989.

Greenlee, David H. "How Is the Gospel Good News for Muslims?" In *Toward Respectful Understanding and Witness among Muslims: Essays in Honor of J. Dudley Woodberry*, edited by Evelyne Reisacher, 205–220. Pasadena: William Carey Library, 2008.

Greeson, Keith. *The Camel: How Muslims Are Coming to Christ.* Richmond, VA: WIGTake Resources, 2007.

Guillaume, Alfred. *Islam.* Middlesex: Penguin, 1954. Reprinted 1990.

———. *The Life of Muhammad: A Translation of Ishaq's Sirat Rasul Allah.* London: Oxford University Press, 1955. Reprinted 1998.

Haddad, Salim. *The Principles of Belief in the Qur'an and the Bible.* Pittsburgh: Dorrance, 1992.

Hakim, Khalifa Abdul. *Islamic Ideology,* 3rd ed. Lahore: Institute of Islamic Culture, 1961. Reprinted 1993.

Hamidullah, Muhammad. *Introduction to Islam.* Paris: Centre Culturel Islamique, 1957. Reprinted by Apex Press, 1980.

Hansen, Carol D. and William M. Kahnweiler. "Storytelling: An Instrument for Understanding the Dynamics of Corporate Relationships." *Human Relations* 46 (1993): 1391–1409.

Hasel, Gerhard F. "The Significance of the Cosmology in Genesis 1 in relation to Ancient Near Eastern Parallels." *Andrews University Seminary Studies* 10 (1972): 1–20.

Hassan, Riffat. "An Islamic Perspective." In *Women, Religion and Sexuality: Studies on the Impact of Religious Teachings on Women*, edited by Jeanne Becher. Geneva: WCC Publications, 1990.

Hiebert, Paul. *Anthropological Reflections on Missiological Issues.* Grand Rapids: Baker Books, 1994.

———. *Cultural Anthropology.* 2nd ed. Grand Rapids: Baker Books, 1983. Reprinted 1990.

———. "Form and Meaning in the Contextualisation of the Gospel." In *The Word among Us*, edited by Dean Gilliland. Dallas: Word Publishing, 1989. Reprinted Wipf & Stock, 2002.

Ibrahim, Ezzeddin and Denys Johnson-Davies. *Forty Hadith Qudsi.* Beirut: The Holy Koran Publishing House, 1980. Reprinted Rabab, 1993.

Iqbal, Muzaffar. *Islam and Science.* Aldershot, UK: Ashgate, 2002.

Jeffery, Arthur. *The Foreign Vocabulary of the Quran.* Baroda: Oriental Institute, 1938.

Jones, L. Bevan. *Christianity Explained to Muslims.* Calcutta: YMCA, 1938. Reprinted 1952.

Juynboll, G. H. A. "Hadith and the Qur'an." In *Encyclopaedia of the Qur'an,* edited by Jane Dammen McAuliffe. 5 vols. Leiden: Brill, 2002.

Kalby, Kais, al-. *Prophet Muhammad: The Last Messenger in the Bible.* Bakersfield, CA: American Muslim Cultural Association, 1991.

Kamali, Mohammad Hashim. *A Textbook of Hadith Studies: Authenticity, Compilation, Classification and Criticism of Hadith.* Leicestershire: The Islamic Foundation, 2005.

Kang, C. H. and Ethel R. Nelson. *The Discovery of Genesis: How the Truths of Genesis Were Found Hidden in the Chinese Language.* St. Louis: Concordia, 1979.

Kateregga, Badru D. and David W. Shenk. *Islam and Christianity: A Muslim and a Christian in Dialogue.* Grand Rapids: Eerdmans, 1980. Reprinted Herald Press 1997.

Kerr, David A. "Christian Mission and Islamic Studies: Beyond Antithesis," in *International Bulletin of Missionary Research* 26, no. 1 (January 2002):8–15.

———. "Islamic *da'wa* and Christian Mission: Towards a Comparative Analysis," in *International Review of Mission* 89, issue 353 (2000): 150-171.

Khan, Israr Ahmad. *Authentication of Hadith: Redefining the Criteria.* London: The International Institute of Islamic Thought, 2010.

Khan, Muhammad Muhsin. *The Translation of the Meanings of Sahih Al-Bukhari, Arabic–English.* 9 vols. Ankara: Hilal Yayinlari, 1974.

Kraft, Charles. *Anthropology for Christian Witness.* New York: Orbis, 1996.

———. *Christianity in Culture.* New York: Orbis, 1979. New edition, 2005.

———. "My Distaste for the Combative Approach." *Evangelical Missions Quarterly* 18, no. 3 (July 1982): 138–41.

Kutty, E. K. Ahmed. "The Six Authentic Books of Hadith." *The Muslim World League Journal*, April-May 1983.

Lapidus, Ira M. *A History of Islamic Societies.* Cambridge: Cambridge University Press, 1988. Second edition 2002

La Sor, William et al. *Old Testament Survey,* 2nd ed. Grand Rapids: Eerdmans, 1996.

Lewis, C. S. *The Four Loves.* New York: Harcourt Brace Jovanovich, 1960. Reprinted 2010.

———. *Mere Christianity.* New York: MacMillan, 1943. Reprinted HarperCollins 2009.

———. *The Screwtape Letters.* London: Geoffrey Bles, 1942. Reprinted 2009.

Malek, Sobhi W. "Allah-u Akbar Bible Lessons: Aspects of Their Effectiveness in Evangelizing Muslims." DMiss dissertation. Pasadena: Fuller Theological Seminary, 1986.

Manji, Irshad. *The Trouble with Islam Today.* New York: St. Martin's Griffin, 2005.

Masih, Abd, al-. *A Question that Demands an Answer.* Rikon, Switzerland: The Good Way, 1993.

McAuliffe, C. S. J. "Forestalling the Pains of Purgatory." *Review for Religious* 5 (1944): 289–96.

Mernissi, Fatima. "Women's Rights in Islam." *In Liberal Islam: A Sourcebook*, edited by Charles Kurzman. New York: Oxford University Press, 1998.

Meyers, Carol. "Temple, Jerusalem." In *Anchor Bible Dictionary,* edited by David Noel Freeman. 6 vols. New York: Doubleday, 1992.

Miller, Darrow. *Discipling Nations.* Seattle: YWAM, 1998. Second edition, 2001.

Moorehead, Alan. *The White Nile.* London: Harper & Row, 1960. Reprinted HarperCollins, 2000.

Moreau, A. Scott. *Contextualization in World Missions.* Grand Rapids: Kregel, 2012.

Morris, Leon. *The Gospel According to John.* Grand Rapids: Eerdmans, 1971.

Nasr, Seyyed Hossein. "God." In *Islamic Spirituality Foundations*, edited by Seyyed Hossein Nasr. New York: Crossroad, 1991.

Nazir-Ali, Michael. *Frontiers in Muslim-Christian Encounter.* Oxford: Regnun Books, 1987. Reprinted Wipf & Stock, 2007.

———. *Islam: A Christian Perspective.* Exeter: Paternoster Press, 1983.

Neill, Stephen. *A History of Christian Missions.* Baltimore, MD: Penguin Books, 1964. Reprinted 1987.

O'Leary, De Lacy. *How Greek Science Passed to the Arabs.* New Delhi: Goodword Books, 1949. Reprinted 2001.

Owen, David. "A Classification System for Styles of Arabic Bible Translations," *Seedbed* 3, no. 1 (1988): 8–10.

Padwick, Constance E. *Muslim Devotions: A Study of Prayer Manuals in Common Use.* London: SPCK, 1961. Reprinted 1969.

———. "The Language of Muslim Devotion," *The Muslim World*, 47 (1957): 5–21, 98–110, 194–209.

Parshall, Phil. *Bridges to Islam.* Grand Rapids: Baker Books, 1983. Reprinted Authentic Publishing, 2006.

———. *Inside the Community: Understanding Muslims through Their Traditions.* Grand Rapids: Baker Books, 1994. Reprinted in 2002 as *Understanding Muslim Teachings and Traditions: A Guide for Christians.*

———. *Muslim Evangelism: Contemporary Approaches to Contextualization.* Waynesboro: Gabriel, 2003.

Parsons, Martin. *Unveiling God: Contextualizing Christology for Islamic Culture.* Pasadena: William Carey Library, 2005.

Patai, Raphael. *The Arab Mind.* New York: Charles Scribner's Sons, 1973. Updated edition, 2007.

Peace, Richard. *Conversion in the New Testament: Paul and the Twelve.* Grand Rapids: Eerdmans, 1999.

Peters, George W. "An Overview of Missions to Muslims." In *The Gospel and Islam*, edited by Don McCurry. Monrovia, CA: MARC, 1978.

Peterson, Eugene. *A Long Obedience in the Same Direction.* (Downers Grove, IL: InterVarsity Press, 2000.

Pfander, C. G. *The Mizanu'l Haqq: The Balance of Truth.* 1835. Revised and updated by W. St. Clair Tisdall in 1910. Villach, Austria: Light of Life, 1986.

Phipps, William E. *Muhammad and Jesus: A Comparison of the Prophets and Their Teachings.* New York: Continuum Publishing, 2003.

Polkinghorne, Donald. *Narrative Knowing and the Human Sciences.* Albany: State University of New York, 1988.

Pritchard, J.B., ed. *Ancient Near Eastern Texts.* Princeton: Princeton University Press, 1969.

Qutb, Sayyid. *Islam and Universal Peace.* Indianapolis: American Trust Publications, 1977. Reprinted 1993.

———. *The Islamic Concept and Its Characteristics.* Indianapolis: American Trust Publications, 1991.

Rahman, Fazlur. *Islam,* 2nd ed. Chicago: University of Chicago Press, 1979.

Ramadhan, Tariq. *The Messenger: The Meanings of the Life of Muhammad.* London: Penguin, 2007.

Redha, Mohammad. *Mohammad: The Messenger of Allah.* Translated by Mohmoud Salami. Beirut: Dar al-Kotob Al-ilmiyah, 2005.

Renard, John. *In the Footsteps of Muhammad: Understanding the Islamic Experience.* New York: Paulist Press, 1992.

Richardson, Don. *Eternity in Their Hearts.* Ventura, CA: Gospel Light, 1984. Third edition, 2005.

———. *Peace Child.* Ventura, CA: Gospel Light, 1974. Fourth edition, 2005.

———. *The Secrets of the Koran.* Ventura, CA: Regal Books, 2003.

Robson, J. "Hadīth." In *The Encyclopaedia of Islam.* New ed., edited by Bernard Lewis, et al. 11 vols. Leiden: Brill, 1971.

Robson, James. *Mishkat al-Masabih,* 2 vols. Lahore: Sh. Muhammad Ashraf, 1975.

Robinson, Anthony. *Transforming Congregational Culture.* Grand Rapids: Eerdmans, 2003.

Robinson, Neal. *Christ in Islam and Christianity.* London: Macmillan, 1991.

Rodinson, Maxime. *Mohammed*. Middlesex: Penguin, 1971. Reprinted Tauris Parke 2002.

Rogerson, John and Philip Davies. *The Old Testament World*. Cambridge: Cambridge University Press, 1989). Second edition 2005.

Ronan, Charles E. and Bonnie B. C. Oh, eds. *East Meets West: The Jesuits in China, 1582–1773*. Chicago: Loyola University Press, 1988.

Samuel, Vinay and Chris Sugden. "Dialogue with Other Religions: An Evangelical View." In *Sharing Jesus in the Two-Thirds World*, edited by Vinay Samuel and Chris Sugden. Grand Rapids: Eerdmans, 1984.

Sardar, Z. "The Ethical Connection: Christian-Muslim Relations in the Postmodern Age," in *ICMR (Islam and Christian-Muslim Relations)* 2, no. 1 (June 1991): 56–76.

Sarwar, Ghulam. *Islam: Beliefs and Teachings*. London: The Muslim Educational Trust, 1980. Reprinted 2000.

Sayyid, S. *A Fundamental Fear*. London: Zed Books, 2003.

Schlorff, Samuel. "Feedback on Project Sunrise (Sira): A Look at 'Dynamic Equivalence' in an Islamic Context," in *Seedbed* no. 2 (1987): 22–32.

Sheba, Abdurrahman, al-. *Muhammad: The Messenger of Allah*. Riyadh: Islamic Propagation Office in Rabwah, 2005.

Shenouda III (Pope). *The Release of the Spirit*. Cairo: Dar el Tebaa el Kawmia, 1990.

Siddiqui, Muhammad Zubayr. *Hadith Literature: Its Origin, Development and Special Features*. Cambridge: Islamic Texts Society, 1993. Reprinted Suhail Academy, 2001.

Siddiqui, Ataullah. *Christian-Muslim Dialogue in the Twentieth Century*. New York: St Martin's Press, 1997.

Smith, Wilfred Cantwell. *Islam in Modern History*. Princeton: Princeton University Press, 1957. Reprinted New American Library 1959.

Speight, R. Marston. *God Is One: The Way of Islam*. New York: Friendship Press, 1984. Reprinted 1989.

Stacey, Vivienne. "Attitudes to Other Faiths," in Mario di Gangi, ed. *Perspectives in Mission* Ontario: BMMF, 1985.

Stewart, Desmond. *Early Islam*. Nederland: Time-Life Books, 1968.

Swartley, Keith. "Course Introduction," in Keith Swartley, ed. *Encountering the World of Islam*. Waynesboro, GA: Authentic Media, 2004.

Taylor, W. R. "Al-Bukhari and the Aggada," in *Muslim World* 33 (1943), 191-202.

Terry, John Mark. "Approaches to the Evangelization of Muslims," in *Evangelical Missions Quarterly* 32, no. 2 (April 1996): 168–173.

Thiessen, Henry C. *Lectures in Systematic Theology.* Grand Rapids: Eerdmans, 1998.

Thomas, David. *Anti-Christian Polemic in Early Islam.* Cambridge: Cambridge University Press, 1992.

Thompson, J. A. "Covenant (OT)," in G. Bromiley, ed., *The International Standard Bible Encyclopedia.* Grand Rapids: Eerdmans, 1979.

Travis, John and Anna. "Contextualisation among Muslims, Hindus and Buddhists: A Focus on Insider Movements," in Charles Kraft, ed., *Appropriate Christianity.* Pasadena: William Carey Library, 2005.

Trimingham, J. S. *The Sufi Orders in Islam.* London: Oxford University Press, 1971. Reprinted 1998.

Trotter, Lilias. *The Way of the Sevenfold Secret.* Cairo: Nile Mission Press, 1926. Reprinted 1933.

Vine, W. E. *A Comprehensive Dictionary of the Original Greek Words with Their Precise Meanings for English Readers.* McLean, VA: MacDonald Publishing Company, n.d. Reprinted Hendrickson, 1989.

Voll, John Obert. *Islam: Continuity and Change in the Modern World.* Essex: Longman, 1982. Second edition 1994.

Watt, Montgomery. *Islamic Revelation in the Modern World.* London: Hodder & Stoughton, 1970.

Walker, F. Deauville. *William Carey: Father of Modern Missions.* Chicago: Moody Press, 1980.

Wehr, Hans. *A Dictionary of Modern Written Arabic,* ed. J. Milton Cowan. Ithaca, NY: Spoken Language Services, 1976.

Wild, Stefan. "Political interpretation of the Qur'ān," in Jane Dammen McAuliffe, ed., *The Cambridge Companion to the Qur'an.* Cambridge: Cambridge University Press, 2006.

Wilson, John W. *Christianity alongside Islam.* Melbourne: Acorn Press, 2010.

Woodberry, Dudley. "Contextualization among Muslims: Reusing Common Pillars," in Dean Gilliland, ed., *The Word Among Us: Contextualizing Theology for Today.* Dallas: Word Publishing, 1989. Reprinted Wipf & Stock 2002.

———. "Missiological Issues in the Encounter of Emerging Islam," in *Missiology* 3 no.1 (January 2000), 19–34.

———. "When Failure Is Our Teacher: Lessons from Mission to Muslims," in *International Journal of Frontier Missions,* vol. 13:3 (July-September 1996), 121.

Youngblood, Ronald. *The Heart of the Old Testament,* 2nd ed. Grand Rapids: Baker Books, 1998.

Zebiri, Kate. *Muslims and Christians Face to Face.* Eugene, OR: Wipf & Stock, 1997.

Zwemer, Samuel M. *The Moslem Christ.* Edinburgh: Oliphant, Anderson and Ferrier, 1912. Reprinted BiblioBazaar 2010.

———. *The Moslem Doctrine of God.* New York: American Tract Society, 1905. Reprinted by Advancing Native Missions 2010.

INDEX